THE OAK KING,
THE HOLLY KING,
AND THE UNICORN

# The Myths and Symbolism
# of the Unicorn Tapestries

HARPER & ROW, PUBLISHERS, New York
Cambridge, Philadelphia, San Francisco, London
Mexico City, São Paulo, Singapore, Sydney

# THE OAK KING, THE HOLLY KING, AND THE UNICORN

John Williamson

FOR MY PARENTS

*Barbara and Paddy*

Grateful acknowledgment is made for permission to reprint:

Excerpt on page 188 from *The Aeneid* by Virgil, translated by Robert Fitzgerald. Translation copyright © 1980, 1982, 1983, by Robert Fitzgerald. Reprinted by permission of Random House, Inc.

Excerpt on pages 69–72 from *Sir Gawain and the Green Knight*, translated by Brian Stone. Copyright © Brian Stone, 1959, 1964, 1974. Reprinted by permission of Penguin Books Ltd.

FIRST EDITION

*Designer: Lydia Link*

Library of Congress Cataloging-in-Publication Data

Williamson, John, 1948–
   The oak king, the holly king, and the unicorn.

   Bibliography: p.
   Includes index.
   1. Hunt of the unicorn (Tapestries).  2. Tapestry,
Gothic—France.  3. Unicorns in art.  4. Art and
mythology.  5. Christian art and symbolism—Medieval,
500–1500—Themes, motives.  6. Cloisters (Museum).
I. Title.
NK3049.U5W55  1986      746.394      85-45242
ISBN 0-06-015530-2    86 87 88 89 90 MPC 10 9 8 7 6 5 4 3 2 1
ISBN 0-06-096032-9 (pbk.)    86 87 88 89 90 MPC 10 9 8 7 6 5 4 3 2 1

# CONTENTS

*Color plates of the Unicorn Tapestries follow page 116.*

# INTRODUCTION

> [Christianity is a synthesis]; its central figure of the
> Redeemer was at least as old as the Tritos Soter of the
> earlier Greeks, and its promise of personal immortality was
> still older, echoing through the history of timeless Egypt.
> From Babylonia came the idea of God as the maker of
> heaven and earth, from Persia the dualism of Satan and
> God, from Egypt the last judgment, from Syria the
> resurrection drama of Adonis, from Phrygia the worship of
> the Great Mother, from Greece and Rome the idea of
> universal law. From sources too ancient to be identified
> came its baptism and communion. From the various
> mysteries came other ritual elements of the mystery of its
> mass, such as incense, vestments, beads, holy water,
> genuflection, and chanting. Without this ancient and
> cosmopolitan heritage, Christianity could scarcely have
> established its claim to universality.
> —Herbert J. Muller, *The Uses of the Past*

T HIS BOOK is devoted to an exploration of the classical blend of pre-Christian and Christian iconography that vivifies the famous set of textiles known as the Unicorn Tapestries—works of art that mirror the startling imagination of the artists, who used plant and animal imagery in order to convey the symbolic meaning woven into the depiction of the hunt and slaying of a unicorn. On the surface and at immediate glance, the Unicorn Tapestries seem like elegantly decorative art of little or no intellectual or religious significance. But if we prolong our exploration of these seven remarkably handsome panels, we gradually begin to discover the unexpected. For the drama that is so richly depicted in the Unicorn Tapestries can only be effectively interpreted when we understand the various symbolic levels of the elusive creature who is at the center of the pictorial drama. The author of *The Survival of the Pagan Gods*, Jean Seznec, has suggested that "myth really possesses its full significance only in those epochs when man still believed himself to be living in a divine world." Clearly, we come face to face with such human beings when we turn our attention back a few centuries to that exceptional time known as the Middle Ages.

Today, there is a growing excitement about the sensibility and lifestyle of the Middle Ages. We have become aware of the somewhat humiliating fact that history is not necessarily progressive, that one era does not necessarily improve upon its predecessor; and so we believe more than ever that the past can teach us something important about our options for the future.

The politicial framework of the past has therefore become a major interest to many people, at the same time that there is no less a preoccupation with the unique pre-Christian culture of Europe, which is viewed, after long neglect, as a vital and realistic aspect of the heritage of our modérn European and American culture. Behind that pre-Christian mentality lies a mystic symbolism that contrasts drastically with the obsolescent "realism" of our nineteenth- and early twentieth-century Western attitudes, but which dominated the minds of medieval artists, theologians, and intellectuals. It is the very remoteness and yet curious familiarity of the visionary sensibility of the Middle Ages that most fascinates us today. Thus we not only find in the past models for our political and economic future, but—perhaps more essentially—we are rediscovering paradigms which provide fundamental alternatives to our world view.

The Unicorn Tapestries, now housed at The Cloisters of the Metropolitan Museum of Art in New York City, are considered by most art historians to be the finest surviving series of pictorial textiles from the late fifteenth century, not only for the technical achievement of the artist or artists who produced the tapestries but for their astounding diversity of imagery and the subtlety of their symbolism.

That symbolism persists in our consciousness, yet until recently it was largely ignored because it did not readily fit into either our decorative notion of art or our naturalistic expectations of pictorial technique. Gradually, however, we have been taught to see works of art in a new way—with new eyes, given to us by modernists whose revolutionary painting and sculpture often borrowed heavily both from earlier periods of history and from primal cultures. In our era, this interaction of the past and the so-called pagan world mirrors the unique amalgamation of pre-Christian, classical Greek and Roman, and Christian icons and images which was at the heart of the mentality of the late Middle Ages. It is this "language of art" that the art historian Ananda Coomaraswamy says we must relearn "if we wish to understand medieval art." Such attuning to the medieval psyche is one of the major efforts of this book, which attempts to lead the reader back through the overlay of centuries to the rediscovery of a rich and much forgotten language of pictorial symbols. Indeed, this book is an odyssey that takes us back to the classical worlds of Greece and Rome, venturing through the eras that saw the birth and evolution of the pre-

Christian deities of Europe and their eventual fusion with Christian ideology during the early centuries of the Middle Ages. As we shall see, the influence of these "pagan" gods upon Christian art and thinking was both enormous and subtly pervasive, affecting every aspect of the succession of cultures which culminated in what we erroneously think of as the insular, self-contained, and culturally unique Western civilizations.

To the contrary, we will find that the most important element of Western civilization is the survival of ancient Indo-European religions and their cosmologies and deities, which have remained unchanged except for their pre-Christian names. Their ideals and rituals, however, have insinuated themselves into every aspect of Western religion and art. Ultimately, we do not know ourselves as Americans or Europeans unless we know from what shadowy and half-forgotten sources our cultures evolved.

For me, the Unicorn Tapestries became a doorway between our world and the world in which my forebears lived their lives. When I was a lecturer at The Cloisters, and while I was researching and designing that institution's Medieval Garden, I became convinced of the need for a thorough study of the unique medieval cosmos that is symbolically revealed in the plant and animal iconography of the Unicorn Tapestries. In order to explain the tapestries in their *full* meaning, they must be seen not only in relation to the epoch that produced them, but also in relation to the extensive flowering of natural symbolism that is visible everywhere in the art and literature of the Middle Ages. This specialized interpretation of medieval art was once a bit remote from public interest, but gradually it has become a less rarefied subject as the symbolism of Blake and Donne, of Bosch and Bruegel, as well as pre-Christian European art have surfaced as strong popular preoccupations. We are hungry for the living, daily reality of the past, and yet we do not have many sources from which to discover more than its dead statistics and facts. As Jamake Highwater has said, "We want the past to be inhabited; and we have found that art has the unusual ability to bring life back to lifeless relics and artifacts, for art is the living part of us that persists when we are gone."

It was both essential and inevitable that the "life" of early "barbaric" Europe should finally find its way into the interpretation of medieval art. Peculiarly, most art historians have not consciously inherited the powerful legacy of Sir James Frazer, Jane Harrison, Gilbert Murray, or such current mythologists as Mircea Eliade and Joseph Campbell, and so their unique perceptions of the life hidden *within* art and myth have not often informed the way we look upon the Middle Ages. I hope to be guided by scholars who have taught us that facts alone cannot inform us, and to use the Unicorn Tapestries as the focus as well as the point of departure for a grand adventure in ideas and images, myths and realities—all those elusive elements from which we gain an intimate view of ourselves, of what we have been and what we are becoming.

My first exploration into this neglected but highly revealing symbolism of the medieval mind was in the form of an article published by *Horizon* (March 1979). My research since then, as well as the extensive discoveries made in regard to both the tapestries themselves and medieval flora and fauna generally, prompted this extensive study of the Unicorn Tapestries. I have come to recognize that all the creatures and flora woven into these elaborate tapestries have a strong correspondence to the emblematic images central to the minds of the Middle Ages. There is, in fact, something of a detective story in unraveling the "mysteries" of the Unicorn Tapestries. Not only are the individual emblems of the panels complexly interrelated to Greco-Roman and Christian allegorical traditions; even the sequence of the seven panels of the Unicorn Tapestries can be concisely and reasonably understood and explained in terms of the plant and animal iconography of the fifteenth century.

The complicated and often contradictory legends and lore depicted in the Unicorn Tapestries and other art of the same period were often regarded as frivolous and nonsensical. Now, however, we have come to realize that such ancient emblems and symbols are an iconographic shorthand for cosmic mysteries and principles of immense depth and seriousness. Through the combination of these symbols, through their embodiment in works of art, and because their impulse and significance were an emotional reality to a vast population, the medieval artist was able to address himself (or herself) to the central ideas of the day by manipulating a whole system of emotionally and philosophically charged images. Thus, in the truest sense, the Unicorn Tapestries contain the entire cosmology of the age that produced them.

This book will center on the Unicorn Tapestries as the nucleus around which many major artworks of the Middle Ages and the early Renaissance may be brought into focus, providing numerous parallels to the iconographic compositions and implications of the series of tapestries at The Cloisters. Although much is still unknown about the origin and provenance of the Unicorn Tapestries, one of the identifiable tangibles is the iconography of flora and fauna in the series, and these elements surely represent a cyclic calendar sequence which has its roots in early European "pagan" cosmologies. It is upon this fascinating premise—of European iconographic roots—that a sound basis for the interpretation of the Unicorn Tapestries may be found. Implicit in the story of these elegant pictorial textiles is the story of Europe itself: of its lost rituals of plants and animals, and of its fabulous allegory of the divine hunt.

I am exceedingly grateful to my editors, Hugh Van Dusen and Janet Goldstein, for their concern and interest, and for their generous efforts in the publication of this book. Gratitude also extends to Samuel Kinser, for reading the manuscript and offering valuable suggestions. I also wish to thank Jamake Highwater for his invaluable inspiration and critique, and Frank Anderson, Honorary Curator of Rare Books and Manuscripts at the New York Botanical Garden, for allowing me to make an extensive photographic survey from the library's comprehensive collection. Mr. Anderson's scholarly research proved especially valuable in bringing to my attention a medieval reference that explains the absence of ears upon the unicorn depicted in the fourth panel of the tapestries. Frank Anderson's enthusiasm and encouragement over the years have been significant factors in my writing this book.

Other exceptional help has been provided by Thomas Todd and James Cromwell of Taurgo Slides, New York. Mr. Todd made an exhaustive photographic survey of the Unicorn Tapestries available to me; he also provided valuable assistance through his extensive knowledge of art history. And I am grateful to Mr. Cromwell, who prepared special photographic materials for me on a number of occasions.

During my years at The Cloisters, encouragement and valuable critiques were given by my friend Nancy Kueffner, the Associate Museum Educator, in whose excellent department I was a lecturer.

Throughout the research for this book I was fortunate to have the assistance of many exceptional librarians. The Bobst Library of New York University was outstanding in its help, and I am indebted in particular to Stanley D. Nash and Rickel Twersky. The staff of The Institute of Fine Arts of New York University also provided valued help as well as an amicable attitude that made their facility one of the most pleasant in which to do research. My thanks, too, to the librarians of the Morgan Library, and to the New York Public Research Libraries, especially the staff of the New York Public Library's Rare Book Room, who provided essential bibliographical data over the years.

Two exceptional librarians at the University of Connecticut at Storrs have furnished me with special material that contributed indirectly to this book. The first is Richard Schimmelpfeng, Head of the Special Collection; the second is Barbara Mitchell. I would also like to thank my dear friend Isabelle Joris, from the University of Massachusetts, who on a number of occasions translated passages from the early French for me.

The identification of birds in the Unicorn Tapestries is based upon a report that appeared in *Natural History* (December 1961). For the identification of the animals appearing in the second tapestry I relied upon the observations of Dr. Richard G. Van Gelder, Curator at the Department of Mammalogy of the American Museum of Natural History, New York. I have departed from one of his findings; the reasons for this digression appear in the Conclusion of the book.

My identification of some plants is based upon an article by J. E. Alexander and Carol H. Woodward, entitled "The Flora of the Unicorn Tapestries," that appeared in the May 1941 edition of the *Journal of the New York Botanical Garden*. This article employed the findings of an earlier researcher, Eleanor C. Marquand, whose paper on "Plant Symbolism in the Unicorn Tapestries" was originally published in *Parnassus* magazine in October 1938. The diagrams identifying the flora of the Unicorn Tapestries that appear at pages 232–238 of this book are based upon the report made in the May 1941 edition of the *Journal of the New York Botanical Garden* previously referred to.

In most instances, quotations from medieval and Renaissance authors have been transliterated into modern English.

Since my themes draw upon a wide range of influences and experiences, I cannot adequately credit all the sources that are reflected in this book. But perhaps the Selected Bibliography at the close will help to highlight some of the major resources that have been essential both to my research and to the formation of my ideas.

# PART ONE

# Seeing Old Art
# with New Eyes

If you do not expect it, you
will not find the unexpected, for
it is hard to find and difficult.
—Heraclitus

# THE HISTORY
# OF THE UNICORN
# TAPESTRIES

I broider the world upon a loom,
I broider with dreams my tapestry;
Here in a little lonely room
I am master of earth and sea,
And the planets come to me.
—A. Symons, *The Loom of Dreams*

T HE UNICORN TAPESTRIES are aesthetically, historically, and icono-graphically one of the most remarkable sets of late Gothic weavings in the world today. They are outstanding for their skill in design, brilliance of color, and for their dramatic and extraordinary portrayal of the hunt, death, and rebirth of a unicorn.

History and time have been harsh with most of the splendid sets of tapestries mentioned in the medieval accounts and inventories, so that few have survived the vacillations of fashion, the wear and tear of centuries, and the turbulence of war.

The Unicorn Tapestries consist of six large panels and two fragments of a seventh. All seven panels unfold the story of the search, hunt, and death of the unicorn; a drama that culminates in the animal's resurrection in an enclosed garden.

Hunting was a common motif depicted in secular tapestries of the late fifteenth and early sixteenth centuries. This sport was an important pastime for members of the high-spirited upper classes. As a way of life for some and a much-needed distraction for most, hunting provided a remedy from the claustrophobic atmosphere of the medieval castle, and a relief from the apparent tedium of feudal society. It is natural that the hunt would therefore be a favorite subject of secular art of the period, and the Unicorn Tapestries are no exception.

These lively hangings would have been one of the prized possessions of a nobleman. So costly were tapestries, and so much in demand, that textiles similar to the Unicorn Tapestries were often part of a prince's or noble's ransom. These glorious panels were easily transported and would travel with their owners when touring scattered estates, during campaigns, or if a commission was accepted in a new region. The tapestries formed an essential adjunct to the nomadic life of the nobility, receiving permanent exhibition only when the lord was in his own domain. One of the great advantages of having tapestries as works of art was their adaptability. They were easily removed from the wall, rolled up, and slung across the back of a pack horse or into a wagon; and upon relocation, they would provide a familiar setting for the owner while he was away in alien surroundings.

The residence of many of the European nobility was a château—a somber building originally taking the form of a fortified castle, an unfortunate necessity during the earlier unsettled centuries of the Middle Ages. Until the end of the fifteenth century, few changes took place in these dark citadels. The stone buildings, with their stout walls, allowed little light to enter the rooms. The monotony of dark stone was relieved only by narrow portals, chimney breasts, and a few scattered windows. When hung in one of these gloomy interiors, a set of tapestries would surely have had a dramatic and pleasant effect on the occupants.

As the medieval historian William Tyler puts it: "Magnificent as decoration, tapestries reflected the taste and preference in the subject matter of the most wealthy and powerful elements in the land. In turn they influenced the ideas and values of those who lived among them and saw them day after day."

The Unicorn Tapestries are just such a set of remarkable hangings. Attesting to this fact is a document that mentions that 180 years after their manufacture, the Unicorn Tapestries were still treasured possessions hanging in a great noble's sleeping quarters. This account, the oldest that mentions the tapestries, is part of the inventory of the estate of François VI de La Rochefoucauld.

Until the Revolution, the tapestries continued to be in the possession of the La Rochefoucauld family, gracing their château at Verteuil, a town some two hundred and fifty miles south of Paris. Then in 1793, during the Reign of Terror, many of the La Rochefoucauld possessions were pillaged or destroyed by peasants from the local village. The tapestries were stolen from the château, but lacking any royal insignia, they were spared destruction by the enraged citizens of the new French Republic.

Nothing was heard of the Unicorn Tapestries for the next sixty years, until the 1850s, when Comte Hippolyte de La Rochefoucauld initiated a search of the area around Verteuil in the hope that some of the family heirlooms might be recovered.

The count's efforts and determination were finally rewarded when news came that in the vicinity of the château some interesting "old curtains" were being used as a protective covering for vegetables in a farmyard barn. These "curtains" were no less than the seven panels of the Unicorn Tapestries. After purchase and repairs, they were reinstalled at the Château Verteuil. There they remained until the 1920s, when they found their way to the Anderson Gallery in New York City.

A few years later, in 1923, they were purchased by John D. Rockefeller, Jr., and ultimately given to the Metropolitan Museum of Art in 1935. The seven Unicorn Tapestries, which once covered the cavernous walls of a medieval castle, had made a perilous five-century odyssey before reaching their final destination in the special room prepared for them at The Cloisters, in New York City. Barely avoiding destruction during the French Revolution, exposed to harsh weather in the nineteenth century, brought to the United States in the 1920s, and then removed to a safe location outside New York City after the bombing of Pearl Harbor, the tapestries have miraculously survived.

Most of the information we have about the Unicorn Tapestries—such as the date of manufacture, the provenance and ownership, as well as their subsequent history—is the result of fairly recent investigation. Both the patron and the occasion or celebration for which they were commissioned are still unknown.* What we have established, based upon their technique and style, is that they must have been produced in workshops, or ateliers, in Brussels. Extensive study of the costumes and weapons shown in the seven panels date the Unicorn Tapestries to around 1500. The most useful feature for dating these textiles is the footwear which is part of the colorful costume worn by the nobles, huntsmen, and peasants depicted in these hangings.

The square toe on the boots and shoes of the male aristocrats and their attendants became fashionable at the end of the fifteenth century, superseding the pointed shoes of previous generations. Contemporary in style and date with such footwear are the swords, with their asymmetrical cross guards. Exactly such a sword hangs from the waist of the hunter who mortally wounds the unicorn in the sixth tapestry of the series. From this evidence, art historians have concluded that the primary sketches, or *petit patrons*, for the Unicorn Tapestries were drawn around 1500. When these drawings were completed, they were customarily handed over to a competent artist, who rendered the primary sketches into full-size *patrons* (or cartoons). These cartoons would then be dispatched to the workshop contracted to produce the actual weavings. There is some doubt among art historians as to whether all seven of the panels of the Unicorn Tapestries

* The hypothesis presented by James Rorimer in "The Unicorn Tapestries Were Made for Anne of Brittany," *The Metropolitan Museum of Art Bulletin* (1942), has very little factual evidence, as Margaret Freeman ably demonstrates in her book *The Unicorn Tapestries.*

were woven at the same time, or even if they all came from the same workshop. The reason for this uncertainty is based on the sharp contrast between the *millefleurs** backgrounds of the first and last tapestries as compared to the naturalistic backgrounds of the other five panels.

Further differences exist between the seven textiles: the first and last tapestries show a similar, stylized medieval formalism in the weaving of plants, whereas the flora in the rest of the series have more realistic renditions. Many of the plants in the two *millefleurs* hangings are extremely rigid and unlifelike, most probably drawn by an artist who had no first-hand botanical knowledge. The most obvious example of this lack of realism is the tree which forms the central motif of the tapestry depicting "The Unicorn in Captivity." In the unicorn's enclosure is woven an *imaginary* tree of no known species, which nonetheless bears very ripe pomegranates and has palm-like foliage. This pomegranate tree appears again in the third panel of the tapestries, but here it is woven with more care and in a form that is botanically recognizable. Of the many explanations put forward to explain these contradictions in both design and weaving, the following seem most probable:

- "The first and last tapestries were designed and woven at a later date and added to the set."†
- Both of these hangings "are of approximately the same date as the others, and . . . they are different mainly because they were planned by different designers."
- "All the tapestries were designed by one man, and such disparities as the stiffness of the figures in the 'Start of the Hunt' and the unreal pomegranate in the 'Unicorn in Captivity' are due to the fact that the tapestries were executed by different and less accomplished workshops of weavers." (Freeman)

Because of the conspicuous but unidentified initials "A.E." originally woven into every one of the seven tapestries, we can assume that they were all part of the same set. It is my opinion that the cartoon designs were conceived at the same time, and then, for unknown reasons, the *millefleurs* hangings were woven in a different and less competent workshop from the rest of the tapestries.

The laborious and lengthy procedure needed to make a set of hangings such as the Unicorn Tapestries started with the patron selecting an enticing story, favorite myth, battle, or historical event. The patron and his retinue

* Literally "one thousand flowers." The term applies to tapestries that depict a great number of plants and flowers as an overall background.

† This is why the Metropolitan Museum of Art has dated these two *millefleurs* hangings later than the other panels of the Unicorn Tapestries.

of artists and scholars—along with all those who enjoyed reinventing and retelling ancient and medieval stories—would spend hours in speculative dialogue before selecting a fable or tale from the vast repertory of current themes and ideas, significant allegories, personal motifs, and the medieval amalgam of classical and Christian myths.

A tapestry was a costly acquisition for the residence of a rich and powerful aristocrat. As Whitney Stoddard points out, "The wealthy dukes and princes who gathered architects, sculptors, manuscript illuminators, and painters into their households to enrich their palaces and to augment their collections of art paid great attention to the tapestry designers and weavers in whose workshops wall hangings were created."

After much deliberation, the designer would sketch the basic idea. Then, upon approval, a competent painter would produce full-size cartoons, either on sheets of linen or pasted strips of paper. These would be dispatched to the atelier chosen to weave the tapestries. In the workshop, many different technicians were employed; the dyers of silk and woolen threads toiled alongside workmen who erected the wooden looms. But the most highly skilled artisans of the workshop were the weavers themselves, who worked side by side, weaving the bobbins of colored wool and silk thread through the thick warp. In the case of a set as large and complex as the Unicorn Tapestries, the manufacture could take many months or even years before completion.

The general consensus among art historians is that the Unicorn Tapestries were woven in Brussels. Most of the ateliers in that city around 1500, the date of the cartoons for the tapestries, used the *basse-licé*—low looms with horizontal warps. Unfortunately, no detailed account exists of how the late fifteenth-century weavers used the *patrons* in duplicating the design from cartoon to textile, though with horizontal looms it would have been most practical to place the cartoon under the loom, thus enabling it to be easily seen through the warp threads.

One fact emerges from the inspiration that molded and enriched the particular myths and icons chosen for the Unicorn Tapestries. This is the certainty that the designer of the cartoons for the tapestries was strongly influenced by other works of art, especially those that were generally known and those that were circulating in Paris at the end of the fifteenth century.

By comparing the Unicorn Tapestries with the woodcuts and metalcuts that were being made in Parisian workshops around 1500, some remarkable iconographic similarities can be discovered. Of the many cuts produced by book illuminators during that period, those of the royal bookseller, Antoine Vérard, seem to have most influenced the anonymous designer of the Unicorn Tapestries. Vérard's illustration of *The Temptation of Adam and Eve* (Fig. 1), published in 1495, has many similarities to the images woven into

Figure 1. *The Temptation of Adam and Eve.* Woodcut in Bible published by Antoine Vérard. Paris, c. 1500. Metropolitan Museum of Art.

Figure 2. Scenes of a stag hunt, in a French book of hours printed by Philippe Pigouchet for Simon Vostre, 1498. Metropolitan Museum of Art.

Figure 3. Trojan War series. Drawing of man with dog. Paris, 1465–70. Musée du Louvre.

the second panel of the Unicorn Tapestries. Each has almost identical fountains, and if we reverse the woodcut, the genet (a type of weasel) and stag appear in almost the same position in both woodcut and tapestry. These similarities and iconographic parallels will be developed in future chapters.

The Parisian engraver Philippe Pigouchet provides further examples of influences from other works of art. The metalcuts that he supplied for a book of hours published by Simon Vostre in 1498 have some interesting relationships to the imagery contained in the Unicorn Tapestries. One of the pages from Pigouchet's book of hours is bordered by a lively stag hunt, an illumination that has some remarkable parallels to the action depicted in the Unicorn Tapestries (Fig. 2). For instance, at the bottom of the page a dead stag has been placed over the back of a horse, an incident that evokes the imagery presented in the sixth panel of the Unicorn Tapestries. There are other similarities: halfway into the right margin, hounds are depicted attacking the stag, a composition not unlike the violent attack by the dogs, prior to the killing of the mythical beast, in the Unicorn Tapestries.

A further example of this artistic "plagiarism" is a rare surviving *petit patron*, drawn for the renowned Trojan War Tapestries that were woven in Tournai around 1474. Some of the figures in these sketches bear a resemblance to those in the Unicorn Tapestries (Fig. 3). Nichole Reynaud, of the Louvre, was the first to bring this similarity to the attention of art historians. Mme Reynaud attributes the *petit patrons* of the Trojan War series to Henri Valcop, the royal "enlumineur" to Marie of Anjou, queen of France, and her son, the future Charles VIII. Reynaud proposes that the style and drawing from the Valcop workshop influenced the designer of the Unicorn Tapestries.

During the research for this book, I was fortunate in finding a set of textiles that contains imagery almost identical to the sixth panel of the Unicorn Tapestries (Figs. 4 and 5). These remarkably similar textiles belong to what is generally known as the *Carrabara Series,* various tapestries that depict events from the nomadic life of gypsies. One of them is entitled "Gypsies at a Château Gate" (Fig. 4). This tapestry is now part of the permanent collection of the Currier Art Gallery of Manchester, New Hampshire, but in the early seventeenth century it hung in the Château d'Effiat, near Clermont-Ferrand, the estate of the Effiat family.

An exhibition catalogue entitled *Masterpieces of Tapestry* (published by the Metropolitan Museum of Art) attributes this particular weaving to a Tournai workshop of the early sixteenth century: "The inventory of one of the greatest Tournai tapestry weavers of the early sixteenth century, Arnould Poissonier, mentions a large number of pieces of the *Histoire de Carrabara dit des Egiptiens.* For this reason, the weaving of this type of work has been attributed to Tournai." (Souchal)

The similarities between this Tournai textile and the sixth panel of the Unicorn Tapestries are indeed striking. In each, a castle is depicted on the right, under which a noble couple contemplate their surroundings. In each, a hoofed animal is killed with the thrust of a spear. The coup de grâce is administered to a stag in the Carrabara weaving, and to the unicorn in The Cloisters tapestry (Fig. 6). In the Tournai panel, a huntsman sounds a horn to announce the death of the stag—an action that is strikingly similar to his counterpart in the sixth hanging of the Unicorn Tapestries, which depicts the demise of the unicorn. In the former panel, the huntsman stands behind the stag, and in the latter a similar figure is placed under the unicorn. The horse in each respective tapestry bears a sharp likeness, especially in the features of the head.

According to many art historians, the coat-of-arms at the top of the Tournai tapestry was added during the early seventeenth century in order to identify the Effiat family. This particular tapestry probably hung in the family château at Clermont-Ferrand, a noble residence completed in the early seventeenth century.

An interesting hypothesis, though one that needs much more research, is a feasible connection between the unidentified monograms "A.E." and

Figure 4. "Gypsies at a Château Gate." Tapestry, Tournai, early 16th century. Manchester, New Hampshire, The Currier Gallery of Art.

Figure 5. Gypsies in front of a castle. Tapestry, Tournai, early 16th century. The Bavarian National Museum.

Figure 6. "The Unicorn Is Killed and Brought to the Castle."
The Unicorn Tapestries. Franco-Flemish, c. 1500. The
Cloisters, Metropolitan Museum of Art.

"F.R." and the Effiat family. (The initials "A.E." appear on all seven of the
Unicorn Tapestries, while the initials "F.R." appear on just the third panel
of the Unicorn Tapestries, the one that depicts the unicorn crossing a
stream.) Furthermore, the tapestry called "Gypsies at a Château Gate" is
so similar to the sixth panel of the Unicorn Tapestries that it is possible
that both this Tournai tapestry and the Unicorn Tapestries were commissioned by the Effiat family. It is therefore not unlikely that this noble French
family, whose heirs bore the title marquis d'Effiat and whose family name
was Ruzé, were the original owners of the Unicorn Tapestries.

In summary, we know from the inventory of the duc de la Rochefoucauld that 150 years after their manufacture there were a total of seven
panels in the Unicorn Tapestries series, all of them in good condition. It is
not too unreasonable to assume that this was the original number of hangings commissioned by the unknown patron. Another probability is that all
of these weavings came from one of the fine ateliers centered in Brussels
at the end of the fifteenth century—a deduction based upon the style of
footwear and swords worn by the hunters and nobles depicted in the
tapestries.

It seems likely, as Genevieve Souchal of the Cluny Museum suggests, that the designer of the Unicorn Tapestries "no doubt played an important part in French art at the end of the fifteenth century." In that case, he would have been living in Paris at least part of the time, a fact that is made evident from the influence of Parisian art on the themes and images of the Unicorn Tapestries. So he would have been involved with both the artistic and intellectual life which was an intrinsic part of the city at this period. Such a master designer, living in the French capital, would have had access to a large number of woodcuts, metalcuts, manuscripts, and cartoons from the numerous renowned workshops of Brussels and Tournai. The Paris of the early sixteenth century was a magnetic center of the rich intellectual and artistic life that epitomized the late Middle Ages. Thus the Unicorn Tapestries arose out of a unique moment of history; in them we can see a perfect reflection of the ideals and culture of the period that produced them.

# 2

# FRANCE
# IN TRANSITION:
# A PERSPECTIVE
# OF THE PERIOD

> The cosmos of culture, like the cosmos
> of nature, is a spatiotemporal structure,
> and in order to understand an art object
> it is imperative to learn as much as
> possible of the circumstances under
> which the objects of study were created.
> —Erwin Panofsky, *Meaning in the Visual Arts*

BEFORE THE RICH IMAGERY of the renowned Unicorn Tapestries can be fully explained, the society and the period in which they were produced must first be understood. For instance, although created in France, the tapestries were not uniquely French, but rather the result of a complex blend of aesthetic European experiences.

Because we do not fully understand their history, it is difficult immediately to grasp the intentions of the early sixteenth-century creators of these remarkable textiles. In fact, the tapestries represent an important turning point in European cultural exchanges. In order to have such an exchange a sumptuous court life had to exist, with its myriad assortment of scholars and patrons. The development of this courtly atmosphere began in the last half of the fifteenth century. It was a time when France was emerging from a period of stagnation and feudal wars, and evolving into a stabilized and centralized monarchy.

The political and cultural period under discussion in this chapter covers the reign of Charles VIII and the early years under the monarchy of his successor Louis XII. It was a crucial point in French history: beginning just after the disastrous Hundred Years War with England, which finally ended in 1453 and left France devastated in both town and country, this was also a time fraught with economic calamities and repeated epidemics.

Clearly, France's problems did not cease after the wars with England.

In fact, just shortly after the conclusion of that turbulent period, the rulers of France were threatened with new hostilities—this time from the wealthy and powerful dukes of Burgundy.

The Burgundian territory was vast, encompassing the Netherlands, Flanders, Artois, Picardy, Franche-Comté, as well as territories within France itself, mainly the duchy of Burgundy. A substantial part of this enormous area was to return to the victorious French monarchs at the end of their latest military exploits. The capture of these lands by the French, and the taking of Burgundy in particular, was to have great influence on the mentality and culture of France of the pre-Renaissance.

Fifteenth-century Burgundy was presided over by the Valois dukes in their capital at Dijon. This young branch of the French royal house had cleverly fought and married its way into a powerful and prestigious position among the monarchs of Europe. The Burgundian courts rivaled those of the king of France himself. And Dijon had become a treasure house of paintings, sculpture, tapestries, and books since the fourteenth century.

This remarkable duchy was finally defeated and dissipated when Louis XI of France, aptly nicknamed "the Spider," used intrigue, skill, and cunning to countermand the political and cultural threat of Burgundy. Eventually he formed a coalition against his Burgundian enemies. In the ensuing war between the two countries, Charles of Burgundy was killed (1477), and Louis XI made claim to the duchy of Burgundy, as well as Picardy and Artois. By the end of Louis's reign, only the duchy of Brittany remained independent of French control; and even this duchy was eventually assimilated by France through the marriage of Louis's successor, Charles VIII, to Anne, the heiress of Brittany.

Thus by the time of the reigns of the much less competent monarchs Charles VIII and his cousin and successor Louis XII, France had already become a politically powerful and stable country. It was under the governments of these two kings that the French people would eventually recover from the calamities of the turbulent past century. This was the period that would consummate the beginnings of the French Renaissance.

The geographical changes brought about by such confrontations reshaped France both politically and intellectually. From the artistic point of view, the royal liaison with Anne of Brittany would also have lasting importance. Both Charles VIII and, thereafter, Louis XII of France were fortunate to have Anne as their queen. She was a young woman of culture and intelligence, who made a lasting contribution to society during her reign as queen of France.

Betrothed to Charles XIII, Anne of Brittany arrived in France in 1496. She brought with her a host of retainers, including musicians, writers, poets and other learned men. Attesting to her literary interest is the fact that shortly after arriving in France she had her father's library transported to the castle at Blois. "Anne," writes the French historian R. Doucet, "was like her father in some characteristics. She was responsible and diligent in studying state affairs, and earned from him the name of 'the least foolish woman in the world.' During those early years, a period of unrest among the aristocracy and among the people, the government felt the effects of her vigorous and far-sighted guidance."

Gradually, this distinguished French court attracted many literary men of the day. A large and sophisticated assembly of intellectuals and retainers became the nucleus of a highly social court, similar to those in certain culturally renowned Italian states.

The true power behind Charles VIII and Louis XII was not Anne of Brittany but the ambitious Georges d'Amboise, archbishop of Rouen. This churchman achieved his greatest power as prime minister, cardinal, and papal legate under Louis XII, and for ten years (until his death in 1510), "he enjoyed almost sovereign authority, directing Italian policy and dictating to the Church in France . . . [and when] his ambitions turned towards Italy . . . he had visions of putting the crowning touch to these ambitions by becoming pope himself." (Doucet)

Whatever Georges d'Amboise's political motives, his interest in art stimulated the domestic French culture, as well as establishing an exchange of ideas with Italy. Unfortunately, the initial contacts between the two countries were not peaceable. Shortly after succeeding to the throne, Charles VIII planned a full-scale invasion of the Italian peninsula.

This ill-fated French monarch caused a contemporary to remark that "in body as in mind, he is of no great value." Another contemporary named Philippe de Commynes stated that the king's "only appreciation was for 'moral and historical' works, and above all for romances and chivalry which provided food for his imagination." (Doucet)

Instead of strengthening his own kingdom as his father had done, Charles's ideas of romance and imagination took hold of his senses, and he turned his attention toward campaigning for a dubious foreign inheritance—the Kingdom of Naples. As a result, some of the foundations for the French Renaissance were unwittingly laid by Charles VIII during the Franco-Italian wars. In Charles's reign the Italian campaigns were short-lived, but they were continued more successfully under the next two monarchs. Even though Charles's ill-fated invasion of Naples ended after only eleven months, it planted the first seeds of the Italian Renaissance in the French consciousness. The retreating French army did not return to France empty-handed; among the pillaged goods was much precious booty, including tapestries, sculpture, books, and other treasures. Charles VIII brought back to France both the literary and the artistic Renaissance in his supply wagons.

The Italian influence on France at the time of the creation of the Unicorn

Tapestries was so great that Italian culture of the late fifteenth century warrants some discussion. At the time of King Charles's campaign, the Italian Renaissance had already peaked, but the peninsula continued to be culturally dominant in sixteenth-century Europe. The notorious discord and strife between the various Italian states stimulated a healthy cultural competition. Each prince and potentate tried to outshine his neighbor, and in so doing both stimulated and dispersed art and ideas. Each kingdom and state nurtured an artistic and intellectual elite, ranging across Italy from the papal court in Rome to the powerful Medici family of Florence, the Sforza of Milan, the Gonzaga of Urbino, the Este of Ferrara, and the princes of Aragona in Naples.

An even stronger and more prolonged contact between France and Italy was established when Louis XII succeeded Charles VIII in 1492 and inherited the French monarchy. During the next eleven years of war with Italy, pillaged artworks trickled into France. This "art booty" had a great effect on the domestic culture. Some of the most notable literary treasures during these military campaigns came from Pavia, an urban center between Genoa and Milan. After capturing the city in 1499, Louis XII carried off the entire library, one of the finest in Europe at the time. This precious collection contained almost a thousand illuminated manuscripts.

The organizer and initiator of this second campaign against Italy was the king's prime minister, Cardinal d'Amboise. The cardinal was not idle during these years; as Franco Simone notes, "the illustrious statesman was collecting there all the treasures of art and literature that he gathered during his more or less extended stays in Italy . . . he negotiated to buy what was left of the Aragonese library, which he did in fact acquire and bring to France. But the manifestations of such a sincere devotion to culture were not limited to Italy, since their most concrete realization was right in Rouen, where the Cardinal did not exactly found, but certainly developed, a scriptorium in which the best copyists sought to collect excellent miniatures in order to emulate the Flemish and the Italians."

Although Italy had a profound influence on every region of northern Europe, France nonetheless created its own distinctive art style. After the death of Charles VIII, the widowed Queen Anne of France married his successor, Louis VII, in 1499. Both of these monarchs and their expanding French court continued to be dominated by the intelligent and paternal Cardinal d'Amboise.

A brilliant and scintillating court was not just a luxury of the era; it also reflected political muscle. The insightful Dutch historian Johan Huizinga made the following comment about Burgundy, but this observation could apply to any European court of the late Middle Ages: "A splendid court could, better than anything else, convince rivals of the high rank the dukes claimed to occupy among the princes of Europe." The French court was no exception.

Among the many outstanding artists and writers of the late fifteenth and early sixteenth century was Jean Lemaire des Belges (1470=1525), a notable poet under Anne of Brittany's patronage. This laureate of the French literary circle became the major popularizer of the myths of classical Greece and Rome. The subject matter of these fables was to have an important influence on the painting and textiles of the period. Lemaire was not only a poet and historiographer, diplomat and traveler, he was also the queen's official secretary and bibliographer. His was an era of the *grands rhétoriqueurs*, witty and verbose versifiers, who flourished in the scintillating courts of Burgundy and Flanders during the second half of the fifteenth century.

Upon the death of Louis XI, Lemaire and other poets and artists entered the French court at the invitation of Charles VIII. These versifiers produced poems and prose, ranging from lyrics of love and chivalry to tracts on statecraft and history. They also produced verses on topics as diverse as art, religion, and morals. This broadly didactic literature is cast in the form of allegories, mythologies, and personifications. The heavy dependence of these men on courtly patrons, avid for entertainment, partly explains the diversity of their sources. Poets and artists traveled widely with their patrons—or in search of new ones. In the process, they both gathered and dispersed cultural ideas and information.

Equally important, and even more effective in stimulating a new intellectual climate in Europe, were the books being turned out by the printers' workshops. This revolution of bookmaking commenced with the invention of the prototype printing press in Mainz around 1455.

Literacy and printing went hand in hand, each stimulating the other. Major works both old and new were printed in Latin—the universal language of the educated of Europe. And this universality of Latin greatly facilitated the exchange of ideas between the important centers of learning in France, Germany, England, and Spain.

The invention of printing also brought about a revolution in the production of books. Frederick Artz notes that "by fifteen hundred, nine million books and pamphlets had been printed, and their price had sunk to one-eighth of what it had been before printing." By means of the press, an abundance of the classics were made widely available. Italy, taking the lead in this field, produced two hundred editions of Cicero and seventy of Virgil before the year 1500.

In France, the first printing press was set up in 1470 by three German printers, who had come to Paris at the invitation of officials from the Sorbonne. In the first few years, this university press alone turned out editions of Cicero, Terence, and Virgil. Paris became the great center in France for the production of printed books because it was triply important as an economic center, the focus of royal administration, and the seat of one of the greatest medieval universities. Paris's domination of French culture increased rapidly in the early sixteenth century, carried on the rising curves of political centralization and economic prosperity. It was in this Parisian milieu that Guillaume Budé was to become the first French humanist scholar to rival in Greek and Latin learning the famed Italians or the Dutchman Erasmus.

This brief profile of the era that produced the Unicorn Tapestries is essential to our grasp of their aesthetic and symbolic purposes. Although there are many ways to comprehend the prevailing ideas that were influencing art, a survey of the books being printed and read by intelligent, informed people is perhaps one of the best clues to the full social context. The philosophies and literature that existed in France during the time of the making of the Unicorn Tapestries can tell us much about their creators and the ideals these textiles embody. The subject matter contained in these books of the sixteenth century had a dynamic and widespread influence on the art of the period. Studying the symbolic references of the literature gives us an intimate insight into the world view of the people who created the dazzling cartoons for the Unicorn Tapestries.

From the research done by a number of French historians, notably R. Doucet and A. H. Schultz,* the following brief survey gives a good indication of the types of books purchased by the literate Parisian of the early to mid-sixteenth century. The most popular volumes include the medieval romances and histories, especially those concerned with Troy and the exploits of the Trojan heroes. The early medieval mythic exploits of Arthur, Lancelot, and other great knights of the Round Table were also in much demand by the literate population. Romantic epics like the adventurous and erotic *Romance of the Rose* came out in many editions; as did the *Dream of Poliphilus*, an amorous work, full of references to the divinities of the ancient world, written by the fifteenth-century Dominican friar, Francesco Colonna.

The religious texts of the period were widely read, including the writings of such Latin Church Fathers as St. Augustine, St. Jerome, St. Ambrose, and Pope Gregory the Great.

But classical writers particularly captured the imagination of the literate people of this period. Beside those authors already mentioned, there was great fascination for the translations into Latin of the works of Plato and Aristotle, as well as the original Latin writings of such Roman philosopher-

* See the discussion by Warner L. Gundersheimer in his *French Humanism—1470–1600.*

statesmen as Seneca. The late fifteenth-century Italian genius Pico della Mirandola had a wide and influential audience for his books. This famous member of the Florentine Academy combined in his own work a refined esoteric eclecticism along with elements from the writings of Plato and Plotinus, as well as ideas taken from the Judaic Cabala and from Christian mystics.

During their research, Doucet and Schultz discovered that some libraries even contained works in Arabic, Greek, and Hebrew—languages that were relatively unknown in the Europe of the period. Also popular were scientific writings, and in the early sixteenth century these included a number of volumes on the occult.

To supply this great demand for printed books, more printers set up their own workshops. Within fifteen years after the first press at the Sorbonne had been established, illustrated books were numerous. The premier French press, owned by Jean Dupré, turned out in 1481 a *Paris Missal*. This was the first illuminated book produced in the capital having full page cuts. Sometime between 1485 and 1515 the dominancy of printing passed to Antoine Vérard. This printer and renowned woodcutter became the bookseller to the French court under Charles VIII.

The aristocracy both stimulated printing and helped by making substantial purchases. The French nobles of the court must have had a strong interest in books, as Vérard was able to publish some three hundred editions in twenty-seven years.

By the reign of Louis XII, the royal library of France was one of the finest in Europe. This vast collection consisted of the combined libraries of Anne of Brittany, her late father Charles VIII, and Louis XII. Although Anne of Brittany was by no means a scintillating intellectual like her more famous contemporary Margaret of Austria, and "could not read Latin," she "liked nothing better than to talk about Livy and to have learned works dedicated to her." (Sichel)

Paris was a stimulating city for the artists and publishers. The published texts available to Parisian buyers were vast and diverse, ranging from the religious to the secular. The latter group included bestiaries and the new German herbals, which provided exciting pictures of both real and imaginary animals and plants. This pictorial and descriptive material was reworked and reused by the Parisian painters, writers, and illustrators, resulting in a resurgence of these images in their art, writings, and textiles.

The Unicorn Tapestries are a good example of this process. They were unquestionably influenced by visual material from the French capital, especially by printed woodcuts and metalcuts from the Paris workshops of the end of the fifteenth century. For instance, similarities exist between many images in the Unicorn Tapestries and the figures from prints made in the workshops of Jean Duvet and Antoine Vérard. This important connection will be explored in the sections dealing specifically with the Unicorn Tapestries.

Without a doubt, the plethora of printed books revolutionized communications, dispersed ideas and philosophies, and made available in vast numbers the pre-Christian classics of Greek and Latin scholars.

Despite popular opinion to the contrary, the Renaissance does not represent a sudden awakening and awareness of the pre-Christian culture and deities. As R. Wittkower points out: "Recent studies have revealed how tenaciously the ancient gods survived the ages. The Middle Ages infused new life into them, and the Renaissance administered that heritage, as is shown by the fact that Boccaccio's *Genealogy of the Gods* remained the principal source book. After the first printed edition of 1472, four further editions were necessary during the fifteenth century, and innumerable more in the course of the sixteenth century."

Medieval scholars had studied the "pagan writings" for the erudition of their Christian texts. Then in the late Gothic and Renaissance period, literate people freed themselves from restrictive doctrines, viewing the classical world for its own sake, not simply as a precursor or adage for the new Christian religion. This humanistic change of attitude toward pre-Christian literature provoked strong condemnation from the Church.

In fact, humanism was condemned by many authorities merely because it focused upon the moral and ethical writings from classical antiquity, and attempted to reconstruct some of these heretical written ideas in late medieval and Renaissance Europe. "Paganism" was not something new. The Church did not consider it a new heresy, for it had survived in many forms among the folk, and the old gods had been perennial, though dormant throughout the whole of the medieval period. But the open intellectual admiration of antiquity was regarded by the Church as a palpable danger.

It is important to understand how "paganism" had survived, and in what guises. For if the ancient gods and their rites had faded from memory, they could not possibly have had such a rich and dynamic impact on the art and literature of Europe, from the Carolingian period through the flowering of the Gothic Age.

Clearly, the pre-Christian pantheon did not die, but remained viable in many subtle guises. Some of the most important disguises were the popular medieval allegories. The impetus of these allegories originated in biblical parables—those integral parts of the New Testament used to simplify profound theological ideas. The Church scholars applied the same allegorical techniques to pre-Christian literature, attempting to moralize the ancient gods and to see Christian teachings in classical literature.

Long before the Middle Ages, this task of demystifying and moralizing the ancient gods had been attempted by the late Greek philosophers. These agnostic men had begun to interpret their deities as metaphors for the forces of nature or of various ethical qualities. Some even extended this form of argument to explain the Olympian pantheon as exceptional mortals raised to a divine state by the legends of later generations. This process of deification was named after Euhemerus, a third-century B.C. mythographer who had discovered that Alexander the Great, just one hundred years after his death, had already been deified. Euhemerism, as Seznec points out, was a vital influence "throughout the Middle Ages, although it underwent a total change of character. The human origin of the gods ceased to be a weapon against them, a source of rejection and contempt. Instead, it gave a certain protection, even granting them a right to survive. In the end it formed, as it were, their patent of nobility."

This wealth of pre-Christian mythology was preserved in Christian parable and allegory, and survived to become highly charged symbols and images for the later medieval artists, poets, and writers. The early encyclopedists, such as Bede and Isidore of Seville, also made use of this wealth of material, and the riches of classical allegory continued in the works of Rabanus Maurus into the ninth century, finally culminating in the High Medieval erudition of such scholars as Vincent of Beauvais, Bartholomaeus Anglicus, and Brunetto Latini. These great encyclopedists became the purveyors of iconography for centuries to come. Thus the pre-Christian gods survived in elite early medieval culture as the incarnation of ideas. Eventually, they were reinstated in the arts and literature of the twelfth century by authors and artists, who with great enthusiasm submerged themselves in the legends and myths of the Latin gods. Christianity also accommodated itself to the pre-Christian religions at the popular cultural level, covering these influences with a veneer of Christian faith.

The process of assimilation has been succinctly expressed by Mircea Eliade in his *Myth and Reality:*

A part of the popular religion of pre-Christian Europe survived, either camouflaged or transformed, in the feasts of the church calendar and in the cult of the saints. For more than ten centuries the Church was obliged to fight the continual influx of "pagan" elements—that is, elements belonging to the cosmic religion—into Christian practices and legends . . . "paganism" could survive only in "Christianized" form, even if at times the Christianization was rather superficial. This policy of assimilating the "paganism" that could not be destroyed was nothing new; the primitive Church had accepted and assimilated a large part of the pre-Christian sacred calendar.

It was the humanism of the early Renaissance, and the strong cultural exchange between European nations, that provided artists and scholars with both the opportunity and the stimulus to free themselves from such camouflaged allegories. They could now see the gods in the full context of their sensuality and significance. And by the early sixteenth century, the poet and mythologer Jean Lemaire was doing just this when he declared that "he who looks carefully may find much allegorical and moral fruit hidden under the colors of poetry." Lemaire further taught that myth "is rich in great mysteries and in poetic and philosophical meanings, containing fruitful substances beneath the rind of fable." (Seznec)

The resurgence of the classical cosmos combined with the Christian mythos, and was finally transformed into one of the most vital and enduring aspects of human expression in the Middle Ages. Far from simplistic, the moral conception of Christian visual symbolism was extremely complex and subtle, representing the focus of a new cosmology at the very moment of its birth from the multifarious layers of prior "pagan" beliefs. This religious and aesthetic iconography has a distinctive, highly legible history, culminating in an art that uses an iconographic shorthand to make visible cosmic mysteries of immense depth and seriousness.

Ultimately, this visual language informs the Unicorn Tapestries, rendering them some of the most artistically and intellectually compelling works of their era. The combination of symbols and their embodiment in works of art became a comprehensible reality to a vast population. This public symbolism permitted the artist to address himself to the central issues of his day, through the manipulation of a whole system of emotionally and philosophically charged images. Thus, in a true sense, the Unicorn Tapestries contain the entire cosmology of the age that produced them.

This cosmology was created by an intelligentsia that was intoxicated with rediscovered myths and symbolism. By the early sixteenth century, artists and learned persons of the French court were crystallizing and assimilating the revolutionary ideas that were evolving in Renaissance Italy. At the same time, these Frenchmen were highly influenced by the multitude of books from the printing presses, and by the abundance of dialogues and discussions of brilliant scholars from the various centers of learning, who traveled widely and exchanged ideas with their colleagues throughout Europe.

The conditions of political and economic stability in the emerging European nations made possible this international exchange of ideas. As Lucien Febvre points out, "After lying so long hidden, all the manuscripts in the world, all the texts of Greek or Roman antiquity could have come to light suddenly at the beginning of the century, but without peace, riches, wellbeing, security, who would have dreamed of devoting himself to study?"

The nadir of the medieval world in France, the art of the Unicorn

Tapestries marks "the climax and close of the late Middle Ages in the north as the ideals of the Italian Renaissance begin to emerge and dominate." Whitney Stoddard comments: "This last flowering of the Middle Ages was the product of a new kind of individual patronage together with a new emphasis on the individual artist and his personal style. Indeed, as patrons, Philip the Bold of Burgundy; Jean, duc de Berry, and later, Margaret of Austria, and Kings Louis XII and Francis I of France, were Renaissance individuals; yet the art they commissioned from French, Dutch, and Flemish artists remained profoundly medieval."

The prevailing medieval attitude—the desire to discard nothing—made possible the amalgamation of pre-Christian and Christian learning. This in turn allowed a fusion of artistic and philosophical images and ideas from diverse, even conflicting origins. And from this unity arose transcendent symbols that bridged the centuries, creating a unique late Gothic art—embodied in the remarkable Unicorn Tapestries.

# 3

# THE FUSION
# OF CLASSICAL
# AND CHRISTIAN
# GODS

> History cannot basically modify the
> structure of an archaic symbolism.
> History constantly adds new meanings,
> but they do not destroy the
> structure of the symbol.
> —Mircea Eliade, *The Sacred and the Profane*

I F WE ARE GOING to interpret complex works like the Unicorn Tapestries beyond the prosaic level, then it becomes essential to understand how the pre-Christian gods, mythologies, and ancient icons survived after the collapse of the classical world, to infuse unexpected meanings into the imagery of the tapestries.

Four main factors guaranteed the survival of these pre-Christian rites and images. The earliest one was the inclination of the "pagans" themselves to humanize their divinities, a metamorphosis that made their assimilation into the Christian mythology of later centuries an easier task than it might have been had the gods retained their supernatural forms. Secondly, like their Roman predecessors, the early Church Fathers were crafty psychologists. Instead of totally destroying the old religions, the Christian ecclesiastics absorbed the alien myths and icons, and rechanneled the power of the old gods to their own advantage.

The Judaic tradition was already a reservoir of many Near Eastern mythic traditions. It also provided, in turn, the foundations of Christianity. The ancient Hebrew religion was largely based upon cosmic parables and myths, gathered from many cultures during the endless nomadic history of the Jews. Judaism provided a framework and intellectual climate for the survival of non-Semitic traditions. These eventually became an intrinsic part of the "pagan" rites and festivals of the Judaic culture, and therefore an essential source for the later Christian texts and rites.

Although Near Eastern cosmologies had a remarkable and cumulative impact on both Judaism and Christianity, the influence of classical Greek and Roman mythology, ever since the collapse of Imperial Rome, had been a subtle but important source of many elements of Christian orthodoxy. In fact, numerous classical writings had been copied through the centuries by scribes. This scholarly activity was a major factor in the perpetuation of the pre-Christian gods. The "textual tradition," writes Erwin Panofsky in his *Meaning in the Visual Arts*, "through which the knowledge of the classical themes, particularly of mythology, was transmitted to and persisted during the Middle Ages was of the utmost importance, not only for the medievalist but also for the student of the Renaissance iconography. For even in the Italian Quattrocento [fourteenth century] it was from this complex and often very corrupt tradition, rather than from genuine classical sources that many people drew their notion of classical mythology and related subjects."

These diverse, complex influences, when blended together, gave the medieval and Renaissance artist and scholar their images and ideas about the ancient gods and mythologies.

To understand these symbols and how they could affect European art so dramatically, we must explore the fusion of numerous pre-Christian and Christian icons and mythologies. This process was already at work during the early centuries of Christianity. The religious fever that transfixed those converts embracing Christianity did not obliterate their pre-Christian reverence for symbols. In essence, it added a new Christian dimension to their prior religion.

For the devoted, the mythos surrounding Christ became a consuming ideal. Yet at the foundation of Christianity were ancient icons—an ancient imagery that was given a new focus and interpretation by Christian scholars. This point is stressed by Eliade when he says that "history cannot basically modify the structure of an archaic symbolism. History constantly adds new meanings, but they do not destroy the structure of the symbol." (1959)

The fusion of classical and Christian mentality enabled the gods of the ancient world to survive the perilous centuries under the unkind scrutiny of an intolerant and proselyting new religion.

In our approach to the Unicorn Tapestries, it is important to know how the classical gods gradually evolved from their original aspect to become metaphors of Christian ideas. When we grasp this knowledge of ancient symbolism, we can then interpret medieval works of art such as the Unicorn Tapestries with imagination, but also with an understanding of their relationship to their own era and the impact on that era of previous powerful symbols.

Long before the advent of Christianity, the classical gods had already changed. This metamorphosis consisted of a process of demystification and humanization, which changed the meaning of the gods from its original metaphysical emphasis to a representation of worldly ideals. Such transmutation helped the gods to survive as aspects of later Judeo-Christian traditions. These transformations were not radical; they began, first, when the Greeks started viewing their gods not as supernatural beings but as the personification of the forces in nature. Only later did worldly ideals and moral creeds replace the natural symbolism of the gods.

For instance, the great Latin poet Virgil viewed the gods as symbols of social conscience. But long before Virgil, Homer had already humanized the gods by making them participants in his grand dramatic sagas. And in so doing, he transformed the quarrelsome family of Olympus into metaphors of spiritual dignity.

This new allegorical treatment provided a revised interpretation of the gods, allowing pre-Christian peoples—who found it disturbing to worship supernatural beings with a brutal, lustful, and elemental nature—to sustain the religion of their ancestors during their more aesthetic and inquiring epoch.

It was the dramatic force of the golden age of Homer, as much as the later medieval essayists and apologists, who made the survival of the old deities permissible. This survival was achieved by making abstractions and metaphors of the gods, enabling the doctrine of the new Christian faith to fulfill itself in the guise of ancient divinities.

From their earliest beginnings, Christianity and Judaism had combined certain important historical events from the chronicles of Israel with various "pagan" seasonal festivals and cyclical myths, which became such renowned celebrations as the Feast of the Tabernacle, Hanukkah, and the Feast of Lights. As Robert Graves observes: "Prophets and psalmists were as careless about the pagan origins of the religious imagery they borrowed, as priests were about the adaptation of heathen sacrificial rites to God's service. The crucial question was: in whose honour these prophecies and hymns should now be sung, or these rites enacted. If in honour of Yahweh Elohim, not Anath, Baal or Tammuz, all was proper and pious." (1963)

It is clear that mythological elements abound in biblical testaments, and that Christianity absorbed many rituals, symbols, and figures of Hebraic and Mediterranean origin. This accommodational inclination was one of the reasons for the triumph of Christianity in the ancient world. "The new faith from the beginning," writes Frederick Artz, "showed an enormous capacity to borrow from other philosophies and religions. Indeed, Christianity is the supreme syncretism of antiquity."

Thus, many non-Christian ethnic ceremonies were converted into

Christian rites. The mystery religions of the East provided needed elements of ceremony and mythology for the emerging Christian religion. During the uncertain early years of the Christian Church, its greatest challenge came from a religion that was centered upon the Persian god of light—Mithras. Mithraism was a faith that was very similar to Christianity: both religions promised immortality, as well as providing ethical and moral codes of behavior. The eventual supremacy of Christianity over Mithraism was not so much a defeat of the Mithras as an effective assimilation of Mithraic ceremonies into the rites of the Christian Church. These included baptism with water and a feast involving a sacred meal of bread and wine. Even the moral connotation of light in contrast to darkness came from this "pagan" cult. The choice of December 25 as the birth date of Christ was not an arbitrary one, but was chosen because that was the time of the great Mithraic feast which celebrated the return of Mithras as the sun god.

The religion of Mithras was also to provide Christianity with many ceremonial objects and rites: bells, candles, the blood symbolism in baptism, a sacred meal that identified with the god, and the setting aside of Sunday as a special day from which all work was excluded.

The rituals associated with the mystery religions became utterly interchangeable with those annexed to Christianity. Thus the Christian theologians chose to celebrate the nativity of Christ on December 25, thereby transferring the devotion of the followers of Mithras to the new Christian god. This December day was the winter solstice—or pre-Christian miscalculation of the winter solstice—a date that since earliest times was believed to be the period during which the sun was reborn. And since Christ, like his Asiatic counterpart Mithras, was a solar god, he would naturally share his nativity with the sun.

By similar methods, the ecclesiastical authorities were able to assimilate the Easter festival of the death and resurrection of their deity into the death and resurrection of Attis, another widely celebrated Asiatic god. The rites of Attis, and his successor Christ, took place at the vernal equinox, a time corresponding to the revival of spring verdure. And as such, Christ, like the Phrygian Attis, becomes a god of vegetation.

Once Christianity had established itself in its Mediterranean cradle, it could gather its resources and direct crusades of conversion into foreign lands. The Church, however, found in these far-flung regions that it had to contend with local religions and heritages, something very different from the Judeo-Christian environment that had so far nurtured the new faith.

The battle for the supremacy of Christianity was fought not so much against the great gods of Olympus—Zeus and Hera—or those of the German pantheon—Odin and Thor in their magnificent Valhalla—as against the myriad lesser European deities. And it was this crucial battle that the

Church lost. The early Christian monks soon realized that various spirits of nature were deeply rooted in the psyche of the people of ancient Europe whom they were attempting to convert. Taking advantage of this knowledge, they channeled the devotional energy of worshippers of the old gods into a new Christian hierarchy of various godlike saints, as well as the veneration of saintly relics. Eventually, the Christian saints assumed the attributes and qualities of most pre-Christian divinities.

So, as Emile Mâle points out, St. John's Day replaced the festival of the sun. "St. Valentine's day, marking the end of winter, became (especially in England) the festival of early springtime. . . . In Provence, St. Caesarius of Arles assumed the power over storms. . . . St. Barbara averted the lightning, and the bells which were sounded during a storm bore her likeness. St. Medardus was the master of the rain. Several saints shared this privilege with him; and irritated by the uselessness of their prayers during long droughts, the people more than once drenched the statue of the saint whom they had vainly invoked."

These transformations of pre-Christian to Christian celebrations were by no means accidental. In fact, Pope Gregory the Great had advised the missionary monks not to interfere with traditional non-Christian beliefs or with religious observances that could be harmonized with Christianity. Indeed, Gregory strongly urged the taking over of sacred places and rededicating them to Christian saints. In following this shrewd and clever directive, the reverence attached to ancient pre-Christian shrines gravitated toward the Church itself.

In Pope Gregory's own words: "Do not pull down the fanes. Destroy the idols: purify the temples with holy waters: set relics there, and let them become temples of the true God. So the people will have no need to change their places of concourse, and where of old they were wont to sacrifice cattle to demons, thither let them continue to resort on the day of the saints to whom the Church is dedicated, and slay their beasts, no longer as a sacrifice but for a social meal in honour of Him whom they now worship." (Sheridan and Ross)

The Christian theologians never provided the saints with any role other than that of mediators between man and the heavenly hosts. They would not and could not suggest so heretical a stance as presuming that the saints were divinities. On the other hand, newly converted Christians made no such distinction. They willingly embraced these new heroes and took them to their hearts, offering them the same homage and reverence that had once been the prerogative of the ancient gods.

During this difficult transitional process, the Church took over indigenous legends and myths, unwittingly creating an amalgam—a new religious mythos far removed from the syncretism of the Gospel. There is little question that a good part of the popular religion of pre-Christian Europe survived either disguised or transformed as part of the festivals of the Church calendar with its curiously non-Judaic cult of the saints.

For example, the early Church was aware of the similarities between the archangel Michael and the Roman god Mercury. Both had an affinity with hills and mountains, and both had the task of conducting to heaven the souls of the departed. The monks used these parallels when trying, in the first centuries of Christianity, to divert the people of Roman Gaul from their long-standing worship of Mercury. To facilitate conversion, they bestowed on St. Michael all the accoutrements of Mercury. The god's temples were usually found on a natural prominence or summit. As the new religion gained dominance, the old pre-Christian temples of Mercury were pulled down, and from the rubble arose churches dedicated to the archangel Michael.

Throughout Europe, in each province, there were "pagan" sacred places that were blessed by some itinerant hermit, bishop, or martyr in the new era of Christianity. The springs or wells that were formerly the sanctuary of a local deity were sanctified by the clergy and rededicated to a popular saint. The saints also marked the cycle of the year, and they inherited the earlier "pagan" influence over nature and the seasons, controlling their progress and marking their return. The seasons not only became a reminder of various traditional monthly labors, but also became associated with the cycle of the Christian year, with its round of liturgical prayers and festivals.

Specific aspects of pre-Christian myths had great appeal to the new mythos of Christianity. For instance, many dragon-slaying divinities or heroes were transformed into the local version of St. George, and numerous fertility goddesses of Europe were assimilated into the cult of the Virgin Mary or those of the chaste female saints. Thus in various guises of Christian saints, the old gods survived and slipped into the ceremonial life of Europe, simply by donning a new mantle and holding a bishop's crosier instead of a sheaf of corn or a lightning bolt. The people never tired of seeing their ancient friends and defenders, whom they felt were more familiar and with whom they felt more at ease than with a distant and omnipotent Judeo-Christian God. Thus, for a whole millennium, the Church was obliged to struggle with and to absorb and adapt many pre-Christian elements belonging to an agricultural and seasonal cult.

As Artz notes, "medieval men saw in the Old Testament a vast collection of stories. They accepted these stories without any feeling for their historical settings. They took these tales to their hearts, allegorized them, and meditated upon them." It was not only the Old Testament stories that were used. The writings and religions from classical Greece and Rome provided too tempting a storehouse of symbols to be ignored by Christian intellectuals.

Proof that these ancient fables were widely used can be judged by the amount of criticism directed toward members of the clergy who employed classical mythology to exemplify and also to simplify philosophical and religious ideas. One of the first Church Fathers to condemn the exploitation of "pagan" fable was St. Augustine. This renowned theologian stated in *City of God* that to use the classical mythologies to exemplify and praise, thus endowing them with a high spiritual significance, was "a shameful and miserable error [made] under cover of imparting a profound truth."

And another Church Father, St. Jerome, a contemporary of St. Augustine, related that while he was sleeping he had been reproached by Christ himself for being a better Ciceronian than a Christian.

A little later, in the seventh century, St. Eloy preached a sermon against the people's continuation of these idolatrous practices:

Before all things I declare and testify to you that you shall observe none of the impious customs of the pagans. . . . Let none regulate the beginning of any piece of work by the day or by the moon. Let none trust in nor presume to invoke the names of demons, neither Neptune, nor Orcus, nor Diana, nor Minerva, nor Geniscus, nor any other such follies. . . . Let no Christian place lights at the temples or the stones, or at fountains, or at trees, or at places where three ways meet. . . . Let no one presume to hang amulets on the neck of man or beast. . . . Let no one presume to make lustrations, nor to enchant herbs. . . . Let none on the calends of January join in the wicked and ridiculous things, the dressing like old women or like stags, nor make feasts lasting all night, nor keep up the custom of gifts and intemperate drinking. Let no one on the festival of St. John or on any of the festivals join in dances or leaping or diabolical songs. (Rohde)

Thus the mythologies, icons, and rituals of earlier centuries were assimilated into the homogeneous Christian religion. Such popular ceremonial influences had a powerful impact on the laity; while it was the literature of antiquity which was to transform the intellectual life of Christendom. For, at the same time that Christianity was being paganized and "paganism" was being Christianized, the languages and literature of the ancients were being carefully and innocently preserved by monks in the monastic scriptoria, where they laboriously copied the ancient texts of Greece and Rome.

After the final collapse of the Roman Empire, Greek learning all but vanished in the West. Those few scholars who had any knowledge of the language were limited to a pathetically small selection of available texts. Most of the Greek scholars followed the Christian emperor Constantine to the old city of Byzantium, where his insular empire became a repository for the civilizing elements of the East—producing a unique Asian and

Greek culture that continued the traditions of the ancient world, now largely lost in the Latin West. But the classical tradition that existed in the Eastern empire was "an incubus rather than a stimulant; classical literature was an idol, not an inspiration. Higher education was civilizing but not quickening; it was liberal but did not liberate." (Artz)

One of the few Western scholars in the early Middle Ages who had any knowledge of Greek was Anicius Boethius (c. 480–525). This brilliant individual was both politician and academician, well versed in Christian philosophy and other disciplines. Boethius translated into Latin most of Aristotle's logical treatises and a few Platonic writings. These intellectually precarious times received from Boethius most of what was then known about Greek philosophy. His self-appointed task was to render the entire works of Aristotle and Plato into Latin. Unfortunately, this project was cut short by his falling into disfavor with Theodoric, king of the Goths, and as a result he was imprisoned and subsequently executed in his forty-fifth year.

Boethius has been called the "last of the ancients" because of his extraordinary knowledge of the Greek language and Greek philosophy. After his death, an understanding of Greek virtually vanished in the West.

In times of controversy, when various Church conservatives objected to the study of classical writings, there was always some daring scholar on hand to allegorize and sublimate the overt sensuality and "paganism" of the literature into acceptable expressions of mystical Christian devotion. Such a man was Fortunatus, an Italian poet who lived most of his life in sixth-century Gaul. It was with Fortunatus that Latin poetry again blossomed. In Poitiers, where he was bishop of the city, he met Radegund, a Frankish queen. This monarch eventually became the object of his abject mystical devotion. His innovative verse, much of it written to honor Radegund, was the beginning of a style that would flower with the poetry and sagas of the troubadours of later centuries.

These versifiers and singers of song would "effect a change," writes C. S. Lewis (*The Allegory of Love*, Oxford: 1938), "which has left no corner of our ethics, our imagination, or our daily life untouched, and they erected impossible barriers between us and the classical past or the Oriental present. Compared with this revolution, the Renaissance is a mere ripple on the surface of literature."

One more scholar who must be mentioned in this survey of "pagan" influences upon Christian aesthetics is the acclaimed Spanish bishop Isidore of Seville, a man who greatly enriched the early centuries of Christianity. He was the paramount anthologer of his age, and over his long life he accomplished the fusion of both Christian and classical components.

The most famous of Isidore's writings was the encyclopedic *Etymo-*

*logiae,* a compilation that blended the entire known spectrum of Western knowledge into its pages. It was the quintessential summary of theology, art, and science of the early Middle Ages. The *Etymologiae* was tremendously influential. No library of any pretensions during the Middle Ages would have been without a copy.

According to the medieval historian Henry O. Taylor, Isidore "by reason of his own habits of study, by reason of the quality of his mind, which led him to select the palpable, the foolish, and the mechanical correlation, by reason, in fine, of his mental faculties and interests," assembled "a conglomeration of knowledge, secular and sacred, exactly suited to the coming centuries."

A third outstanding and influential work of the sixth century was written by the Latin grammarian Fulgentius. The *Mythologiae* consisted of seventy-five brief extracts from classical mythology, which were to be much used, admired, and quoted over the following centuries. During the twelfth century, a scholar commenting on Fulgentius wrote: "A reader is awestruck by the acumen of a mind which refers to the whole series of myths, philosophically related, either to the natural order or to man's moral life." (Seznec)

In the *Mythologiae,* Fulgentius condenses the most popular Latin fables, and provides for each one an interpretation that accords with Christian doctrine. In the well-known myth of the Judgment of Paris, for example, the three goddesses who are contesting for greatest beauty became symbols for the active, amorous, and contemplative life. In another, the three ages by which death enters the world—infancy, youth, and old age—are personified as Cerberus, the triple-headed dog who guards the entrance to Hades.

Thus a few renowned encyclopedists, notably Bede and Isidore of Seville, popularized and developed these mythologies during the early period of Christianity. Once established, this tradition continued into the Carolingian period, when the successor of Bede and Isidore, a scholar named Rabanus Maurus, inherited their immense task of compiling myriad histories and commentaries derived almost exclusively from Christian sources. Although Maurus valued classical learning, he condemned its religious aspects. "One should use the treasured experience and accumulated wisdom of the ancients," he wrote. "But one should shun their vain as well as their pernicious idolatries and superstitions." (Barnes)

The result of this marvelous, complex amalgam of vastly different mythologies and aesthetic traditions gave a unique impetus to the mentality and art of the late Middle Ages and Renaissance. We can be thankful to all of these medieval scholars, moralists, and theologians for the survival of the pre-Christian gods and values during the transient years of Christianity. These few scholars absorbed the classical gods into their writings, and in so doing they cleared the medieval conscience by sanctifying classical literature. As a result, Church doctrine became more flexible and more acceptable to the Christian laity as well as to the unconverted. This departure from the rigidity of Church doctrine into a greater flexibility and acceptance of alien icons and ideas not only enabled the early Church to survive but made its expansion far easier. And, as importantly from the iconographic point of view (though unwittingly achieved), the Church evolved into "a store house of the unconscious of the people—the lumber-room, as it were, in which were bygone, ancient, half-forgotten, half-formulated beliefs and superstitions, customs and folklaw. The authorities would seem to have been remarkably tolerant of these, and by countenancing such bric-à-brac the Church has effectively preserved to an astonishing degree a great deal of our ancient past." (Sheridan and Ross)

A few remarkable scholars and poets had preserved in the pages of their manuscripts a great heritage—one that would entrance and intoxicate artists of future centuries. These learned men not only recorded the rich philosophy, literature, and science of the ancient world, but its whole pantheon of gods, goddesses, and heroes. And with this noble entourage came a marvelous symbolic trove of magical animals, trees, plants, and monsters—many of which would make their startling appearance in artworks such as the Unicorn Tapestries.

By the twelfth century, when allegory became, as Seznec says, "the universal vehicle for pious expression," this accumulated classical knowledge and "mythological exegesis . . . grew to astonishing proportions." In fact, a mystic union of Christian and pre-Christian ideals began to take shape, producing a peculiar and fantastic visionary mentality.

One of the greatest theologians of the Middle Ages was Peter Abelard. A radical genius, Abelard was a great admirer and proponent of Greek thought. In what he knew of the philosophies of the Greeks, Abelard found all essential Christian doctrine, discovering to his own satisfaction God, the Trinity, and the Incarnation. His studies led Abelard to conclude that there were closer parallels between the Hellenic doctrines and the Gospel than existed between the Old Testament writings and the New Testament teachings. As a result of this research, he was to proclaim that it was unjust that the "pagan" thinkers should be denied eternal salvation simply because they had not known of Christ.

His visionary search for inner meaning and multiple interpretation, in both the scriptures and the literature of the ancients, was the beginning of new dimensions in academic thought. Abelard's declaration of the dialectic method ("I doubt in order to understand") marked the dawning of what his contemporary, Abbot Suger, described as the whole of the universe shining "with the radiance of delightful allegories." (Panofsky, 1971) Such mystical idealism heralded the beginning of a virtual mania for disguised and fantastic imagery and complex iconographies that would produce a rich symbolism in art.

The myths of the ancient Greeks and Romans were not only being written about but were also appearing on canvas and in stone during the High Middle Ages. Although these images of the gods had been drawn and painted for generations, by the eleventh century the classical deities were no longer depicted in classical attire. The gods were now clothed in what is best described as a type of Oriental costume that was part invented and part imagined. For example, in High Gothic art, Venus was often portrayed as a young lady of fashion, and presented by medieval artists either playing an instrument or smelling a flower. And when Jupiter was included in a composition, he was often depicted as a judge. Mercury suffered a similar fate, being transformed into a bishop or an old scholar. Even landscapes were anachronistic, especially in scenes drawn from classical stories. When Alexander the Great was represented in a High Gothic composition, for example, he was removed from his classical time frame and portrayed in the context of the medieval world.

The removal from their historical context and period made persons, events, and gods more accessible and familiar to a non-classical audience. In the art of both France and Italy in the twelfth and thirteenth centuries, there is a direct deliberate borrowing from classical motifs. The theme remains the same, but, as Panofsky states, we see in the art of this period the prototypical Hercules "dragging Cerberus out of Hades, used to depict Christ pulling Adam out of Limbo." The mind of the Middle Ages, as Panofsky explains, "being unaware of its historical distance from antique mentality, was consequently undisturbed by the idea that antiquity was a cultural cosmos concentrated about its own center of gravity. It was therefore capable of assimilating the classical elements artistically as well as philosophically and scientifically." (1962)

In the paintings, tapestries, sculptures, and narratives of the High Gothic period there appears a homogeneous mixture of history, fable, and myth. Indeed, it is impossible to tell where one ends and the next begins. Joseph Campbell has described this remarkable process—a cross-cultural amalgamation of mythologies and symbols—in a passage of great clarity:

With the passing of the gallant days of the great crusades, the artistic taste for verse romance declined. . . . Prose compendiums of traditional lore began appearing, filled with every kind of gathered anecdote and history of wonder— vast, immeasurable compilations, which the modern scholar has hardly explored. A tumbling, broad, inexhaustible flood of popular merry tales; misadventures; hero, saint, and devil legends; animal fables . . . riddles, pious allegories, and popular ballads burst abruptly into manuscript and carried everything before it. Compounded with the themes from cloister and the castle, mixed with elements from the Bible and from the heathenness of the Orient, as well as the pre-Christian past. This wonderful hurlyburly broke into the stonework of the cathedrals, grinned from the stained glass, twisted and curled from the humorous grotesque in and out of illuminated manuscripts, appearing in tapestries, on saddles and weapons, on trinket-caskets, mirrors and combs. This was the first major flowering in Europe of the literature of the people. From right to left the material came, to left and right they [sic] were flung forth again, sealed with the sign of the late Gothic, so that no matter what the origin, they were now the recreation of the European folk. (1969)

As Campbell stresses, it was during the High Gothic period that secular authors became fired with the inspiration to write books that would capture the earlier tales of magic and saints, unicorns and adventure.

Perhaps the most outstanding piece of literature of the thirteenth century, and one that will be mentioned in connection with the Unicorn Tapestries, is the epic poem entitled *The Romance of the Rose*. Begun by Guillaume de Lorris around 1237 and completed by Jean de Meun in about 1277, *The Romance of the Rose* is "like a Gothic cathedral, it includes the grotesque and the sublime, the profane and the sacred." (Dunn) Huizinga comments that the "pagan spirit displayed itself as amply as possible" in *The Romance of the Rose,*

not in the guise of some mythological phrases . . . but in the whole erotic conception and inspiration of this most popular work of all. From the early Middle Ages onward Venus and Cupid had found a refuge in this domain. But the great pagan who called them to vigorous life and enthroned them was Jean de Meum. By blending with Christian conceptions of eternal bliss the boldest praise of voluptuousness, he taught numerous generations a very ambiguous attitude towards Faith.

It was the development of such ambiguity in the later centuries of the Middle Ages, along with an increasing interest in classical mythology, that enabled the pre-Christian symbolism associated with the venerated oak to surface in late medieval art.

By the early sixteenth century, when the Unicorn Tapestries were created, the use of classical renditions and interpretations was a common practice in both Italy and France. As F. Funck-Brentano puts it: "We no longer find Christians writing of Christianity but Greeks of the time of Alcibiades, Romans of that of Cato. Paradise is once more Olympus, the saints are deities. When a poet describes a storm and the following calm, he summons Neptune and Aeolus, who calls the winds to heel and locks them securely in their kennel. Mars is the arbiter of battles, and the King of France fights like a Hercules. All the rest in the same vein."

For the Olympians and their kin, Fortuna's wheel had gone full circle. The ancient gods, heroes, animals, and plants—their stories and sacred lore—had survived by this remarkable process of assimilation, guise, and mystic allegory, along with an evolving widespread delight in fantastic imagery.

In this poetic and intellectual vortex, says Seznec, "profound symbolism, profound speculation, and gallant gestures were intertwined . . . and blended with legends from the old cosmologies. The painter's whole entourage, his clients and protectors, friends and advisors, formed a coterie of *littérateurs* and pedants, men who delighted in the spinning of far-fetched theory." Freed from Christian abstractions, the pantheons of Greece and Rome, the menageries and gardens of mythical flowers could once again appear as they had before the domination of Christianity—not as an adage or extrapolation of another religion, but as "realities" that could delight and influence artists, writers, poets, and philosophers by their own powers. By the second half of the fifteenth century, under the tutelage and guidance of this coterie of thinkers and artists, the mythic gods, animals, and plants were being interpreted as the inner core of an ancient cosmology, annexed with Christianity—but having its own centrality.

It had been a long and perilous journey for this rich and ancient symbolism, which had only managed to survive behind multifarious guises and through the apologetic reasoning of a few rare scholars. Huizinga stresses that "There is no real contrast between medieval allegory and Renaissance mythology. There is rather a fusion."

Originally, the mythic metaphors of classical times were used as innuendos for the edification of pre-Christian truth. On the other hand, Christian allegories were not simply moral abstractions of the gods; they brought the poetic and mystical aspects of such divinities to life, rendering them familiar, graceful beings. The fables of the gods did not change, but the cast of characters was replaced, so that a magical animal or venerated tree—stolen from its original pre-Christian owner—was relocated, and became a new attribute of Christianity, part of the Holy Family or one of the saints.

This allegorical current of the Middle Ages, far from ebbing, grew into an ever-widening river, engulfing in its onrush all that lay before it. At precisely this historical moment, the Unicorn Tapestries were conceived. That remarkable conception was in complete accord with the love of fantasy and the intoxication with classical myth that consumed the artists and patrons of the period.

In these early years of the sixteenth century, creators of enigmatic imagery flourished—those who delighted and tantalized brilliant or aspiring intellectuals, providing riddles and composing hieroglyphs understood by only a few. Gone were the days of valiant classical deeds, real or imaginary; past were the years of chivalry and chastened love so splendidly sung by the troubadours. This was the age of the versifiers, the composers of witticisms and cryptic messages, who flourished behind the potpourri of orthodox piety and "paganism." And it was this same generation that set its stamp upon the splendid images in the Unicorn Tapestries—those astonishing textiles produced in an age that was climaxed by the fusion of "pagan" and Christian icons.

From this vantage point, we can see the Unicorn Tapestries as far more than the depiction of the hunt of a fabulous beast—a creature that had haunted the human imagination for centuries. Nor, as some medieval scholars insisted, are the tapestries simply an allegory of Christ's death and ultimate resurrection. The Unicorn Tapestries are an amalgam of a much older and more intricate imagery. Thus, powerful ancient images provide the underlying meaning of the tapestries.

As Boccaccio maintained, myth has four layers of meaning: literal, moral, allegorical, and metaphysical. Each of these meanings must be investigated if the Unicorn Tapestries are to be properly understood.

# 4

## ICONOGRAPHY

## AND ITS

## MEANING

> True symbolism holds too large a
> place in medieval art to make it
> necessary to look for it where it
> does not exist.
> —Emile Mâle, *Gothic Image*

> Medieval man thought and felt in
> symbols, and the sequence of his
> thought moved as frequently from
> symbol to symbol as from fact to fact.
> —Henry D. Taylor, *The Medieval Mind*

W HEN VIEWING the Unicorn Tapestries for the first time, the experience is pervaded by a rich display of medieval imagery, excitement, and pathos. We encounter characters, animals, and flowers that look vaguely familiar, but astonish us by their strangeness. And ultimately these splendid tapestries evoke more questions than answers. Many people wonder why the unicorn is killed. Why is he depicted next to a fountain? Why is he chained to what looks like a pomegranate tree?

In order to answer these questions and many more, we have to go beyond the pictorial content and view the culture from which the Unicorn Tapestries emerged. Only when we know something of the rich symbolism that not only directed the lives of the people but had a profound effect upon their art will the world of the French pre-Renaissance become visible through its paintings and tapestries. Then and only then will we grasp the multitude of meanings and interpretations that have echoed through all the years since the Unicorn Tapestries were created.

Often, when we view dramas woven into tapestries or depicted in painted paradises in their gilded frames, we concentrate upon the decorative elegance and beauty. But, unfortunately, the symbolic interpretation of such works easily escapes us, for it exists in a historical and social context no longer accessible except through research. Long forgetfulness has made us see the abundance of plants and animals in early paintings and textiles as purely decorative emblems. This lost grasp of the original intention of the iconography in the art of the Middle Ages has deprived us of much of its meaning and emotion. One of the purposes of this book is to recapture the original metaphoric intent of these splendid images, and to reveal the iconographic impact of the brilliant age which saw their creation, reawakening in the modern viewer the vividness of their symbolic imagery. We must relearn something that has been lost for many centuries, the meaning and impact of deeply rooted icons—those symbols that Eliade calls "transconscious" images, ancient and fixed emblems that always remain aspects of the subconscious. Yet when such symbols become conscious, they are inevitably interpreted in the prevailing genre of each era.

We may expect little more than an effusive aesthetic pleasure from the arts of different time and different cultures unless we attain some comprehension of the icons which underline the society that produced them. As Don Cameron Allen points out: "Modern man, who has abandoned all allegory and invented his own private symbols, might not easily understand an imaginative mind of . . . centuries ago unless he knows its traditional symbolism."

In order to grasp the symbolic nature of the Unicorn Tapestries, we must turn to both ancient and medieval writings, the scriptures and the classics, which provide a basis for the rediscovery of doctrines and icons that we have lost. For example, we must recognize that in medieval art and literature saints and sinners, gods and goddesses were often symbolized by animals and flowers. "Close to the heart of the Middle Ages was its love for allegory and symbolism," comments Artz. "Behind every object and every event lay a spiritual implication of which the immediate experience was merely the imperfect reflection. God gave man two sources of knowledge, the Book of Scripture and the Book of Nature. Behind each are hidden meanings to be searched out; the universe is a vast cryptogram to be decoded."

Church doctrine of the Middle Ages conceived of good and evil as embodied in nature, animals, and plants, and eventually all natural elements were segregated into those that had good properties and those that had bad properties. The virtuous characteristics of flora and fauna were compared to Christ and his assembly, while all others were attributed to Satan and his wicked entourage. St. Basil explained this when he wrote in the *Exegetic Homilies* that "all poisonous animals are accepted for the representation of the wicked and contrary powers, for the Lord says: 'I have given you power to tread upon serpents and scorpions, and over all the powers of the enemy.' "

As "Christian" as this curious "natural history" of the animals and plants may seem, it actually originated long before the advent of Christianity, and may be discovered in the writings of such Greek and Roman naturalists and physicians as Aelian, Dioscorides, and Pliny. By the Middle Ages, this classical approach to science had turned into folklore. "The medievals cared not a whit to know anything about animals and plants for the sake of curiosity; they wanted to find in them something useful to the body or something profitable to the soul. They wanted folklore and they abhorred experiment." (Smith)

Symbolism based on imperfect observation, superstition, and theology was a central aspect of the art of the early Church. During the first two centuries of Christianity, pictorial representations of the fisherman and the shepherd, the dove, the fish, the ship, the anchor, and the lyre were common images. To complement this rudimentary pictorial decoration, the early Christians took over motifs from the debased Hellenic art—cupids bearing garlands, birds, grapevines, flowers, and all kinds of purely ornamental imagery.

This repertory of images proved very useful in elucidating the biblical Testaments and explaining Church doctrine. By the fourth century, Christian theologians were defining Creation as a symbolic act in which every person and event assumed a moral symbolism. As the art historian Mirella Levi D'Ancona says, they had "an authoritative source for this symbolic interpretation of the world in the Bible itself." (1977)

But of what advantage was this highly dramatic interpretation of a complex and abstract theology? The advantage was pedagogical: the use of images and icons were forms of visual parable, an expressive and direct means of communication with simple and largely illiterate people. A vocabulary of icons was used both to explain complexities of doctrine and to replace indigenous, non-Christian symbols.

As Christianity spread northward from the established Mediterranean centers, it took with it the oral tradition of the New Testament: the Christian mythology of miracles, of Christ restoring the dead, of his own resurrection, and the promise of eternal salvation for believers, as well as vivid descriptions of the hell awaiting those who refused conversion to the new faith.

H. R. Ellis Davidson comments that "The believer in the old religion would find a great deal in Christianity which would seem to him familiar and right. The idea of the dying god was already known to him from the fertility cults, and the lament for Christ's death on Good Friday followed by rejoicing in the Resurrection on Easter Day would follow a familiar pattern of death and renewal. The cycle of the Christian year was something to which he was already accustomed. Even the idea of God himself hanging upon a tree as a sacrifice was foreshadowed in the image of Odin upon Yggdrasill. Welcome also must have been the teaching that his new god would speak to him 'as a man speaks with his friend,' for he had grown up with the idea that it was natural to seek council from Thor or Freyr, or to visit the seeress who spoke out of trance, uttering words of wisdom from great powers to guide his steps in life."

In this newly established northern center of Christianity, a new symbolism developed. It was not invented, but was a complex amalgam of icons from many religions: "pagan" images that were salvaged from the collapse of the antique world, and symbols that had been absorbed into Christian iconography long before the missionaries ventured from their Mediterranean homelands. Into this symbolic vortex went the icons of the northern tribes, rudimentary Christian glyphs, and complex classical images—themselves a composite borrowed from many mythologies.

The symbols that form the pictorial basis of medieval and Renaissance art are derived from rich and diverse cultures, each giving and taking from the other in such a way that it is difficult to see where one starts and the other ends. These images come from the Judeo-Christian writings of the Bible, the Apocrypha, and the Christian theses of the Church Fathers. The non-Christian sources include classical and northern mythologies, as well as early "scientific" texts comprised of both real and imaginary plant and animal descriptions from antiquity.

John Speirs points out that the medieval people must have been "taught to see and, by way of the symbolism, to think and feel largely by means of the paintings and sculptures in the churches. These images in color, stone and wood were an essential part of their visible and . . . imaginative world, and are mostly allegorical or symbolical, multiplex in meaning. The symbols are often highly sophisticated and elaborate, some in forms (such as the Tree and the Wheel) of ancient types, having a long and involved cultural history. By means of these symbols, and with the aid of the preachers who expounded them, the audiences . . . must have been made accustomed to symbolism and expert at symbolical, not merely literal, interpretation. The medieval mind must have been filled by these images and symbols, and shaped by them."

To clarify this wealth of Christian and non-Christian imagery, we must explore its numerous sources in ancient, classical, and medieval literature. This trove of vivid writings provided a unique symbolism that has become an integral part of European culture—so intrinsic, as a matter of fact, that the significance of such symbolism has often lapsed from our consciousness.

THE BIBLE

The Bible has a wealth of parables, many of which incorporate plant and animal metaphors to provide a moral interpretation. For instance, wormwood, a bitter herb, symbolizes injustice and false doctrine. Hence in the book of Deuteronomy, we read: "Lest there should be among you a root that bearest gall and wormwood." (Deuteronomy 29:18) The herb's bitter taste accounts for wormwood being associated with gall as a symbol of calamity and sorrow. In another example, the Book of Amos reads: "ye have turned judgment to wormwood, and leave off righteousness in the earth." (Amos 5:7)

In some instances, plants may be part of a story, as in the case of the gourd that is described in the Book of Jonah: "And the Lord God prepared a gourd, and made it to come up over Jonah, that it might be a shadow over his head, to deliver him, from his grief. So Jonah was exceedingly glad of the gourd." (Jonah 4:6) Because of this particular biblical myth, the plant became a symbol of salvation and resurrection. If the gourd occurs in medieval and Renaissance art, then there is a good probability (depending on its juxtaposition with other symbols) that it is intended to convey forgiveness and rebirth. Its appearance is neither casual nor purely decorative.

In the Bible there is a whole menagerie that provides a basis for allegorical interpretation. Sometimes animals have more than one interpretation. For instance, the lion stalking its prey was analogous to Satan searching for lost souls: "Your adversary the Devil, as a roaring lion, walketh about seeking whom he may devour." (1 Peter 5:8) On the other hand, because of this animal's majesty, power, strength, and courage, Christ was called "the lion of the Tribe of Judah, the Root of David." (Revelation 5:5)

Besides deriving allegory from the animals and plants of the Bible, medieval scholars also believed that the numbers mentioned in the Testaments could divulge secrets. According to this doctrine, the numbers mentioned in the scriptures were connected to the mystic and mathematical science of the universe, and were therefore of great significance. (This is a subject of sufficient importance to be discussed later under a separate subheading.)

## THE APOCRYPHA

These religious writings were an intrinsic part of the medieval scriptures. The Apocrypha from the Old Testament originated as part of the literature contained in the Greek version of the Jewish Bible, the holy book used by the early Christians in their teachings and devotions. This Greek Bible contained all the apocryphal writings that are associated with the Old Testament. The stories of Tobit, Judith, and Susanna were part of the scriptures contained in this non-orthodox version of the Jewish Bible. About A.D. 400, St. Jerome translated the Greek scriptures into Latin, and finding that the orthodox Hebrew Bible did not contain these stories, he called them *Apocrypha*—meaning hidden or secret books. St Jerome's translation became the Vulgate or Authorized Bible, the holy text that was to be used in Western Christendom for the next thousand years. It was not only the Old Testament that contained apocryphal writings. The later gospels, epistles, and apocalypses: stories from the Gospel of James, pseudo-Matthew and pseudo-Melito texts, were also part of the apocryphal writings that were loosely connected to the New Testament. As we shall see, the Christian Apocrypha affords much material for the interpretation of the Unicorn Tapestries.

These biblical supplements provided very explicit iconography. For instance, to make Mary aware of her impending death, we read in the Gospel of pseudo-Melito that the archangel Gabriel presented the Virgin with a palm branch. "And behold, the Angel stood before her. . . . Here, he said, is the palm branch that I brought to you from the paradise of the Lord." (D'Ancona, 1977) The Apocrypha offers an abundance of such emotionally charged symbols.

## CHRISTIAN EXEGESES

These theological writings produced by the early churchmen had an enormous influence on the Middle Ages, becoming a source of authority almost on a par with the scriptures. The Church Fathers believed that by meditation on tangible objects and personages, a greater understanding of the universe could be achieved. The first Christian to voice this idea was St. Augustine, when he said in the *Epistolae:* "Apt similitudes often lead our thought from visible to invisible things." (trans. D'Ancona, 1977)

Mysticism and metaphorical ideology occur throughout Augustine's writings. In one instance he compares Christ's death on the Cross to a marriage bed: "Like a bridegroom, Christ went forth from his chamber, he went out with a presage of his nuptials into the field of the world. He ran like a giant exulting on his way and came to the marriage bed of the cross, and there in mounting it he consummated his marriage. And when he perceived the sighs of the creature, he lovingly gave himself up to the torment in place of his bride, and joined himself to the woman forever." (Campbell, 1969)

## CLASSICAL MYTHOLOGY

Images from classical mythology were one of the first sources of icons to be exploited by the emerging Christian faith. This vast storehouse of images was quickly and eagerly absorbed into the Christian religion. The ancient writings were a major inspiration for scholars and poets alike, extending their influence on art, theology, and philosophy from the early

Middle Ages to the Renaissance. For example, a perennial classic with both the clergy and the laity was Ovid's *Metamorphoses,* one of the most widely read Latin works in western Europe during the Middle Ages. In Ovid's pages were demigods, heroes, and mortals transformed into animals and birds, plants, and trees, as well as rivers, streams, and mountains. In the hands of medieval artists these magical metaphors would find their way from the pages of Ovid into stone, onto canvas and tapestry.

## NORTHERN MYTHS

As Christianity penetrated into the remote regions of the north, the missionaries came into contact with religions that were drastically different from those existing in the warmer regions of the south. Permanent communication between these two cultural regions occurred only after the sixth century, when Christian refugees fled to the remote northern territories of the Empire to escape the "barbarians" that were descending upon Rome.

By the next few centuries, Western Christianity had established a precarious foothold in central and northern Europe, and its policy of converting the numerous "pagan" tribes that were native to the region flourished. These early missionaries employed symbolism as a method for explaining their doctrine and beliefs. They made effective use of a symbolic language that was a powerful tool of Christian conversion—such as the use of images like the cross and the lamb to illustrate Church doctrine. These simple Christian glyphs were accepted by the northern "pagans" because they could readily add their own beliefs and religious iconography to the fundamental imagery of the Christian missionaries.

As Christian myths met head-on with strong northern imagery, Christianity was to undergo a mutation. It had to contend with the heroes and sagas of the old religion, which stayed alive in the hearts of the people even after their conversion to the new faith. Holy grails replaced magical cauldrons of inspiration and fertility; the "pagan" land of Avalon became the mythical realm where King Arthur ventured; and although suitably carved into rough stone crosses, the ancient veneration of large stones persisted. These northern lands produced works of art like *The Book of Kells,* which—though a Christian text—was embellished with images that had been alive in the imagination of the non-Christian Europeans for centuries. Biting, clawing, and snapping monsters, having nothing to do with the Christian traditions, decorated the margins of *The Book of Kells.* This symbolism was uniquely northern and an intrinsic part of the rich Celtic cosmology. *The Book of Kells* could not have been produced by an eighth-century Byzantine scribe, nor by any other monks of the period. It was the northern land—with its harsh climate, distinct seasons, and unique mythologies, gods, and heroes—that ultimately supplied the alloy for the Christian mold.

## CLASSICAL BOOKS ON SCIENCE AND NATURAL HISTORY

The major classical writings on science and husbandry known to the Middle Ages included the *Natural History* of Pliny, *The Nature of the Universe* by Lucretius, Aelian's *On the Characteristics of Animals*, and the agricultural treatises of Varro and Columella. These ancient texts provided botanical and zoological information, both real and imagined, and each author expanded his narrative with interesting myths and legends. Precious insights into Greek and Roman life were absorbed into the medieval writings, giving rise to further symbolism in the encyclopedias, bestiaries, and herbals of the Middle Ages. For instance, when Pliny wrote of the peony, he considered it a plant with supernatural properties that "prevent the mocking delusions that the Fauns bring on us in our sleep." (Vol. VII, Book XXV)

Many influences from ancient writers were adopted by medieval and Renaissance authors, who transformed such material into fable in the service of Christianity. In the writings of the medieval author Bartolomeo Ambrosini, for example, the peony became one of the herbs of salvation, a protector from evil.

## HERBALS

A medieval herbal was a treatise on the plant kingdom, but it also dealt with the medical properties of animals, stones, minerals, and other organic substances. The term "herbal" was not in common use until the sixteenth century; in the medieval period, "herbals" were much less specialized. Frank Anderson, the curator of Rare Books and Manuscripts of the New York Botanical Garden, has pointed out that herbals were something like medieval natural histories, "not limited to their medical and botanical content. . . . [But they contain] tracts on animals, and trace superstitious practices to their origins in Rome, Greece, and the Orient. Because they are such rich repositories of learning, lore, history, and exploration, they present a close-up view of the manners and beliefs of the Classical and medieval worlds." (1977)

Classical fables, superstitions, and lore became part of the oral tradition in the West, and much of this material was fortunately preserved in the pages of the medieval encyclopedias and herbals. A small herb called *aron*, *draconitum*, or in modern Latin nomenclature, *Arum dracunculus*, is one example of this. Pliny describes the properties of this herb in his *Natural History*, saying that "serpents are kept off if the body is thoroughly rubbed with aron in oil of bay. For this reason it is also considered beneficial for snake-bites if one takes aron in a draught of dark wine." (Vol. VII, Book XXIV) Centuries later, the Englishman Bartholomaeus Anglicus, using Pliny's lead, wrote in his own compilation, *De Proprietatibus Rerum,* that "draguntea [*Arum dracunculus*] . . . driveth and chaseth away serpents with the smell, and a beast that is bawmed [anointed] with the juice thereof, shall not be hert of a serpent." (1582) As we shall see, because of the antiviperous properties of this plant, its image was symbolically used in one of the panels of the Unicorn Tapestries.

In the fourteenth century, a German bishop, Conrad von Megenberg, wrote the *Buch der Natur* (*Book of Nature*). Similar to the encyclopedic layout of Bartholomaeus' work, Von Megenberg's book includes many subjects of both a spiritual and a secular interest. The following segment on finches is a combination of natural history and religious interpretation:

It is a great wonder that the bird sings so beautifully although it feeds on the sharp spines of the thistle. It is thus a symbol of the good preacher on earth who has to endure greatly, yet even among the thorns of this world joyfully serves God. O, God . . . Thou art well acquainted with meals of thorns; yet thou too hath sung on earth unto the bitter death. (Freeman)

Beside the "herbals," a wealth of botanical and animal symbolism from the Middle Ages is found in the pages of the *Hexameron,* a book written in the fourth century by St. Ambrose, in addition to the material in the sixth-century *Etymologiae* of Isidore of Seville, in the ninth-century *De Universo* of Rabanus Maurus, in the eleventh-century *Gregorianum* of Garnerus St. Victor, and in the fourteenth-century *Repentorium Morale* by Petrus Berchorius. The first three of these medieval authors will be extensively quoted in the sections dealing with the Unicorn Tapestries.

## BESTIARIES

By the end of the twelfth century, a new form of popular book had developed under the generic name of "bestiary." These compendia, in keeping with the encyclopedic mania of the period, absorbed into their pages nearly all known ancient and medieval animal lore. To the stories of beasts, allegorized tales of stones and plants were added. The bestiaries contained fables that originated in Hebrew myths as well as the mythologies of India and Egypt. These tales passed into Greek and Roman folklore, poetry, and art. Then "scientific" writers such as Pliny, Ctesias, and Aelius handed down many of these legends to the early Christian world. They were mixed with the mystical commentaries of the early Christian writers to become a collection of morality tales of animals, plants, and stones—a conglomeration of natural history, fables, legends, and mythology shaped to convey an understanding of the scriptures and conduct of a good Christian.

One book, called the *Physiologus,* was immensely popular throughout the medieval period. It symbolically associated the natural habits and traits of birds and animals with the heroic struggle between the Christian forces of good and evil—a battle which greatly preoccupied the theatrical mentality of medieval theologians. As Curley says: "The anonymous author of the *Physiologus* infused these venerable pagan tales with the spirit of the Christian world and mystical teachings, and therefore they occupied a place of special importance in the symbolism of the Christian world." The *Physiologus* provides one of the most important iconographic interpretations for the animals woven into the Unicorn Tapestries.

## ETYMOLOGY

Symbolism is sometimes based upon etymology, especially from the Latin and Greek, in addition to the major European languages. For example, the Latin for both apple and evil is the word *malum,* a pun that was responsible for the frequent selection of an apple tree as the symbol of the Fall in both medieval and Renaissance art. In Greek, the name for a carnation, *dianthos,* translates as "the flower of God"—hence artists and iconographers of the Middle Ages used this delicate flower to portray Christ's Crucifixion. (D'Ancona, 1977)

## NUMEROLOGY

Frequently occurring numbers in biblical and classical literature were interpreted by thinkers of the Middle Ages as profound, and deserving special consideration. It was believed that specific digits and binumerals governed the whole spectrum of life and religion. As the French historian Emile Mâle stresses, medieval scholars of this period "never doubted that numbers were endowed with some occult power . . . St. Augustine considered numbers as thoughts of God. 'The Divine Wisdom is reflected in the numbers impressed on all things.' . . . The science of numbers, then, is the science of the universe, and from numbers we learn its secret." One of the main characteristics of medieval iconography is its "obedience to the rules of a kind of sacred mathematics. Position, grouping, symmetry and numbers are of extraordinary importance."

From the study of the literature of St. Augustine, theologians designated the numeral twelve to represent the universal Church. The ecclesiastical line of reasoning was based upon Christ having twelve disciples. The clergy argued that twelve is the multiple of three and four, three being the number of the Trinity and four the number symbolizing the elements (earth, air, fire, and water).

Thus in the iconography of the Middle Ages, specific numbers and their multiples play a vital symbolic role "in this reduction of the diversity of the universe to unity," as Seznec comments. "In many cases, the relations established between the themes dear to medieval learning are purely numerical. Like the twelve Prophets and the twelve Apostles, the seven celestial spheres and the seven gifts of the Holy Spirit, the four Elements, the four or seven Ages, the nine Worthies and the nine Muses lend themselves to symmetrical treatment, to balanced combinations which seem, after the fact, to bear testimony to profound inner relations, and to manifest a secret harmony between the truths of the faith and those of nature and history. This 'sacred mathematics,' a renewal of Pythagoras, would itself account for the integration of mythology in the encyclopedic system of knowledge."

The number seven was regarded as the most mysterious of all numbers, being composed of four (the numerical digit of the body) and three (the number of the soul)—an image of the Trinity. According to this system and the rules of sacred geometry, seven is the number of humanity, and all that relates to man is ordained in a series of sevens. Human life is divided into seven ages; the seven planets govern human destiny; and the seven ages of man are under the influence of one of the planets.

The twelve signs of the zodiac were connected with specific parts of the body. All of these celestial influences were correlated with the four elements, the four humors, the four qualities, the four winds, and the four seas. "No branch of medieval thought entirely escaped this interest in number symbolism; it affected theology, science, literature, art and music." (Artz)


PLANT FOLKLORE

A great abundance of interpretive material was available to medieval iconographers. They were surrounded by the visual arts of the great masters: all their lives they heard the oral folklore of the people, and could read the various manuscripts and books that had become a storehouse of icons, symbols, and myths since the collapse of Rome.

Since prehistory, plants had been intrinsically involved in man's religious customs and rituals, as well as in his medical practices and eating habits. This relationship between humanity and plants was complex: medieval man believed that the mind and spirit was as much nourished by plants as was the body. The subtle and dramatic, conscious and unconscious ideas and images of flora helped to produce a unique visual art—the art of the High Gothic and Renaissance.

In all the great iconographic art of the Middle Ages, the evocative colors of flowers held special meaning. The untainted white of the Madonna lily elevated it to a paramount position among floral symbols, while the sorrow that pierced the Virgin's heart became, according to the Christian iconographers, transfixed as the red drop at the center of the wild cyclamen. By extension, the ideas and values as well as the virtues and vices portrayed in early works of art are represented in a wide spectrum of flowers and trees, depicted by artists not merely for their visual beauty but also for their metaphoric significance.

Equally important was the medical use of plants. From the medieval period to the Renaissance, the herbs of the field provided the main remedies for a range of afflictions and diseases. This knowledge of herbal medicine passed from generation to generation, evolving into vivid aspects of both religious and artistic mythology. For instance, it was widely believed that the touch of a magical tree or plant had the same mystical effect as the touch of a sacred relic of a saint, which presumably brought the supplicant in direct contact with the heavenly spheres. In many cures as well as curses, a tactile bond between humans and plants had to be made. Thus the flora itself was strongly interwoven with the lives and destinies of the people.

Some plants had a deadly touch. In northern mythology, an arrow of mistletoe fashioned by the evil god Loki was instrumental in the death of the Nordic hero Balder. Frightened nymphs, like Daphne and Menthe, escaped amorous pursuers by being transformed into plants. And just as incense placated the pre-Christian gods, so the aroma of scented and narcotic flowers evoked in the human mind strong visions of joy and mysticism. The touch of Christ, through drops of his blood upon the crucifix, brought new foliage to the withered "Tree of Life," an important observation, as we shall see in later sections. A strongly scented flower that was popular in medieval art and that often appears in the Unicorn Tapestries is the pink, or carnation. The smell of this simple blossom is much like the aroma of cloves. Cloves are shaped like small nails, so they became symbols of the Crucifixion; because of its similar smell, the carnation in turn was closely associated with the Crucifixion.

The disguised symbolism of the late Middle Ages can be understood by examining a biblical event that provided inspiration for generations of artists. In an address to the Virgin, Simeon prophesied the Crucifixion and Mary's agony: "A sword would pierce through thy soul also." (Luke 2:35) As Erwin Panofsky points out, the artist of the thirteenth century would depict the fulfillment of this prediction by showing the "Mater Dolorosa, her heart transfixed by a sword." When in later centuries artists like Dürer "wished to allude to the same prophesy, [they] showed the Madonna in the happiness of her motherhood, overshadowed by a big iris the ancient name of which was gladiolus, or 'sword-lily.' " (1971)

The development of iconographic tradition in the West makes it clear that the inclination to view the art of the late medieval and Renaissance period for its aesthetic pleasure alone is not enough; we need to interpret the images with specific relevance to the contemporary iconography. At the same time, we must ask ourselves just how much imagery in a particular composition the artist and designer intended to be symbolic. This is no easy question. As Panofsky has suggested: "If every ordinary plant, architectural detail, implement, or piece of furniture could be conceived as a metaphor, so that all forms meant to convey a symbolic idea could appear as ordinary plants, architectural details, implements, or pieces of furniture: how are we to decide where the general, 'metaphorical' transfiguration of nature ends and actual, specific symbolism begins?" (1971)

To demonstrate his point, Panofsky calls our attention to an early fifteenth-century Flemish masterpiece by Robert Campin, *The Mérode Altarpiece* (Fig. 7). Noting the Madonna lilies that are so conspicuously placed in this painting, he states:

the pot of lilies is perfectly at ease upon its table, and if we did not know its symbolic implications from hundreds of other Annunciations we could not possibly infer from this one picture that it is more than a nice still-life feature. . . . [Yet] we are safe in assuming that the pot of lilies has retained its significance as a symbol of chastity; but we have no way of knowing to what extent the other objects in the picture, also looking like nice still-life features, may be symbols as well. There is, I am afraid, no other answer to this problem than the use of historical methods tempered, if possible, by common sense. We have to ask ourselves whether or not the symbolic significance of a given motif is a matter of established representational tradition (as is the case with the lilies); whether or not a symbolic interpretation can be justified by definite texts or agrees with ideas demonstrably alive in the period and presumably familiar to its artists (as is the case with all those symbols revolving around the relationship between the Old and the New Testament); and to what extent such a symbolic interpretation is in keeping with the historical position and personal tendencies of the individual master. (1971)

To further develop this complex point, we might notice that in the same painting, *The Mérode Altarpiece*, Joseph is depicted making mousetraps. These unobtrusive objects are also found in other paintings, such as Lorenzo Lotto's *Nativity* (National Gallery of Art, Washington). But why are mousetraps important in religious art? The art historian Meyer Schapiro discovered the explanation in an ecclesiastical sermon by St. Augustine: "The devil exulted when Christ died, but by this very death of Christ the devil is vanquished, as if he had swallowed the bait of the mousetrap. The cross of the Lord was the devil's mousetrap." (Quoted in Friedmann, 1980)

Figure 7. Robert Campin, *The Mérode Altarpiece*, c. 1425. The Cloisters, Metropolitan Museum of Art.

The problem of interpretation is always a complex one in art. In order to grasp the original significance of images, we must, as Mirella Levi D'Ancona points out, "know the line of thought behind each symbol depicted by the artist, and, to interpret the symbol correctly, we must establish a certain congruence between the thought and the object depicted. To do this, we must examine the context in which the object is placed. Symbols are often ambivalent, the same object meaning sometimes one thing and sometimes another, and even sometimes its opposite. To find among the many contradictory ideas the one that applies to our particular case is not an easy matter. Moreover, in the case of plant symbolism, as in many visual symbols, we must establish whether an artist chose a certain plant, flower, or fruit because of its particular hidden meaning or rather because it made a pretty picture." (1977)

The late Curator Emeritus of The Cloisters, Margaret Freeman, discussed this problem of interpretation with specific reference to the Unicorn Tapestries. "There can be no doubt that a large number of the plants in the tapestries relate to the religious and secular themes of the Hunt of the Unicorn . . . many of these were undoubtedly mysterious even in their own day, for medieval people, especially in the fifteenth century, delighted in cryptic letters, secret ciphers, and devices to be understood by a few persons only." Miss Freeman suggests that it would be unwise to assume "that all of the many [iconographic] meanings were in the minds of the seigneur who commissioned the tapestries, the designer who drew the tapestries, and the weaver who wove them so expertly and lovingly. But it would be equally unwise to assume, as some have done, that except for a very few symbolic plants, the trees were to be enjoyed by the medieval viewer for their decorative values only."

Panofsky believes that the art historian must "make adjustment by learning as much as he possibly can of the circumstances under which the objects of his study were created . . . he will also compare the work with others of its class, and will examine such writings as reflect the aesthetic standards of its country and age . . . he will read old books on theology or mythology in order to identify with its subject matter. . . . He will observe the interplay between the influences of literary sources and the effect of self-dependent representational traditions, in order to establish a history of iconographic formulae or 'types.' And he will do his best to familiarize himself with the social, religious and philosophical attitudes of other periods and countries, in order to correct his own subjective feelings for content. But when he does all this, his aesthetic perception as such will change accordingly, and will more and more adapt itself to the original 'intention' of the works." (1955)

To interpret the Unicorn Tapestries, we need to follow Panofsky's directive by emerging ourselves in the world that produced these remarkable textiles. We must consider the time and place of conception, the overall iconography, the major motifs in each of the tapestries, and the prevailing social, religious, and philosophical attitudes of the period that produced them.

## SOCIAL, RELIGIOUS AND PHILOSOPHICAL ATTITUDES

By the early sixteenth century, the secular patronage of the artist had greatly increased, and his education improved along with his status in the community. This resulted in a much greater freedom of choice of subject matter in compositions, and a much wider use of symbolism. The Church was no longer the dominating authority as it had been in the thirteenth century—a period when artists had an official system of iconography. Along with the diminishing of Christian faith and the lessening of ecclesiastical bonds came a change in European architecture. This was to have a great effect upon all the fine arts. Architects in the stable and secularized society of the fifteenth and sixteenth centuries no longer had to design huge communal churches and military fortifications. They now could turn their energies to the creation of private, princely homes.

For architects at the end of the fifteenth century, the major ideal was the creation of beauty. With the building of these elegant new houses, there arose an increasing demand for art that would adorn the massive walls with grandeur. The late fifteenth- and early sixteenth-century painter could respond to the prevalent taste of the time by utilizing humanistic and classical subjects rather than religious ones, painted in a way that showed that beauty was worth cultivation for its own merits, rather than simply as a universal language for the propagation of the faith. This situation gave artists a wider and less restrictive range, permitting the creation of secular works instead of paintings totally concerned with religious topics.

The artists of this period were more cultured and better educated than their forerunners. Their close proximity to the humanists brought about a heightened interest in the classics. As a result, the ancient myths of Greece and Rome exerted an ever-increasing influence upon their works. Thus the Renaissance was not merely a rebirth of art. Art was never stronger or more significant than in the centuries just preceding the Renaissance. As Herbert Read stresses, the period witnessed "the paganization, the secularization of an art too vital any longer to submit to religious control. Just as the philosophy of this same period shows the slow emancipation of reason from the control of supernatural dogma, so art is emancipated from ecclesiastical control. It may be used to express an individual religious sentiment, but that will not be its exclusive function. The whole realm of nature is thrown open to the artist, and there he may wander free to select and idealize and portray what he will." (1966)

If the overall iconography in a work of art points to a single interpretation, then it is likely that the buildings, animals, and plants have the same iconographic thought. And if the identification and interpretation of animals and plants provide a logical framework, then we may assume that the artist used the flora and fauna depicted in the composition to enhance the overall symbolic intention.

When a designer or artist places one emblem predominantly in a work of art, it seems very possible that the particular emblem was selected for its symbolic connotations. For instance, in the Unicorn Tapestries the orange (in the fifth tapestry) and the pomegranate (in the seventh tapestry) were chosen because they are both connected with fertility. The accompanying flora and fauna of these two panels support this theme of fecundity. A certain number of trees and plants, especially the oak and the holly, occur in nearly all the tapestries. These have specific iconographical meaning that provides a cyclical calendar for the seven panels of the Unicorn Tapestries.

It should be made clear that some of the original significance of the emblematic flora and fauna of medieval art has largely been lost, much as the implications of the ritual dances of the Middle Ages (hopscotch, ring-around-the-rosy, and so on) have been forgotten. Therefore we may speak in the same ethnographic terms when dealing with art of the Middle Ages as we do when discussing the iconographic implications of the culturally alien arts of Africa, Oceania, or the Orient. What this means is that research into the meanings of many of the plants and animals is difficult insofar as such information is not always available to us. Where written sources of data concerning the imagery of early tapestries, paintings, sculpture, love caskets, and other artworks is meager, we must rely on folklore. In fact, the folk name of a plant can carry many of its explicit folk uses and beliefs. Folkloric methodology will be used a number of times in this book for the symbolic interpretation of some of the plants woven into the Unicorn Tapestries. It is both essential and inevitable that the ethnosymbolism of early and medieval Europe should finally find its way into the interpretation of medieval art.

The later Middle Ages delighted in complex symbolism, using one image to convey two totally conflicting interpretations or to convey both a secular and a religious significance. For instance, in the second Unicorn Tapestry the lion represents such a paradox, symbolizing both the sin of pride and Christ's resurrection. Thus the lion is seen as the "devil" and the "divine."

The symbols are often influenced by their juxtaposition. As Don Cameron Allen says, "when the same animal companions another beast or attends a human being, one or more of its symbolic attributes rubs off on its associate. The other creature may alter the lion's quality as easily as the lion changes that of the other creature. The meaning may be also shifted by posture, color, ornament, implement, garment, or the fashion in which garments are worn. When to this individual or group motion is applied, allegory begins; and when some other symbolic figure or figures are the object of this motion, allegory merges into myth. At this point since sustained allegory cannot be maintained for long, literalism enters and myth is created."

There are, however, limits to iconographic interpretation. An icon that has existed for many centuries may acquire a different meaning with the passage of time; and if the meaning survives, it may be conveyed by a different visual interpretation. In the High and late Middle Ages, when borrowing from classical sources, sculptors, painters, tapestry weavers, book illuminators, and printmakers almost always presented classical figures in non-classical forms. Erwin Panofsky, the expert iconologist, terms this phenomenon the "principle of disjunction," and presents the following argument: "whenever . . . a work of art borrows its form from a classical model, this form is almost invariably invested with a non-classical, normally Christian significance: wherever in the high and later Middle Ages a work of art borrows its theme from classical poetry, legend, history or mythology, this theme is quite invariably presented in a non-classical, normally contemporary form." (1969)

In concluding this brief survey of iconography, it is helpful to keep in mind Emile Mâle's remark about artists of the Middle Ages, who "took everything in a literal sense," and in whatever media they worked, "loved to clothe the most abstract thought in concrete form."

The Unicorn Tapestries are considered by many art historians to be the finest surviving series of pictorial textiles from the late fifteenth and early sixteenth centuries, not only in their technical achievement but also in their diversity of imagery and the subtlety of their symbolism. The whole series of tapestries conveys visible traces of a brilliant, emblematic medieval mysticism: a product of its particular time and place. The rich and varied icons that abound throughout the Unicorn Tapestries need explanation, although more than once they have been dismissed simply as "decorative motifs." Doubtless the aesthetic appeal of the plants and animals is great, but it is unlikely that they were made as mere embellishments. Not only was considerable time spent in selecting the iconography, but the images chosen would not, upon closer examination of their individual meaning, make much apparent sense in scenes depicting the hunt, capture, death, and resurrection of a unicorn.

"Renaissance artists," says Sir Kenneth Clark, "by combining symbols, wove elaborate, complicated allegory into these pictures . . . the elements of a picture made not only a unit of design but contain a unity of meaning, sometimes not immediately recognizable."

In fact, as we shall discover, the symbolism of the Unicorn Tapestries is a superb fusion of the pre-Christian concepts with those of Christian mysticism.

# MYTHS OF DEATH

# AND RESURRECTION:

# THE OAK KING,

# THE HOLLY KING,

# THE WILD MAN,

# AND CHRIST

The Lion-sun flies from the rising
Unicorn moon and hides behind the
Tree or Grove of the Underworld;
The Moon pursues, and, sinking in
Her turn, is sunslain.
—Robert Brown

I was brought up a Catholic, and it
didn't take me long to recognize that
there were deaths and resurrections,
virgin births, and all those other
familiar motifs of mythology.
—Joseph Campbell

SOME YEARS AGO, when I was a lecturer at The Cloisters, I was struck
by the predominance of certain species of trees, especially oak and holly,
in the Unicorn Tapestries. Perhaps the most perplexing observation, and
the one that needs most clarification, is that the oak and the holly assume
a central, significant place in most of the tapestries. A similar situation is
true of the arboreal motifs of another important late Gothic set of tapestries
entitled "The Lady with the Unicorn."

After exhaustive study of unicorns in medieval art, an interesting pictorial relationship became apparent between the capture of this exotic animal and the depiction of specific trees. So fundamental is the symbolism
linking the unicorn to trees that we must explore this remarkable relationship, for it suggests an association between various myths of death and

resurrection, as well as the annual cycle of the seasons, with the drama of the hunt, capture, death, and resurrection of the unicorn.

According to medieval texts, a unicorn could only be captured by a virgin, who had to entice the beast into her lap. This pacified him, so that he could be easily killed or captured. After studying numerous examples of medieval art that depict the capture and killing of unicorns, a curious fact began to emerge. In many instances the coup de grâce is delivered by an armed hunter, hiding or concealed under the leafy boughs of an oak tree (Figs. 8, 9, and 10). But before attempting any explanation for this curious association between the unicorn and the oak, we must digress to consider the general importance of the oak to both pre-Christian and medieval people.

The early Indo-Europeans revered the oak as the paramount tree in the forest. So entrenched was the oak in their cultural cosmos that by the Middle Ages the oak had become the tree of kings, and was immortalized in cathedrals, and was carved on benches, portrayed in stained glass windows, and painted in the margins of Bibles and books of hours.

Sir James Frazer's monumental study, *The Golden Bough,* was not published until the end of the nineteenth century. It preserved a reservoir of European folklore and mythology, much of which is connected with the "religious awe" that has long surrounded the oak tree. For this reason I will quote and paraphrase extensively from Frazer.

The central theme of his landmark study is an explanation of the legend of the "Golden Bough," a myth that was first recorded by Virgil in *The Aeneid.* The hero of this epic breaks a branch from a sacred tree before descending into the underworld. This bough grows upon a special tree that is part of the sacred grove of Diana at Aricia. The priest of the grove is a man who has accomplished two things: breaking a branch of the "Golden Bough" and then slaying the earlier priest. In *The Golden Bough,* Frazer posits that the sacred grove consisted of oaks, and that the "Golden Bough" itself was the golden green mistletoe that grew upon these trees. This parasitical mistletoe was given great reverence by the ancients because it grew upon the venerated oak and also because it was green in winter when the oak lost its leaves.

To grasp the immense importance of the oak to pre-Christian Europeans, we must understand that "long before the dawn of history, Europe was covered with vast primaeval woods, which must have exercised a profound influence on the thought as well as on the life of our rude ancestors who dwelt dispersed under the gloomy shadow or in the open glades and clearings of the forest. Now, of all the trees which composed these woods the oak appears to have been both the commonest and the most usefull." Thus, it was natural enough that the oak should loom so large in the religion

Figure 8. Oak depicted beneath speared unicorn. Marginal decoration, Ormesby Psalter, early 14th century. Oxford, Bodleian Library.

Figure 9. Unicorn being killed by man hidden in oak tree. French enamel, 14th century. Munich, Bayerisches Nationalmuseum.

Figure 10. Ivory casket (end panel). Paris, mid-14th century. Metropolitan Museum of Art.

of a people who "lived in oak forests, used oak timber for building, oak sticks for fuel, and oak acorns for food and fodder." (Frazer, 1911)

From earliest times, the oak has been an icon of strength. Because of this fact, Zeus, Jupiter, and Thor all were identified with the oak, a tree that became their sacred emblem. As fathers of their respective pantheons, these three "rain" deities had exclusive rights to wield the fearsome thunderbolt. The fact that the oak is a natural lightning conductor was taken as a manifestation of that power.

To an agrarian society, trees were manifestations of the gods, and therefore both trees and deities became identified with the various seasons of the year. For instance, the oak came to represent the time of year when the days begin to lengthen and brighten, after the darkness of winter. The "defeat of winter" led to spring, when Zeus, Jupiter, and Thor released the fertile rains on the barren winter landscape, making the earth green and sprinkling it with flowers. These special months that herald spring commence after the winter solstice in December. It is the time in the solar year when the sun has passed its lowest point and begins to ascend to its zenith at the June solstice, when the oak blossoms. To the primal people of Europe, this midsummer flowering supported the relationship of the oak with Zeus, Jupiter, and Thor. The spring/summer cycle is followed by the winter, or waning cycle, when the power of the sun weakens and the great solar body descends to its lowest point at the December solstice. Since the seasons were closely connected with various trees, the oak became identified with the fecund period. The worship of the oak was very widespread; even in Palestine the reverence given by non-Semitic peoples to the oak is condemned in the Old Testament: "But ye shall destroy their altars, break their images, and cut down their groves." (Exodus 34:13)

The book of Hosea is more specific about what sort of trees were revered by the idolators: "They sacrifice upon the tops of mountains, and burn incense upon the hills, under oaks, poplars, and elms." (Hosea 4:13) The visionary Isaiah, speaking of the coming of the Messiah's kingdom, singles out the oak as exemplifying the wicked of Israel—those who worship other gods beside Jehovah: "For they shall be ashamed of the oaks which ye have desired, and ye shall be confounded for the gardens that ye have chosen." (Isaiah 1:29)

The oak was not the only venerated tree. To a primal agrarian society, the sight of evergreen trees like the holly during the winter months must have been a striking contrast to the naked oaks. But why was such widespread importance given to the holly, especially considering that the forests of Europe had many other evergreen trees, such as pines, fir, and juniper. It is not enough to note that holly was the most outstanding evergreen in the winter forest. There is, however, a very simple explanation for the reverential attitude toward holly, once we recognize that it is a tradition inherited from the attitude toward a holly-like plant of the south.

In the Mediterranean region, where the Hellenic and Latin religions evolved, there is an indigenous type of evergreen oak called the *kermes*, or holly oak (Fig. 11). This holly oak bears a leaf that is almost identical to the foliage of the northern European true holly. In classical times and long thereafter, the Mediterranean peoples revered the holly oak because—unlike the deciduous oak—it remained green during the winter months. From this pre-Christian sanctity of the Mediterranean holly oak came a diffusion of influences from the south, resulting in the same reverence for the look-alike hollies of northern Europe. The people there, however, did not differentiate between the holly and the evergreen oak, but considered the holly to be the winter counterpart of the deciduous, summer oak. This seasonal contrast, and the fact that the holly flowers after the oak, made holly the symbol of the waning year and the oak's seasonal successor.

Neither holly nor oak originally had any connection with Christianity, but they were gradually absorbed into the lore that surrounded the life and death of Christ. The holly was a tree that since earliest times had been considered to have "manna," or power. Pliny, in the first century A.D., wrote that "a holly tree planted in a town house or a country house keeps off magic influences . . . and a holly stick, cast at any animal, even if . . . it falls short of the quarry, will of its own accord roll nearer the mark, so powerful is the nature of this tree." (Vol. VII, Book XXIV) This advice was

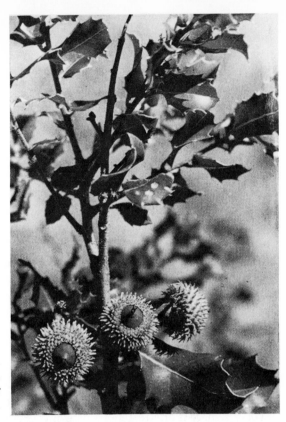

Figure 11.
*Quercus coccifera* L.
Kermes Oak or
Holly Oak.

carried down through the centuries. John Parkinson, in his 1640 herbal *Theatrum Botanicum*, writes that "the branches with berries are used at Christ-tide to decke our houses withall, but that that should defend the house from lightning and keep themselves from witchcraft, is a superstition of the Gentiles, learned from Pliny."

In the Middle Ages, these adages were not considered fictitious, but were regarded as true insights into the miraculous powers of holly. One medieval poem warns of the dangers that will befall anyone who harms this special tree:

> Here comes the holly that is so noble
> To please all men is his intent
> But Lord and Lady of this hall
> Who so ever against holly do call
> Who so ever against holly do cry
> In a loop shall he hang full high
> Who so ever against holly do sing
> He may weep and his hands wring.
> —Chambers, 1966

The name "holly" is derived from the Anglo-Saxon "holegn" and from the old Norse "hulfr." From the latter word arose the Middle English name that was used by Chaucer, "hulver." It was a simple matter for the Church to change the name of this evergreen to comply with the Christmas season or "holy season." (Incidentally, holly had been employed centuries before Christianity as a festive decoration. The bright winter foliage was widely used by the Romans during their December Saturnalia.) The natural physical characteristics of holly aided subsequent Christian symbolists. To them, the white flowers signified Christ's purity; the red berries became drops of his blood; and, of course, the thorny leaves were identified with the crown of thorns. Also attesting to holly's major importance as a Christian symbol is the medieval *Holly-Tree Carol:* "Of all the trees in the green wood, the holly bears the crown." And finally, the fact that holly is ever-green added to its capacity to inspire awe.

Behind the seasonal cycle and the veneration of both the holly and the oak was an ancient European religion that focused much of its symbolism upon fertility. In agrarian societies, trees portrayed the seasons and were identified with the "earth mother" in her three roles: bride, mother, and crone. These aspects of the pre-Christian Mother Goddess were represented by spring, summer, and winter. In the earliest matriarchal societies, the earth mother was often embodied as a priestess. And the oak and the holly were regarded as two Divine Kings, one representing the waxing half and the other the waning season. In the societies where they existed, these Divine Kings, and priestess's consorts, were alternately sacrificed on midsummer and midwinter days. The legacy of the two divine trees outlived the Mother Goddess cults, but her influence was still strongly felt in medieval Europe despite her demise.

It was Frazer's controversial opinion that the great Mother Goddess was "the personification of all the reproductive energies of nature . . . worshipped under different names but with a substantial similarity of myth and ritual by many people of Western Asia. Associated with her was a lover, or rather a series of lovers, divine yet mortal, with whom she mated year by year, their commerce being deemed essential to the propagation of animals and plants, each in their several kind; and further, that the fabulous union of the divine pair was simulated and, as it were, multiplied on earth by the real, though temporary, union of the human sexes at the sanctuary of the goddess for the sake of thereby ensuring the fruitfulness of the ground and the increase of man and beast." (1911)

Many of our primal ancestors believed that the well-being of the people and, even more important, the safety of nature itself were inextricably connected with the life of one of the seasonal kings. And, as such, it was proper that the people took the utmost care of his life, and in so doing believed that they ensured their own well-being. "But no amount of care and precaution will prevent the man-god from growing old and feeble and at last dying." (Frazer, 1911) To primal societies that were matrilineal and in which Divine Kingship was integral, this realization of mortality posed considerable concern, for these people believed that the course of nature was dependent on the man-god's life. They were fearful of what great calamities might result from the gradual weakening of his vitality and powers. Frazer points out that there was only one way "of averting these dangers. The man-god must be killed as soon as he shows symptoms that his powers are beginning to fail, and his soul must be transferred to a vigorous successor before it has been seriously impaired by the threatened decay." Therefore, it is "necessary to put the king to death while he is still in the full bloom of his divine manhood, in order that his sacred life, transmitted in unabated force to his successor, may renew its youth, and thus by successive transmissions through a perpetual line of vigorous incarnations may remain eternally fresh and young, a pledge and security that men and animals shall in like manner renew their youth by a perpetual succession of generations, and that seedtime and harvest, and summer and winter, and rain and sunshine shall never fail." (1911)

At the sacred oak grove at Nemi, it is generally believed that the king was held to be an incarnation of a tree spirit—the spirit of vegetation. Such a position, in the view of his worshippers, would have endowed him with the divine powers of fertility over crops, fruits, and animals. Based on these beliefs, it would have been natural that in the ritual dramas designed to defeat winter and bring back spring, the emphasis would be placed upon vegetation and fertility. Thus in these magical enactments trees and plants figured more predominantly than beasts and birds. Yet the vegetable and the animal, the two sides of life, were not disconnected in the minds of those who participated in these ceremonies. Indeed, they generally believed that the connection between the animal and the vegetable kingdoms was even closer than it is in reality. Because of this belief, people often combined the representation of the revival of plants with a real or ritualistic union of the sexes, in an effort to influence the fecundity of animals, fruit, and human beings. The principles of life and fertility, both animal and vegetable, were inseparable.

These fertility festivals in ancient Europe took place in spring and summer. Such reenactments were not simply symbolic or allegorical rituals—rustic dramas performed to amuse or instruct a pastoral audience. Rather, they were homeopathetic (imitative) rituals, performed by mummers (actor/mimes), and intended to make the woods verdant, the grass sprout, the barley and wheat germinate, and the flowers bloom. It was proper to presume that "the more closely the mock marriage of the leaf-clad or flower-decked mummers aped the real marriage of the woodland sprites, the more effective would be the charm." (Frazer, 1911)

In spring, early summer, and on midsummer day, it was a widespread custom in the Middle Ages* to go out into the forest, fell a tree, and carry it into the village, where amid much general rejoicing it was erected upon the green. In some instances, the people cut down branches in the woods and attached them to every dwelling. The purpose of these customs was to lure home to the village, and to each house in the community, the benevolence of the tree spirit.

This tree spirit, like the spirit of all vegetation, was believed in these societies to be manifest in the Divine King. And as already mentioned, the death of the king of the woods was therefore considered necessary to avoid his physical decline into old age and to ensure the fertility of nature. This was a necessity because these people upheld the idea that the king was mortal as well as divine. Although he was held in great awe as the very personification of a god, the mortal representation of the oak spirit and of Zeus himself, the Divine King could not hope for the miraculous rejuvenation and resurrection of which only the gods were capable. Thus the king in these cultures attained immortality by passing his powers to a succession of Divine Kings, whose powers were transmitted from one to another at the prime of life. Then they were sacrificed. In this way, these ancient primal European cultures hoped to ally themselves with the powerful gods of fertility.

Such a god was Adonis of Greece. This ancient Mediterranean deity was associated with death and the decay of nature in autumn, and also with its mysterious revival in spring. Adonis, like his later, European counterpart, who was personified as the king of the woods, was the partner of an immortal "Mother Goddess." These people believed that both Adonis and his mortal counterpart had to die in order to preserve the reproductive powers of nature.

The widespread motif of a "dying god," or vegetation deity, who is sacrificed or sacrifices himself for the benefit of mankind, is basic to the seasonal motifs of agrarian societies. Seasonable change is mirrored in a dramatic and mythological interpretation of the landscape: the goddess mourns the death of her lover in the autumn and rejoices at his return in the spring. This earth mother is the triple goddess, representing the three stations of the year, spring, summer, and winter, personified as bride, mother, and crone. Demeter and her daughter Persephone are identified with these three stations of the year. Both goddesses are "the personification of the corn." (Frazer, 1911)† The mother, Demeter, represents last year's

* In some rural parts of Europe, the custom still persists today.

† The corn mentioned in the text is not the Indian maize of the Americas, but European grains such as barley, rye, oats, and principally wheat.

corn, and her daughter, Persephone, the corn of the present year.

According to mythology, Persephone is both bride and crone. This dualistic nature is accounted for by the fact that the young goddess was abducted by Hades, and although finally rescued by the intervention of Zeus, Persephone had been tricked into eating some fruits that were growing in the underworld during her captivity. As a result of ingesting these pomegranate seeds, the goddess had to remain six months with Hades in the gloomy regions of Dis, and in this station she is a crone, the death aspect of the winter. Then in the spring, Persephone becomes the bride again when she returns to the earth. As Frazer writes, Persephone is "the goddess who spends three or, according to another version of the myth, six months of every year with the dead under the ground and the remainder of the year with the living above ground." In her absence, fields lie bare and fallow. When the divinity returns in the spring to the upper world, the grain pushes up from the soil and the earth is verdant with foliage and blossoms. Thus the goddess is "nothing else than a mythical embodiment of the vegetation, and particularly of the corn, which is buried under the soil for some months of every winter and comes to life again, as from the grave, in the sprouting cornstalks and the opening flowers and foliage of every spring." (Frazer, 1911)

Many scholars believe that Persephone's annual death and Demeter's mourning is a mythological account of seedtime and harvest. Long after the decline of Greece and its religious rites, a variation of this agricultural drama—the annual cycle of death, decay, and rebirth—was reenacted by Europeans as an act of sympathetic magic in which the Oak King was the personification of vegetation and of the fertile earth.

The successor of the Oak King was the Holly King. The Middle English poem *Sir Gawain and the Green Knight* can help us to understand this transformation from the symbol of oak to the symbol of holly. *Sir Gawain and the Green Knight* is a fourteenth-century poem that has its origins in Celtic mythology, and it provides an invaluable insight into the relationship between the evolution of the kings of the oak and the holly as European spirits of vegetation. In this epic poem, Sir Gawain, as mythologers point out, fights "a holly King, the Green Knight (a winter deity)." (Jobes) The whole adventure is set in a winter landscape. Commenting on *Sir Gawain and the Green Knight*, John Speirs, Professor of English at the University of Exeter, states that this particular literary work is "clearly a mid-winter festival poem. The seasonal theme is the poem's underlying, and indeed, pervasive theme."

By the twelfth century, Celtic myths were well known on the continent due to their constant retelling by Welsh-speaking Breton knights. The fables were adapted by the troubadours of the aristocratic French courts, and became enormously popular as oral romances. They extolled the knightly virtues of courage, devotion to duty, charity to the weak, and generosity to peers.

Frederick Artz points out that these romances "centered on the stories of Charlemagne . . . on the tales chiefly of Celtic origin and on subjects like King Arthur, Parsifal, or Tristan and . . . the whole mythology and history of Greece and Rome from the Trojan War down, all mixed together. The first chivalric romances were written in northern France in the twelfth century, in the same area in which Gothic art was arising. From there the new styles of literature and art spread until they reached Iceland, Norway, and Ireland, and, to the south and east, Spain, Italy, and the Holy Land. . . . The richest vein for romances proved to be the body of Celtic stories, especially those about Arthur and the Round Table. These legends have only slight historical foundation in events of the fifth and sixth centuries in England and in Brittany. They had been elaborated in Ireland and Wales and mixed with ancient Celtic tales, the whole having been given a strong coloring of Christianity and of magic: the grail, for example, was originally a heathen talisman in an Irish fairy palace, and finally it became the cup out of which Jesus drank at the Last Supper."

In *Sir Gawain and the Green Knight,* the Green Knight of the title is an immortal giant who wields a club made of holly. The Green Knight and Sir Gawain "make a compact to behead one another at alternate New Years—meaning mid-summer and mid-winter—but, in effect, the Holly knight spares the Oak Knight." (Graves, 1966)

This dramatic antagonism between the oak and the holly knight occurs in numerous instances in medieval literature, in poems, ballads, and carols. In the medieval ballad *Sir Gawain's Marriage,* King Arthur goes on a journey. He comes over a moor, where he sees a lady seated "between an oak and a green hollen [holly]. . . . This lady, whose name is not mentioned, would have been the goddess Creiddylad for whom, in Welsh myth, the Oak Knight and the Holly Knight fought every May first until Doomsday. Since in medieval practice St. John the Baptist, who lost his head on St. John's Day, took over the Oak King's titles and customs, it was natural to let Jesus, as John's merciful successor, take over the holly-king's." (Graves, 1966)

Another medieval poem, *The Quest of the Holy Grail,* tells how Hector has a dream in which he and Lancelot set off on horseback to search for the Grail. They "wandered for many days till Lancelot fell from his horse, struck down by a man who stripped him of all he wore. And when he stood naked the man arrayed him in a robe all spiked with holly, and set him on an ass." (Trans. Materasso)*

In Sir Thomas Malory's *Le Morte d'Arthur,* one of the knights of Arthur's

---

* During the Roman Saturnalia, an ass was sacrificially killed with a holly club.

court, Sir Marhaus, fights with a powerful giant. Sir Marhaus first sees the giant "under a tree of holly, and with many clubs of iron and gisarms [battle-axes] about him." The knight kills the giant and releases twenty-four knights and twelve ladies from the giant's dungeons. The killing of the giant and the release of the knight and ladies is an allegory of driving away winter, the holly giant. The males and females released from the castle of winter are a metaphor for the appearance of verdure in the spring. The giant is not killed by the knight's sword: "For the giant was a wily fighter, but at last Sir Marhaus smote off his right arm. . . . Then the giant fled and the knight took after him, and so he drove him into water. . . . And then Sir Marhaus made the Earl Fergus' man to fetch him stones, and with those stones the knight gave the giant many sore knocks, till at the last he made him fall down into the water, and so was he there dead."

Sir James Frazer, in a chapter of *The Golden Bough* entitled "The Killing of the Tree Spirit," states that "the effigy of death is drowned by being thrown into the water," and he cites numerous examples of this "drowning ritual" in folk ritual. Frazer continues: "the carrying out of death is generally followed by a ceremony, or at least accompanied by a procession, of bringing in summer, spring or life."

The anonymous fourteenth-century author of *Sir Gawain and the Green Knight* describes a battle between Gawain, the Oak Knight, and the Holly Knight. This encounter is symbolically central to the theme of death and resurrection and its association with the concept of vegetation deities, which is why *Sir Gawain and the Green Knight* is worth examining in some detail. The poem provides a remarkable insight into the survival of pre-Christian rituals which, under Christian allegorical cover, survived in medieval literature. (All the following extracts from *Sir Gawain and the Green Knight* are drawn from the modern translation of Brian Stone.)

The poem begins in the New Year, "The year being so young that yester-even saw its birth." The New Year is being celebrated at Camelot with a feast, and the whole court sits down to a banquet. These joyful revelries continue uninterrupted until the Green Knight arrives unannounced, making a dramatic entrance amid the lively company:

When there heaved in at the hall door an awesome fellow

--------

That he was half a giant on earth, I believe;
Yet mainly and most of all a man he seemed,

--------

Men gaped at the hue of him
Ingrained in garb and mien,

A fellow fiercely grim,
And all a glittering green.

- - - - - - - -

About himself and his saddle on silken work.

- - - - - - - -

Embossed and embroidered, such as birds and flies,
In gay green gauds with gold everywhere.

- - - - - - - -

Yet hauberk and helmet he had none,
Nor plastron nor plate-armour proper to combat,
Nor shield for shoving, nor sharp spear for lunging;
But he held a holly cluster in one hand, holly
That is greenest when groves are gaunt and bare,
And an axe in his other hand, huge and monstrous,
A hideous helmet-smasher for anyone to tell of;
The head of that axe was an ell-rod long.
Of green hammered gold and steel was the socket,

- - - - - - - -

The assembled folk stared, long scanning the fellow,
For all men marvelled what it might mean
That such a horseman and his horse should have such a colour
As to grow green as grass, and greener yet, it seemed,

- - - - - - - -

For astonishing sights they had seen, but such a one never;
Therefore a phantom from Fairyland the folk there deemed him.
So even the doughty were daunted and dared not reply.

Silence reigned in the great hall until King Arthur welcomed this
strange knight and asked the uninvited guest his purpose. The Green Knight
replies:

"Sir, I crave in this court a Christmas game,

- - - - - - - -

As to strike a strong blow in return for another,
I shall offer to him this fine axe freely;
This axe, which is heavy enough, to handle as he please.
And I shall bide the first blow, as bare as I sit here.
If some intrepid man is tempted to try what I suggest,
Let him leap towards me and lay hold of this weapon,
Acquiring clear possession of it, no claim from me ensuing.
Then shall I stand up to his stroke, quite still on this floor—

So long as I shall have leave to launch a return blow
Unchecked.
Yet he shall have a year
And a day's reprieve, I direct.
Now hasten and let me hear
Who answers, to what effect."

Of all the assembled knights, it is Sir Gawain who takes up the challenge:

Then Gawain at Guinevere's side
Bowed and spoke his design:
"Before all, King, confide
This fight to me. May it be mine."

And the Green Knight bends his head so Sir Gawain can deal the blow with the ax.

On the ground the Green Knight graciously stood,
With head slightly slanting to expose the flesh.
His long and lovely locks he laid over his crown,
Baring the naked neck for the business now due.
Gawain gripped his axe and gathered it on high,

- - - - - - - -

And slashed swiftly down on the exposed part,

- - - - - - - -

The fair head fell from the neck, struck the floor,

- - - - - - - -

Blood spurted from the body, bright against the green.
Yet the fellow did not fall, nor falter one whit,
But stoutly sprang forward on legs still sturdy,
Roughly reached out among the ranks of nobles,
Seized his splendid head and straightway lifted it.
Then he strode to his steed, snatched the bridle,
Stepped into the stirrup and swung aloft,
Holding his head in his hand by the hair.
He settled himself in the saddle as steadily
As if nothing had happened to him, though he had
No head.

- - - - - - - -

For he held the head in his hand upright,
Pointed the face at the fairest in fame on the dais;
And it lifted its eyelids and looked glaringly,

And menacingly said with its mouth as you may now hear:
"Be prepared to perform what you promised, Gawain;
Seek faithfully till you find me, my fine fellow,
According to your oath in this hall in these knights' hearing.
Go to the Green Chapel without gainsaying to get
Such a stroke as you have struck. Strictly you deserve
That due redemption on the day of New Year.
As the Knight of the Green Chapel I am known to many."

So far, the narrative of *Sir Gawain and the Green Knight* has taken place in the dead of winter, just one day after the midwinter solstice: "The year being so young that yester-even saw its birth." The Green Knight holds in one hand a holly bush, described as "greenest when groves are bare."

John Speirs makes some extremely insightful observations on the characters presented in this Middle English poem. The Green Knight, states Speirs, has a green beard which "is like a bush, and together with his long green hair covers his chest and back all round down to his elbows." He carries a branch of holly "in one hand . . . and in the other a huge axe (a thunder weapon, like Thor's hammer). He is as green as green verdure. It would indeed be singular not to feel that he is an up-cropping in poetry of the old vegetation god."

According to Speirs, the first section of the poem describes "the indestructibility and perpetual renewal of life. Arthur's castle is placed in history as one of the phoenixes of Troy, the utterly destroyed city—'The battlements broken down and burnt to ashes'—from which so many new cities and kingdoms of the Western World have sprung. . . . The youthfulness of Arthur and Arthur's folk—'For this fine fellowship was in its fair prime'—introduces the theme of youth in contrast to age which is an aspect of the spring–winter (or New Year–Old Year) theme. The poem thus launched is sustained right through as a Christmas–New Year festival poem."

The symbolic association of green in the poem refers to "the color of spring and vegetation," and when verdure is combined with gold ("Of green hammered gold . . ."), it becomes "symbolic of youth." (Stone, 1959) The sacrifice of the Divine King, as we have already seen, took place not during his declining years but at his prime. These are the major attributes of ancient and pre-Christian fertility gods. They are also the attributes of the highly disguised vegetation deities of Christian mythology.

There is, however, still another mythic guise in which the vegetation deity appeared in the Middle Ages. Ultimately, the Holly Knight is transformed into a mysterious and rather bizarre form, known as a "Wild Man." This manifestation becomes clear when we consider that the Green Knight's coloration, strength, energy, and especially his hairiness, "incline us irrevocably to think of two common medieval types, one an outcast and the other a rural deity. The Wild Man of the woods . . . was often an outlaw who had taken to the woods and then developed sub-human habits and the fierce unpredictable behaviour of a wild beast. The Green Man, on the other hand, was a personification of spring." (Stone, 1959).

These two creatures, the "Wild Man" and this "Green Man" mentioned by Brian Stone, were not only clearly linked but in European folklore were often interchangeable. Quite apart from all their other similarities of appearance and manner, the Holly Knight also carries a club of holly while the Wild Man is described as carrying an uprooted tree. Clearly the Green Man relates to the Holly Knight and to the entire dramatis personae of vegetation deities; while the Wild Man apparently represents a fiercer and more Dionysian form of fertility and unbounded nature.

In his book *The Wild Man,* Timothy Husband points out that the "wild habitat, hairiness, supernatural powers, and wanton raucous behavior" of "sirens, fauns, centaurs, satyrs, and other woodland demons and deities . . . were inherited by the medieval Wild Man."

The Green Knight, Holly King, and the Wild Man are all the same person. The Green Knight's offer to let any knight behead him, in return for the promise that he will be able to reciprocate the deed twelve months hence, is interpreted by mythologers in the following way: Gawain is an oak knight, a sun hero, and the Green Knight is the Holly King—a winter deity. The pact and subsequent beheading of the Green Knight represents the reign of the Oak King, and a battle between winter and summer—seasons that "regularly behead each other." (Jobes) Thus the Green Knight (the verdure of winter, like mistletoe) and Gawain (the Oak King and summer) are the personifications of the alternate seasons of fertility.

Many scholars are of the opinion that with the passage of time, a gradual change overtook the fertility knights, the Divine Kings, and the consorts of the Mother Goddess. Exercising a greater power, the male principle embodied in the king is able to alter his status quo. No longer is the inevitable sacrifice acceptable to him. A substitute victim is found in the form of a stranger, a child, or a slave. This "temporary king" was given a mock reign for a few days, then underwent the sacrifice needed to placate the gods and ensure the fertility of the land. Still later an animal substitute, or "scapegoat," was used in the sacrifice—hence the modern significance of that term.

Human sacrifice became a symbolic rather than a literal act. The scapegoat replaced the Divine King as an offering. Ceremonies were drastically changed. And yet the mythic purposes of the ritual sacrifice of a vegetable god to assure abundance persisted throughout the Middle Ages: in symbolic literature, in rural pre-Christian practices, and (as we shall see) even in the metaphor of Christ's sacrifice on the Cross.

Because the withering and decay of vegetation in winter was readily interpreted by many primal people as the weakening of the spirit of vegetation, the decapitation of the Green Knight was a ritual necessity. It was believed in these societies that the spirit of the knight who represented abundance and fertility had grown old and weak; to reverse this process, the mortal personification of the vegetation god had to be slain and then brought back to life in a younger and more vigorous person. Thus the killing in spring of the representative of the Divine King, the Holly Knight, or the Wild Man—all of whom symbolize tree spirits—was regarded as a means to promote and quicken the revival of vegetation. "For the killing of the tree-spirit is associated always (we must suppose) implicitly, and sometimes explicitly also, with a revival or resurrection of him in a more youthful and vigorous form." (Frazer, 1911)

In the same ceremonial context, we may now grasp that the beheading of the Green Knight by Sir Gawain completes the solar year with the death of winter at the end of the waning cycle. The Green Knight, according to the story, miraculously survives the decapitation and carries away his own head. Thus many researchers believe that the whole drama mirrors the annual death and rebirth of nature in a vigorous literary form.

John Speirs sums up this argument: "The Green Knight whose head is chopped off at his own request and who is yet as miraculously or magically alive as ever, bears an unmistakable relation to the Green Man—the Jack in the Green or the Wild Man of the village festivals of England and Europe. He is in fact no other than a recrudescence in poetry of the Green Man." Who the Green Man is is well established. He is the "descendant of the Vegetation or Nature god of (whatever his local name) almost universal and immemorial tradition whose death and resurrection mythologizes the annual death and re-birth of nature."

In other medieval romances, Sir Gawain is connected with the quest for the Holy Grail. He appears in some versions as the knight who heals the sick "Fisher King" (fertility), the result of which inevitably leads to the regeneration of the "Waste Land" (winter). The task of Gawain in his role as sun hero is to be the agent who revives spring, restoring the frozen land to its former verdure—symbolically removing the curse of impotence from the listless and wounded "Fisher King." Jessie Weston is the renowned authority in this field, and she is particularly perceptive when she points out that the sun hero (spring) "played the role traditionally assigned to the Doctor, that of restoring life and health to the wounded or sick representative of the spirit of vegetation." (1920) In other words, he is the personification of spring.

In many parts of Europe a pantomime still exists in which a Wild Man is chased out of the woods, killed, then is restored to life by one of the mummers acting as a doctor. After his miraculous resurrection, the Wild

Man is bound and paraded around the village. Frazer compared this vernal ritual with those that took place at Nemi in classical times. As we shall see, in the Unicorn Tapestries the unicorn, like the Wild Man of the woods, is captured, killed, and then resurrected.

The Wild Man had another important anthropomorphic quality. People believed that they could transfer misadventure, natural calamity, and evil forces to some object, whether plant, animal, or human. This became a new use of the "scapegoat." Thus more than declining fertility could be cast out through a surrogate. Evil was first transferred to the scapegoat and then he was killed. The sacrifice of the Wild Man took place after the death of nature had been transferred to him. The evil of old age and barrenness died with him; the powers of fertility were reborn in a new king.

In the spring festivals, the Wild Man became a scapegoat for the ill-fortunes that daunted the prosperity of the people. "His terrifying nature made him the focus of a broad range of anxieties and, in the folkloric context at least, the scapegoat for unexplained calamities or quirks of nature. Frustrated farmers often blamed failed crops on the rampages or supernatural machinations of the Wild Man." (Husband)

Christ, like the Wild Man, was a symbol and icon of fertility and fecundity. Christ was seen by the people of the Middle Ages as the hero who after his death upon the Cross descends into the underworld and harrows Hell, then leads the imprisoned hordes of virtuous and penitent to restored life in Paradise. Christ's close association with Dionysus and Adonis—gods who return to the earth with the spring verdure—is contained in a medieval carol of divine mystery. Here the nativity of Christ is likened to the germination of grain:

> On Christ's day, I understand
> An ear of wheat of a maid sprang,
> Thirty winters on earth to stand,
> To make us bread, all to His pay.
> —Rickert

The unicorn, like Christ, was ritually killed and then miraculously resurrected. Both figures are associated with the waning year, with the Holly King as well as the Wild Man. The Mother Goddess was also transformed—into Mary, the mother of Christ. All these powerful and mythic figures represent the spirit of vegetation, which is sacrificed at the New Year or at the rites that celebrate the defeat of winter.

The unicorn itself is a lunar creature, and as such it constantly fights with the solar lion. As Odell Shepard points out, the unicorn is "most readily associated with the new or crescent moon, which might indeed seem to dwellers by the sea to be leading the stars down to the water and to dip its own horn therein before they descend. The crescent moon has been used for ages to represent both celestial motherhood and virginity, whether of Ishtar, Isis, Artemis, or the Madonna. . . . Old alchemical charts commonly designated the figure of Luna by placing in her right hand a single horn."

Yet the lunar unicorn is in perpetual conflict with the solar lion. One of the oldest reports of their antagonism occurs in the early Greek translation of the Hebrew Bible (known as the Septuagint), in which an immense mythic beast called a reem is identified with a unicorn. In one Hebrew tale of the young King David, he leads his father's sheep up what he thinks to be a mountain, but which is in fact a huge sleeping reem. Suddenly the monster awakes and starts to rise to its feet. "David clasped the reem's right horn, which reached to heaven, praying: 'Lord of the Universe, lead me to safety, and I will build You a temple one hundred cubits in span, like the horns of this reem.' God mercifully sent a lion, the King of Beasts, before whom the reem crouched in obeisance. Since, however, David was himself afraid of the lion, God sent a deer for it to pursue. David then slid down from the reem's shoulder and escaped." (Graves, 1963)

There is a set of tapestries at the Cluny Museum entitled "The Lady with the Unicorn" which not only invoke the rivalry of the unicorn and the lion, but make a clear symbolic association between the unicorn and the holly tree on the one hand, and the lion and the oak tree on the other. The curator of the museum, Alain Erlande-Brandenburg, mentions that some scholars, such as Mme Reynaud, have recently tried to attribute "The Lady with the Unicorn" Tapestries to an "artist whom she calls the 'Master of Anne de Bretagne' . . . [and] she believes him to be responsible for the models of the most famous tapestries of the end of the century: 'The Perseus' (private collection), 'Illustrious Women' with 'Penelope' (Boston), 'Life of the Virgin' (Cathedral of Bayeux), the Cluny tapestry, and, above all, the famous tapestries in The Cloisters Museum representing 'The Hunting of the Unicorn.' Mme Souchal has repeated and amplified these conclusions in her study of this artist, whom she named 'The Master of the Hunting of the Unicorn.' "

Both the Unicorn Tapestries and "The Lady with the Unicorn" Tapestries have the oak and the holly tree as major motifs, and these two trees are presented as major emblems. Five of the six panels of "The Lady with the Unicorn" have been identified as corresponding to the five senses. In the panel ascribed to "Sight," the Lady is set between a lion sitting under an oak and a unicorn placed under a holly tree (Fig. 12). This imagery summons to mind the woman in a medieval ballad who sits "between an oak and holly." It is my opinion that in both the Unicorn Tapestries and

Figure 12. "The Lady with the Unicorn." "Sight" tapestry, about 1500. Paris, Musée de Cluny.

"The Lady with the Unicorn" Tapestries, the Oak King (who is synonymous with the sun, with the waxing year, and with the lion) alternates with the Holly King (who is associated with the moon, as well as with the waning year, and with the unicorn). Upon this premise, the complex iconography of both tapestries may be seen as a profound celestial and fertility representation of decline and renewal. Furthermore, the unicorn and the lion can then be seen as the basis of a cosmic drama in which aspects of the seasonal cycle, death and resurrection, and the power of celestial bodies, provide a rich symbolic battleground of ideas and concepts. This interaction of images eventually becomes a central motif in the Unicorn Tapestries, and one of its most curious yet apparent manifestations is in the imagery of trees.

Otto Weiner (in Shepard) proposes that in some original myths, the unicorn was captured by the tree itself. In other variants of the unicorn's capture, the lion takes the place of the hunter and a tree takes the place of the virgin. "Unicorned animals are often found on Assyrian cylinder-seals grouped with a single conventionalized tree in symbolic arrangement. This tree of the cylinder-seals is usually called the Tree of Fortune, but it seems to be ultimately indistinguished from the Cosmogonic Tree, the Tree of the World, springing from the darkness and holding the earth and heavenly bodies in its branches, familiar in the myths of many peoples but best known to us by the Scandinavian name of *Yggdrasill.* If the lion and the unicorn are to represent the sun and the moon, they will need no less a tree than this [Tree of the World] as the scene of their encounter." (Shepard)

In the Judeo-Christian tradition, the Cosmic Tree or Tree of the World evolved into two components—the Tree of Knowledge and the Tree of Life. And as we interpret the Unicorn Tapestries, we shall find that the Tree of Life is the arboreal symbol that identifies with the pomegranate— a plant that forms the central element of the seventh and final panel, the tapestry which depicts the enclosure that holds the unicorn captive.

We have come a long way from the ancient rites of the Mother Goddess and her dual consorts with which we began this survey of the Oak King, the Holly King, the Wild Man, and Christ. We have seen that the unicorn is just one guise of a multitude of astounding figures epitomizing the mystery of life and earthly abundance. It is little wonder that over the centuries the unicorn and the Unicorn Tapestries have given rise to many possible interpretations. When symbolizing male potency, the unicorn is a fertility god. To Christians, he was the resurrected Christ. And to many people he remains the untamed spirit of the wilderness.

All of these interpretations are valid, and all of them will be considered when we explore each panel of the Unicorn Tapestries and discover the unifying drama that interrelates each of the seven textiles in a single powerful metaphoric statement. For when we view the Unicorn Tapestries in the context of their landscapes and animal imagery, their plants and trees, we realize that the unicorn is the synthesis of icons that have haunted human beings throughout history: the Divine King, the scapegoat, the Wild Man, and the Holly King of our European heritage. But the unicorn also becomes the symbol of death and resurrection, of fertility and abundance— of the ancient gods (Attis, Adonis, and Dionysus), and ultimately of Christ himself, the redeemer who brings new springs from old winters.

# PART TWO

# The Unicorn
# Tapestries

# AN UNFOLDING
# DRAMA OF
# THE SEASONS

Although much research has been focused upon the Unicorn Tapestries, many scholars have failed to view the flora and fauna contained in these textiles in the context of the medieval psyche. Unnecessary confusion has confounded such modern scholars when they have attempted to understand why the plants of one season are shown in juxtaposition with those of another. The medieval designers of the tapestries were not as concerned with the correct, literal seasonal context of botanical images as they were with the overall metaphors and iconographic messages they could impart. The tapestries are devoted not only to a different artistic method but also to a different artistic reality. Analysis of the symbolism of the major motifs and the supporting flora woven into these seven tapestries has led me to the conclusion that all the identifiable plants depicted in the Unicorn Tapestries fit into the matrix of a carefully selected mythology.

The unicorn is the central figure in all the Unicorn Tapestries with the exception of the first, and even the first panel contains iconographic motifs which relate to the unicorn by proxy. Another predominant image in all but two of the tapestries is the central representation of a tree. The first of the two panels without a tree is the second tapestry of the series. In this panel the central emblem is a fountain, but at the top—forming the main jet—is the image of a stone pomegranate, an important iconographic detail in this work. The other tapestry that does not have a central tree motif is the sixth panel in the series, depicting the killing of the unicorn. In this particular tapestry, two dramatic actions are depicted. The main one, the death of the unicorn, occurs in a grove of trees—an arboreal symbol that is extremely relevant to the iconography of the Oak King–Holly King cycle. The botanical motif of this tapestry is centered upon the dead unicorn, depicted with a garland of oak leaves around its neck.

The key to fully comprehending the Unicorn Tapestries lies in understanding its plant symbolism. This iconographic approach is justified for many reasons, but most essentially because there was a strong belief in the mythical power of vegetation during medieval times. It is thus very unlikely that plant symbols were used simply as ornamentation. The placement of a central tree in most panels, and the depiction of myriad small plants in all the panels, are not accidental or decorative. These served as major elements used to enrich the story of the unicorn's capture, death, and resurrection, and to transform this visual drama into a cosmic metaphor of redemption.

The unicorn, the essential figure in the tapestries, was thought of in the medieval period, and for many centuries thereafter, as a living though somewhat rare creature. The classical authors had made mention of the unicorn on numerous occasions. The accuracy of these ancient writings was not challenged until the Renaissance, when empirical thinkers began to question the observations and reports made by ancient authorities. So strong was this belief in the existence of the unicorn in the Middle Ages that a fifteenth-century book entitled *Defensorium inviolatae virginitatis Mariae* utilized the unicorn as a means of proving that miracles were scientifically valid events, and to promote the feasibility of immaculate conception.

To understand how the unicorn became associated with the Virgin Mary and Christ, we need to know the history and myths that surrounded this mythical beast. During antiquity, the image of unicorns probably arose from stories that originated in India. These tales evolved over the centuries, becoming a unified mythology by the early Middle Ages.

The unicorn is first mentioned by a Greek physician named Ctesias who, around the year 400 B.C., was in residence at the Persian courts of Artaxerxes and Darius II. His book *Indica* describes the unicorn and gives special emphasis to its horn:

There are in India certain wild asses which are as large as horses, and larger. . . . They have a horn on the forehead which is about a foot and a half in length. The dust filed from this horn is administered in a potion as a protection against deadly drugs. . . . Those who drink out of these horns, made into drinking vessels, are not subject . . . to poisons if, either before or after swallowing such, they drink wine, water, or anything else from these beakers. . . . The animal is exceedingly swift and powerful, so that no creature, neither horse nor any other, can overtake it. (Quoted in Shepard)

Around A.D. 170 to 235, a Roman author named Aelian added to the unicorn legend by insisting that the horn of the creature was spiral in shape and that this spiral form was an indication of divinity and immortality.

Biblical texts also provided the basis for many religious allegories associated with the unicorn. For instance, the inclusion of this mythical beast in the Old Testament is attributed to a group of Hebrew scholars—men living in Alexandria around the third to second centuries B.C., who translated the existing Hebrew scriptures into the Septuagint, or Greek Bible. In this rendition, the beast known as the "reem" was transliterated into the Greek word *monoceros,* meaning unicorn.

When St. Jerome translated the Septuagint into the Vulgate, or Latin Bible, in the fourth century, he changed some of the passages that cited the *monoceros* into the word "rhinoceros," while in other chapters he simply used the Latin word for unicorn, *monocornus.*

By the third century, the unicorn had been completely absorbed as a Christian icon, becoming a symbol of Christ. An early Roman Christian, Tertullian, was intrigued by a passage from Deuteronomy: "his horns are like the horns of unicorns," and he explained its hidden meaning as follows: "the unicorn is Christ, and his horn is Christ's cross." (Freeman) In the fourth century, St. Basil, Father of the Eastern Church, expanded upon this symbolism even further, maintaining that Christ "will be called the Son of Unicorns. For, as we have learned in Job, the unicorn is a creature irresistible in might and unsubjected to man." St. Basil noted that the horn of the unicorn is identified in scriptures with glory, power, and salvation; and so he concluded that "Christ is the power of God; therefore, He is called the unicorn on the ground that He has one horn—that is, one common power with the Father." (*Exegetic Homilies*)

In a copy of the *Physiologus* written around the ninth century, we learn that by this early date the unicorn myth was well established:

There is an animal that is called a *monoceros* in Greek and in Latin truly a unicorn. The *Physiologus* says that the unicorn has this nature. He is a small animal, like a kid, but exceedingly fierce, with one horn in the middle of his head; and no hunter is able to capture him. Yet he may be taken in this manner: men lead a virgin maiden to the place where he most resorts and they leave her in the forest alone. As soon as the unicorn sees her, he springs into her lap and embraces her. Thus he is taken captive and exhibited in the palace of the king. In this way Our Lord Jesus Christ, the spiritual unicorn, descended into the womb of the Virgin and through her took on human flesh. He was captured by the Jews and condemned to die on the cross. Concerning him, David . . . says, 'But my horn shalt thou exalt like the horn of a unicorn.' And Zacharias says, 'He hath raised up an horn of salvation for us in the house of his servant David' [Luke 1:69]. . . . Moreover the one horn that he has on his head signifies the words of the Saviour: 'I and my Father are one' [John 10:30]. . . . They say that he is exceedingly fierce, and this means that neither Principalities nor Powers nor Thrones . . . nor the most subtle devil nor Hell could hold him against his will. Moveover they say that he is a small animal and this is because of the humility [of Christ] in his incarnation; concerning this he said, 'learn of me, for I am meek and lowly in heart' [Matthew 11:29]. . . . Only by the wish of the Father did he descend into the womb of the Virgin Mary for our salvation. (Freeman)

The twelfth-century mystic Hildegarde of Bingen, in her treatise on natural history, the *Physica*, includes the unicorn. Like all the other "scientific" literature on the Middle Ages, her book contains contemporary ideas rigidly based on the writings and concepts set down by the classical authors. Medieval people believed that the horn of the unicorn comprised, in essence, all the qualities of the animal, and could be used as a prophylactic, a panacea, or an aphrodisiac—more than sufficient motive for capturing and killing this elusive beast.

In surveying the iconographic meaning in each panel of the Unicorn Tapestries, we discover that much more than a simple hunt for an exotic and potentially valuable capture is the basis of this masterpiece. All the panels will be explored in the context of a calendrical sequence—a cycle that is based upon aspects of the seasons, and upon the universal motif of the sacrifice of the dying vegetation god whose death benefits mankind by renewing fertility. The drama of the Unicorn Tapestries, like the seasons themselves, is cyclical.

An important point, and one that bears repeating before proceeding with our interpretation of the Unicorn Tapestries, is the general consensus of art historians as to the nationality or domicile of the designer of these textiles. The dramas and seasonal rites that are central to this argument are indigenous to northern Europe. The late Margaret Freeman, Curator Emeritus of The Cloisters, concluded in *The Unicorn Tapestries* that the designer was "undoubtedly working in France." Whatever his heritage, one thing is certain—his familiarity with the northern European flora.

The plants and trees depicted in the Unicorn Tapestries are, with few exceptions, all native to northern Europe. Furthermore, the two main trees woven into these textiles, holly and oak, are predominant in the forests of that region. And since the designer of the tapestries was familiar with the flora of northern Europe, he would have known about their rich iconographic heritage. This important premise is also stressed by Margaret Freeman, when she states that the mastermind behind the Unicorn Tapestries "must have been imbued with . . . the 'language' of trees and flowers." Even if the designer lived in the city, which seems most probable, he would have been well acquainted with the various seasonal anthropomorphic rites that were common in both town and country. The French historian Lucien Febvre explains that the people of "the France of Charles VIII, of Louis XII . . . were not urban, they lived on the land. . . . The city was permeated by the country . . . the city, filled with orchards, gar-

Figure 13. Detail—"The Unicorn Is Killed and Brought to the Castle." The Cloisters, Metropolitan Museum of Art.

dens, and green trees was nothing but a slightly more densely populated countryside."

One other point must be clarified before we can approach this first panel of the Unicorn Tapestries: an understanding of its relationship to the sixth and seventh panels that precede it.* In the sixth hanging of the tapestries, the hunt ends with the brutal death of the majestic creature (Fig. 13). Mortal wounds are inflicted by huntsmen who thrust their spears into the unicorn's chest. Two of the most important iconographic elements in this action are the depiction of a holly tree directly above the head of the unicorn, and the representation of an oak tree directly behind the woodsman

---

* Since the seventh tapestry, "The Unicorn in Captivity," is not part of the hunt, the preceding tapestry, "The Unicorn is Killed and Brought to the Castle," provides the dramatic climax of the tapestry series. The seventh and last panel is actually an epilogue that stands apart from the main body of the set, though it is, indeed, part of the cyclical significance of the Unicorn Tapestries.

delivering the coup de grâce. As we shall see, the iconography of the sixth panel of the Unicorn Tapestries corresponds to events connected with the midwinter Saturnalia: the ritual during which the Holly King dies and the solar deity or Oak King becomes his successor.

The cycle is now complete, and "The Start of the Hunt" is symbolically the next panel in the sequence. This first tapestry reflects in its images the beginning of the year, the awakening of the earth, and the rebirth of nature.

# THE START
# OF THE
# HUNT

O N A NARRATIVE LEVEL, the first panel of the Unicorn Tapestries is concerned with the beginning of the hunt for the unicorn (Plate I). Set against a *millefleurs* background, we see three nobles standing in front of a cherry tree that is heavy with fruit. Acting as the vanguard for the hunting party are two hunters, or lymerers, holding at bay their canine charges. Partly concealed and taking advantage of the elevation is a lookout, hidden in a grove of plum and ash trees (Fig. 14). The lookout summons the noble party in his direction.

So much for the pictorial and narrative content of the first panel, which is entitled "The Start of the Hunt." On a more profound and symbolic level, the first panel of the tapestries has as its central theme rebirth, spring, and cosmic renewal. Almost every iconographic element of the panel is related to this central motif of the inception of spring. Besides the fruitful cherry tree, there are ash, birch, and plum trees—all carefully selected by the tapestry designer in order to provide specific symbolism that relates to the inception of the fecund season. In addition to these important arboreal icons, there are a variety of supporting plants identified with the rebirth motif intrinsic to the symbolism of the work.

The central tree, the cherry, is a seasonal emblem for the beginning of spring and is connected with the nativity of Christ. As this is the first tree of spring to bear fruit, the cherry became identified with the renewal of nature. The plural "cherries" is identical with *cheres*, meaning "orb of the sun" in Hebrew (Bayley), so this scarlet fruit came to symbolize the rebirth of the sun after the gloomy winter months.

The other main botanical motifs in the first panel of the Unicorn Tap-

Figure 14. Detail—
"The Start of the Hunt."
The Unicorn Tapestries.
Franco-Flemish, c. 1515.
The Cloisters, Metropolitan
Museum of Art.

estries also support the iconography of rebirth. For instance, the ash is the predominant tree in the left-hand margin (with the initials "A.E." woven into its uppermost branches), and it was a very special tree in European folklore. Ash is the tree of rebirth, sacred to Poseidon and Woden, both major deities in their respective pantheons. The ash was also connected with fire, lightning, and rain—all elements vital to the fertility motif of agrarian societies. Lightning strikes the ash with a frequency second only to the oak, which explains the couplet:

> Avoid the Ash,
> It courts the Flash.

Since only the major gods wielded the lightning bolt, this privilege was seen by primal people as a symbol of the power and importance of the tree. The Latin name for the ash is *Fraxinus,* which translates as "fire-light," revealing a long-standing connection of the ash tree with fire, which has played an important ritualistic part in homeopathetic ceremonies that celebrate the birth of the sun. In both Roman and Norse mythologies, the ash appears as the ancestor of the human race, thus symbolizing both fertility and creation. The legends of both races are similar: the gods breathe upon the ash to create the first human beings. The *Prose Edda,* an account written around 1220 by an Icelandic scholar, Snorri Sturlason, records that the first man, named Askr, was created from Ash and that the first woman was made from the Elm. An elm can be seen in this first Unicorn Tapestry just under the oak tree. The *Prose Edda* relates that the great ash that was sacred to Woden was called *Yggdrasill;* the name is derived from the other name for this mighty god, Yggr. This ash was a tree of prodigious dimensions, known as the Tree of Life, so huge that its roots reached down to the kingdoms beneath the earth and its branches engulfed the universe.

In the various European mythologies, the ash tree had connections with divine infancy (which associates it with birth). According to Greek mythology, when Zeus was a child, he was fed honey made from the flowers of the sacred ash. The early Christians therefore linked this tree with the nativity of Christ. And in parts of Europe, the Yule fire was made from an ash log. The Yule Festival took place after the winter solstice. It was essentially a celebration of the rebirth of the sun after the long winter months, a symbolic event that eventually became associated with the birth and infancy of Christ—thus combining both the ash-honey fed to Zeus and the pre-Christian rebirth of the sun. The use of ash as the fuel of the Yule celebration is recorded in the following English verse:

> Thy welcome Eve, loved Christmas, now arrived,
> The parish bells their tuneful peals resound,
> And mirth and gladness every breast pervade.
> The ponderous Ashen-faggot, from the yard,
> The jolly farmer to his crowded hall
> Conveys with speed; where, on the raising flames
> Already fed with store of massy brands . . .
> —Folkard

Another significant tree in the first panel of the Unicorn Tapestries is the birch. An example is woven directly under the hand of the lookout, and provides a perch for a bird (see Fig. 14). A number of attributes make the birch iconographically important. With the exception of the alder it is the first tree in spring to put forth new leaves, and so is readily associated with the beginning of the New Year—those first months when the days begin to lengthen again after shortening to their extreme limit. In northern mythology, the birch was sacred to Thor. The early leaves put out by this tree coincide with the spring rains, and insofar as Thor was a rain god, the tree came to symbolize his return to earth during the early months of the year.

The other important tree in this tapestry is the palm, which appears

Figure 15. Altar tapestry. Swiss, c. 1480. Zurich, Landesmuseum.

as small shrubs at the base of the ash tree. The palm provides a further iconographic clue to this first panel of the Unicorn Tapestries. It was venerated as an immortal tree because it never loses its leaves; on the contrary, it gets new branches every month. And because the palm bears fruit until it dies, it is often identified as the Tree of Life. Another vivid association with the palm is the phoenix; in fact, the generic name for the tree is identical to that of the mythic bird. As the encyclopedist Bartholomaeus Anglicus states: "Palm . . . is a tree noble and famous. Always fair and green, a long time beautiful with branches both in winter and in summer . . . it endures and is green for many days, therefore by its likeness to the bird phoenix that lives a long time, the palm is called phoenix amongst the Greeks . . . when the palm is so old that it faileth all for age, then oft it quickneth and springeth again of itself. Therefore men suppose, that the phoenix a bird of Arabia, has the name of this palm in Arabia. For he dieth and quickneth and liveth as oft, as the foresaid palm does." (1582)

The next tree occurring in "The Start of the Hunt" is iconographically important although not a dominant image in this particular panel. It is an oak. A fine specimen is woven above the spear of the lymerer in the upper left part of the tapestry.*

As already mentioned, the oak was the sacred tree of Zeus, Jupiter, Thor, and Hercules. Virgil says that the roots of the oak are equal in length

---

* "The Start of the Hunt" is the only hanging in the actual hunt sequence that does not have a holly woven into its design. The last tapestry, "The Unicorn in Captivity" is not part of the actual hunt of the unicorn, and contains neither the oak nor the holly.

Figure 16.
Detail—Altar
tapestry. Zurich,
Landesmuseum.

to the branches, thus symbolizing Zeus' power in both lower and upper regions of the earth. "For the roots go down as far into the underworld as the cresting boughs go up." (*Aeneid*)

In the art of the Middle Ages there are many examples that connect Christ with the oak. For instance, in a Swiss altar tapestry woven around 1480 (Fig. 15), images are depicted that interrelate the oak with both Christ and the unicorn. This interesting textile shows an enclosed garden in which the Virgin Mary is surrounded by her numerous symbols, including a unicorn. Also depicted as being with Mary in the enclosure are Adam and Eve. Above the Virgin is an image of the Christ child, accompanied by a large branch of oak, both of which radiate toward her (Fig. 16). And placed in the left of the enclosed garden is a large oak tree bearing many acorns.

Again, a German woodcut dating from the fifteenth century (Fig. 17) presents the Virgin accompanied by female saints in a walled enclosure. Upon her knee sits the Christ child, while behind him there are two large oak trees.

Clearly, the oak was highly venerated, doubtless because it was closely associated with the major deities of the old religion. Christianity, in its search for long-standing iconography, readily allied Christ to the oak.

The tree has a particularly interesting relationship to Hercules. In antiquity, Hercules, after being deified, became the guardian of the door of the gods, like his Latin counterpart the two-faced god Janus. Both Hercules and Janus are identified with the winter solstice—the door to the New Year. In representations of Janus he is depicted with two faces, one turned toward the Old Year and the other facing the New Year. This "pagan" imagery of January depicted by the two-faced Janus was not uncommon in medieval art (Fig. 18).

Hercules, the Greek guardian of the door, was also a sun hero, and like all solar deities was born during midwinter. The first remarkable task performed by Hercules as an infant was the strangling of two serpents that had managed to find their way into his bedchamber. In mythology the serpent, among other interpretations, represents the spirit of winter. So this episode of the infant Hercules is an allegorical drama depicting the defeat of winter by the spirit of the New Year.

The ash tree, as we have already established, was a glyph of the New Year, and as the following examples illustrate, was viewed by the people of the Middle Ages as antivenomous. As such it was identified with the defeat of winter by such solar deities as Hercules.

The unicorn, on the other hand, was a pre-Christian, lunar symbol. Its qualities were so remarkable that the Church theologians reinvented the "pagan" unicorn as a symbol of their Messiah. Christ was also associated with the oak, and this relationship of the oak with Christ identifies him as a solar power. But, as we have seen, the early Christian theologians compared the lunar unicorn with Christ. Although this antagonistic juxtaposition constitutes a dilemma in that it merges the solar Christ with the lunar unicorn, the apparent contradiction is not unique, but may often occur when one religion supersedes another. In this instance, the Christian iconographers and allegorists simply changed the significance of the original symbolism, and so the lunar unicorn became identified with the solar Christ. Thus the Christian allegorists added one more level of myth to the fables of the unicorn.

Christ was further identified not only with the oak but also with the holly, as Robert Graves explains: "Since in medieval practice St. John the Baptist, who lost his head on St. John's Day, took over the Oak King's titles

Figure 17. "Virgin with Virgins." 15th-century German woodcut.

Figure 18. Janus depicted for the month of January. Manuscript mid-12th century. Oxford, Bodleian Library.

and customs, it was natural to let Jesus, as John's merciful successor, take over the Holly King's. The holly was thus glorified beyond the other forest trees. For example, in the *Holly-Tree Carol:* 'Of all the trees that are in the wood/The holly bears the crown.' " (1966)

Before concluding this discussion of the first panel of the Unicorn Tapestries, we should examine the smaller plants in this *millefleurs* hanging. Although some of the plants in these tapestries, as in other textiles of the Middle Ages, are presented solely for decorative value, many are important iconographic motifs.

A botanical specimen in this first tapestry that must not go unnoticed is the white campion, woven between the legs of the noble silhouetted against the cherry tree. The white campion belongs to a group of plants from the carnation family. Although only an inconspicuous white flower, iconographically the white campion is very important, providing a specific symbolism to "The Start of the Hunt" and other panels in the Unicorn Tapestries. In English, French, and German the white campion has a remarkable number of names, giving an insight into the folklore that surrounds it. A few of the English names that also have equivalents in other European languages illustrate the malevolent associations of this plant: snake's flower, thunder flower, cuckoo flower, robin, and devil's flower. To the people of the Middle Ages the white campion was no ordinary herb, but a sinister flower protected by adders and supernatural beings, and connected with the devil, the goblin, Robin Goodfellow, and death.

In his excellent book *The Englishman's Flora*, Geoffrey Grigson mentions that in some English counties, the white campion is called mother Dee, because "picking the flowers brought death to your Mother. . . . A North German name for white campion is *Totenblume*, 'death-flower.' . . . And in Luxembourg the red variety of this flower is called *fleur de tounouar* [thunder flower], and children believed that they would be killed by lightning if they picked it." Grigson suggests that these plants belonged to the mischievous Robin Goodfellow, and his counterparts in the French and German. "The name Robin, a diminutive of Robert by way of French, seems innocent in its attachment to flowers, but most of the Robin flowers appear to have been linked to goblin, robin, and evil . . . all these plants share Robin names . . . and by other names as well they are all, or several of them, associated with snakes, death and the devil."

The snake as a symbol, especially in the Christian context as an icon for evil, is present in a number of instances in the Unicorn Tapestries, and in each example is represented by the white campion. In "The Start of the Hunt," the white campion is present as a serpent icon, because of the snake's connection with "the darkness of night and of winter," as Gubernatis puts it.

Figure 19. Detail—"The Start of the Hunt." The Cloisters, Metropolitan Museum of Art.

In concluding the iconography of this first tapestry, one small plant that must be mentioned is the blue cornflower, which is woven between the left hand of the lymerer at the bottom of the tapestry and the head of the hound looking to the left (Fig. 19). Cornflowers were considered repellent to snakes and beneficial to the eyesight. The antivenomous qualities of this plant, like those of the ash tree, were perhaps included in this tapestry as an opposing icon to the white campion, the botanical icon of adders. (Medieval artists delighted in placing conflicting and antagonistic symbolism in one composition.) Attesting to the cornflower's toxicity to serpents, the Roman poet Lucan mentions the cornflower in his *Pharsalia* as one of the plants that upon being burned would drive away snakes:

> Beyond the farthest tents rich fires they build
> That healthy medicinal odours yield . . .
>
> - - - - - - - -
>
> There centaury [cornflower] supplies the wholesome flame . . .
>
> - - - - - - - -

The monsters of the land, the serpents fell
Fly away, and shun the hostile swell.
　　—Folkard

From ancient times, the cornflower as an herbal medicine was also believed to improve the eyesight. In fact, a famous eyewash called *Eau de Casselunette* has long been made in France. Bartholomaeus Anglicus stated that cornflowers "cleareth sight." (1582) When we consider that the theme of this tapestry is the search for the unicorn, it is interesting to note that the designer placed the cornflower—a plant that improves eyesight—in direct relationship to the two main hounds leading the hunt. Such small iconographic details occur in many of the Unicorn Tapestries.

Upon initial examination, "The Start of the Hunt" seems to be concerned with little more than the search for a unicorn by a group of royal hunters and their retainers. But under scrutiny and a careful interpretation of iconography, the overriding motif begins to surface: the awakening of the earth in early spring, and the cosmic preparation for a time of growth and abundance. These images portray the beginning of the waxing cycle, the time when Hercules has strangled the serpents of the old year. The powerful ash and other smaller members of the plant kingdom help exile these reptiles of evil and winter. As a reminder of the ever present malevolence of winter, hardship, and evil, numerous botanical motifs (cornflower and campion) connected with serpents are woven into this panel.

The tapestry also focuses on the phoenix which is reborn upon the palm, a tree that is associated with the births of Apollo, Aphrodite, Artemis, and Dionysus, and which, in Christian legend, is connected, like the cherry, with the nativity of Christ. Much subtle classical and Christian imagery is contained in these botanical images. The birth of gods and mortals is protected by prophylactic plants and trees, which secure their safe delivery and protect the vulnerable young.

The spirit of the old has been slain in order to make way for the rejuvenating, waxing cycle, and many powerful talismans are visually invoked to ensure survival. This chronology of the waxing oak cycle continues in the imagery of the next panel of the ingenious series of tapestries. And the varied, explicit imagery in "The Unicorn at the Fountain" allows a more complete understanding of the rich iconography contained in the next part of the work.

PLATE

II

# THE UNICORN
# AT THE
# FOUNTAIN

I N THE SECOND TEXTILE of the Unicorn Tapestries (Plate II), the unicorn appears for the first time, as he gracefully kneels and dips his horn into the stream of water that is woven in the forefront of the scene. In the center of this panel is a beautiful Gothic fountain, surmounted by a jet that is carved into the form of a pomegranate. And from a carved lion's head in the side of the fountain, a stream of water gushes, flowing into the stream at the bottom of the panel. Flanking the fountain is a thick border of fruit and oak trees, and on the outside of this arbor are twelve hunters. These men, both servants and aristocrats, stand in awe of the unicorn as he dips his horn into the water of the fountain. Behind them are positioned a number of trees, including holly and oak. Of these two principal trees, the oak predominates in this particular tapestry; it is woven mainly to the right of the fountain.

In front of the stream, four different carnivorous species of animals appear. As we shall shortly see, they all play a vital role in the iconography of this tapestry. Included in the group are a lion and lioness, a panther, a genet (weasel), and a scowling wolf. On the other side of the stream we see a stag, two frisky rabbits, and a number of hounds. Besides these animals, the fauna includes a few birds: on the rim of the fountain are two brightly colored pheasants and a pair of goldfinches, while a lone nightingale perches on the blue plum tree to the left of the fountain. And on the stream itself, two ducks and a woodcock are depicted.

From the interpretation of the iconography of the first tapestry, we learned that "The Start of the Hunt" is centered upon the inception of the New Year and the reawakening of fertility associated with solar deities such as Christ, Zeus, and Hercules. The plants depicted in that panel identify it with the start of the fecund season and the waxing year.

The second tapestry in the series, "The Unicorn at the Fountain," reveals associations with spring—the actual blossoming of vegetation—as well as strong motifs of fecundity. Underlying these themes are the images which suggest the return to earth of vegetation deities like Christ, Adonis, and Narcissus, and their female counterpart, Persephone. Curiously, however, the strongest icons in this second panel are not symbols of abundance and fertility, but representations of the sacrifice which gives rise to rebirth: the Easter drama of the Crucifixion. The iconography is associated with the death and descent of Christ into the underworld to defeat the devil, a victory that is followed by his resurrection (rebirth), which is identified with the return of spring. The animal and plant icons that are particularly rich in this tapestry reflect Christ's battle with Satan and the dualism of Christianity, which declares the polemic existence of good and evil.

Another essential set of symbols in the second tapestry is related to the barrenness and negative powers of winter, which must be overcome in order to make way for spring and rejuvenation. Such negative images, as we shall see, include serpents, poisoned water, and, ultimately, the withered Tree of Life that resulted from original sin and the exile from Eden. The symbols are clearly Christian; but underlying this Christian message are far older mythologies.

The story of this particular tapestry centers upon the unicorn and the fountain. The association of these two images suggests an idea that was well known to the people of the Middle Ages: the belief in the unicorn's ability to purify water from the contamination of poison because of his miraculous horn. According to the story, the venom was produced by serpents that came to streams and rivers at night. This fable developed from the Greek version of the *Physiologus*, which states that when various animals assembled beside a stream in the evening to drink, they were unable to quench their thirst because a serpent had left its venom floating upon the surface of the waters. The animals, apparently, could see or smell the poison. When the unicorn arrived, he waded into the water and made the sign of the Cross over the surface in order to neutralize the venom.

Such legends of the unicorn came from pre-Christian sources, stories that provided the Christian iconographers with an ideal analogy of Christ releasing mankind from the burden of original sin. When interpreting the unicorn, iconographers took this symbolism even further, explaining the ability of the unicorn to purify water by saying that the animal's single horn represented the holy Cross, that the serpent represented the devil, and that the poisoned waters symbolized the sins of the world.

Another pre-Christian legend, and one that is important to this tapestry, is related to the stone pomegranate carved on top of the fountain. The pomegranate in classical myth was connected with the release in spring of vegetation gods and goddesses from the underground kingdom. And the fact that the pomegranate forms one of the fountain's outlets identifies the water with that which issues from the underworld and flows from the fountain to nourish the land. This is an allegorical reference to the release of the verdant forces of spring, and a mythological symbol of these deities' return to earth.

To help explain the connection between the unicorn and the fountain in a Christian context, we are fortunate in having a woodcut that is contemporary with the Unicorn Tapestries. Although this particular print was mentioned briefly in an earlier chapter, a more detailed account of its symbolism is helpful here. The woodcut, entitled *The Temptation of Adam and Eve* (see Fig. 1), was first printed in Paris around 1495 by Antoine Vérard. The central portion depicts Satan in the guise of a serpent coiled around the Tree of Knowledge of Good and Evil. At the right of the tree is a fountain similar to the one depicted in "The Unicorn at the Fountain" tapestry. The parallel does not end there, for the Vérard woodcut also contains a unicorn and a stag, and a genet at the bottom of the tree (similar to the one in the Unicorn Tapestries), which is staring at the dramatic scene that leads to the Fall of mankind and the withering of the Tree of Life. However, the woodcut also depicts a monkey, an animal which is not shown in the Unicorn Tapestries. In the Vérard woodcut, we see that the imagery is iconographically balanced: the stag and the genet are placed so as to represent enemies of the serpent and to suggest the eventual redemption of mankind. The fruit-eating monkey to the left of Eve is a familiar symbol of the devil.

The fountain in the woodcut represents the "Waters of Life" that flow next to the "Tree of Life," according to biblical texts. These waters, which are depicted pouring from the central fountain, have been polluted by the devil/serpent, and so must be purified by the horn of the unicorn, or in terms of Christian symbolism, by the death of Christ—a sacrifice that atones for the original sin committed in the Garden of Eden.

The association of the fountain with Christ is mentioned in the thirteenth-century bestiary of Guillaume le Clerc:

> Jesus Christ, our saviour,
> When he burst the gates of hell
> And destroyed the devil.
> In him wells up the clear fountain,
> Which is full of wisdom,
> Of which the devil cannot endure
> The word nor abide it.

It was believed that these befouled waters, like the withered Tree of Life, could only be cleansed of evil by the symbolic sacrifice of Christ. This doctrine of the descent of the god into the water in order to purify it from evil is still a part of the Roman Catholic liturgy. On Holy Saturday, the waters of the baptismal font are blessed. The priest touches the waters with his hand and prays that it may be cleansed of the malice of Satan. Making the sign of the Cross over the surface, he divides the water with his hand, then throws some toward each of the four corners of the world. The Pascal candle is dipped into the water and the priest repeats: "May the virtue of the Holy Ghost descend into all the waters of the font." Breathing on the water, he adds: "And make the whole substance of this water fruitful for regeneration." (*Catholic Daily Missal*, English trans. D. E. Lefebvre) The assisting priest then sprinkles the congregation with the blessed water. A similar action is repeated by the unicorn over the poisoned waters of the fountain.

In the early fourteenth century, Jean Pucelle, a Parisian book illustrator, wrote an explanation of his illustrations in the *Belleville Breviary*. In these commentaries, he identifies the "Waters of Life" with the blood of Christ:

And since the scriptures can be set forth in several ways, I am showing the crucifixion differently: I am putting it in the earthly Paradise, in the garden of delight, symbolized by the river that was in the paradise of delights and that came forth and divided itself into four parts to water the garden of paradise. It is Jesus Christ who came forth from paradise and who was extended in four directions on the cross to water the garden of paradise; because it was so dry that no fruit would grow, no soul could be planted there; therefore, he watered it with His Precious Blood. (Holt)

In many instances, especially in the art of the north, the medieval and Renaissance artists identified the withered Tree of Life with the oak. According to Christian myth, this tree becomes verdant only after the Crucifixion: an expression of the ancient belief that the blood of the sacrificed god restores life to land and vegetation. This rejuvenation of fertility is an important point, for as we shall shortly see, "The Unicorn at the Fountain" tapestry is a reference to this same restorative power of Christ.

The restoration of a "withered oak tree" by blood sacrifice is well illustrated in a woodcut by the German artist Lucas Cranach the Younger, which represents *The Fall and Redemption of Man* (Fig. 20). On the left side of the panel, Adam and Eve are seen in the world of the Old Covenant, eating the apple from the Tree of Knowledge offered to them by the serpent of death. Also on the left (Old Covenant) side of the woodcut is Moses holding the Ten Commandments. Behind him are various prophets from the Old Testament. Near Moses we see Death and the Devil pushing a figure, representing all the peoples of the Old Covenant, into the hell fires.

Figure 20. Cranach the Younger, *The Fall and Redemption of Man.* Woodcut, after 1530.

On the right side of the same panel of the Cranach woodcut, we see the representation of the New Covenant: a diminutive Christ child bearing a cross radiates toward the Virgin, placed by the artist high on a hill. The crucified Christ spurts blood from a wound made in his side by a spear, and the gushing blood falls upon the head of a professing sinner. At the bottom right, in front of his open tomb, is the risen Christ. In celebration of his victory over Death and the Devil, Cranach depicts Christ standing upon a dragon and skeleton.

These two aspects of the woodcut are divided—right from left—by an oak tree. The left side of the oak is bare, while on the right the tree sprouts green leaves. The oak on this occasion is identified with the Tree of Life.

According to Christian theology, no man could enter Paradise until Christ himself had descended into Hell and defeated the devil. This concept of regeneration by divinity, both pre-Christian and Christian, is also reflected in the icons woven into the fountain panel of the Unicorn Tapestries. For instance, the pomegranate that surmounts the central fountain symbolizes the rebirth of "pagan" mythologies; hence this fruit becomes an emblem of resurrection and immortality.

Nor was this pomegranate motif solely associated with pre-Christian gods. Christian iconographers, like Bede and Cassiodorus, stated that the pomegranate may also "signify Christ. Just as one must open [the pomegranate] and look into the interior, where such precious fragrant juice and scent flows forth, so must one also penetrate into the inner suffering of the Redeemer, in order to contemplate the boundless soul-suffering of the heart of God whose blood flows over all mankind." (Freeman)

Another important churchman, Rabanus Maurus, identified the red juice of the pomegranate with the blood of Christ, thus associating the pomegranate with the Crucifixion. As we develop the iconography in this second tapestry, we shall see that the images woven into this textile are connected not only with spring but also with the death and resurrection of vegetation gods like Christ, Adonis, and Narcissus.

The last-named divinity is often depicted as a beautiful youth, who stares at his own reflection in the waters of a pool or fountain. The pheasant became associated with Narcissus because for centuries this bird was caught by placing a mirror in a cage. A book from the fourteenth century, *Livre de chasse du roy Modus*, gives a description of how a pheasant was presumably trapped by this method. When the pheasant sees his own reflection, he believes "that he is seeing a rival"; he immediately attacks the mirror and is easily taken by the hunter. (Tilander) Another textile not only of the same date but considered by some art historians to be from the same workshop that produced the Unicorn Tapestries is the so-called Narcissus Tapestry (Fig. 21). In this fine late medieval work the central figure, Narcissus, stares enraptured at his own reflection. A cock pheasant stands on the rim of the fountain—a parallel that is seen in the second panel of the Unicorn Tapestries, where a pair of pheasants are conspicuously placed on the rim of the central fountain, imagery meant to connect this work with the Narcissus myth. And it is surely an appropriate association, insofar as Narcissus is identified with Hyacinth and Adonis, and all three are vegetation gods representing spring.

Christ, like these vegetation gods, sacrificed himself for mankind. After his preordained death, he was resurrected, and with that resurrection, verdure was restored to the land. In Christian myth (as, for instance, in the Cranach woodcut), the withered tree is restored to life. This "ritual death and resurrection, this new birth in Christ" is derived from an archaic symbolism invested in the ritual of baptism, "a descent into the abyss of the waters for a duel with the marine monster; the model is Christ's going down to the Jordan. . . . For the Christian, baptism is a sacrament because it was initiated by Christ." But, as Mircea Eliade stresses, it also "repeats the initiatory ritual of the ordeal (= battle with the monster), of the symbolic death and resurrection (= birth of the new man)." (1982)

Figure 21. "Narcissus Tapestry." French, c. 1500. Boston, Museum of Fine Arts.

Figure 22. Deliverance of man from the power of the dragon. *Codex Palatinus Latinus*, 15th century. Biblioteca Apostolica Vaticana.

A fifteenth-century illustration in the *Codex Palatinus Latinus* (Fig. 22) depicts this Christian myth, the idea that the Crucifixion delivers man from the power of the "dragon." Christ is shown in glory above the Cross, with the aid of angels lifting souls toward Heaven, and away from the monstrous dragon coiled around the base of the Cross.

The death of Christ purifies the "Waters of Life" from sin. The Easter iconography presented in the second panel of the Unicorn Tapestries attests to the fact that the waters that issue from the fountain will be freed from corruption. In the Vérard woodcut, the symbolism of original sin was much more obvious: Adam and Eve are seen in the act of precipitating the Fall. They are placed in front of the "Fountain of Life" beside the Tree of Knowledge, around which is coiled a serpent. In the second panel of the Unicorn Tapestries, no actual reptile is present. But considering the iconography so far discussed—spring renewal and the release of mankind from evil—we should be able to find some imagery that identifies the evil serpent. And upon careful examination of the animals and plants in this tapestry, such an identification proves possible.

Under the right foot of the unshaven lymerer (Fig. 23), woven to the left of the fountain and pointing toward the unicorn and lions, is a white campion. This is a very important iconographic arrangement, inasmuch as the white campion, and other species of this family, had an evil reputation (as we have seen) and were the flowers of adders, goblins, and death. This seemingly innocuous white flower appears in other textiles that are contemporary with the Unicorn Tapestries, and is included in these hangings for its association with evil. From the many available examples of the campion's association with sin, a late fifteenth-century tapestry (Fig. 24) depicting the Last Judgment will suffice to illustrate the plant's malevolent symbolism. In the right-hand corner, the damned are shown cringing as they are driven into Hell by the figure of justice. Beneath the falling bodies are woven white campion, nettle, and violet, all three sharing an evil reputation. Rabanus Maurus suggested that the nettle symbolized lust, as did the violet, a flower that was thrown by the personification of the Vices in their battle with humans representing the Virtues. Finally, completing this satanic trio of plants, is the campion itself.

In the fountain tapestry, the white campion is woven under the foot of the young lymerer, depicted behind the lion, in a direct reference to a biblical quotation. One of the Psalms of David specifically cites the wickedness of the lion and the snake: "Thou shalt tread upon the lion and the adder: the young lion and dragon shalt thou trample under feet." (Psalms 91:13) This psalm must have been in the mind of the artist who executed the cartoon for this tapestry, as the pointing hunter behind the lion is literally stepping upon the plant. Medieval illustrations of Christ treading on the lion and the adder occur in works of art from the Carolingian to the late Gothic period. (Fig. 25 is one example.)

We can conclude that even if we do not have an actual snake or botanical icon of a serpent woven into the waters that issue from the fountain, the fact that the unicorn has placed his horn in the water indicates that reptiles have already exuded their venom there. The presence of the stag and genet reinforces this argument.

According to medieval sources, the genet belonged to the Mustela family, which included the weasel and the ermine. Members of this family were believed to be the enemy of all serpents, destroying these reptiles whenever possible. In Edward Topsell's *History of Four-Footed Beasts* (a translation of an earlier mid-sixteenth-century work by the Swiss naturalist Conrad Gesner), the author comments about the weasels: "They live in hatred with the serpent . . . for by eating of rue they drive them out of houses wherein they inhabit."

Figure 23. Detail—"The Unicorn at the Fountain." The Unicorn Tapestries. Franco-Flemish, c. 1500. The Cloisters, Metropolitan Museum of Art.

Figure 24. Detail—"The Last Judgment." Tapestry, Flemish, 1500–25. Paris, Musée du Louvre.

Figure 25. "Christ Triumphant." Carolingian ivory book cover, early 9th century. Oxford, Bodleian Library.

In the Vérard woodcut *The Temptation of Adam and Eve,* the genet is depicted in an alert attitude, as he stares at the evil serpent that is wrapped around the Tree of Knowledge. And though there is no actual serpent in "The Unicorn at the Fountain," it is important to note that the genet is depicted in the panel because of its long-standing animosity toward snakes. There is yet another suggestion of serpents in this second panel of the Unicorn Tapestries: above the genet is the image of the herb rue (Fig. 26). Unfortunately, because of a repair in this section of tapestry, only a small segment of rue is left, but a sufficient part of the plant has survived to make an identification possible. According to the medieval authors, members of the weasel family could restore their dead young to life with the aid of rue—"The weasel is so skilled in medicine that if she finds her babies dead, she can make them come alive with a certain herb she knows." *(Ortus Sanitatis)*

Another animal that is an adversary of the serpent is the stag, and this animal too is depicted in the second tapestry. The stag has a clever technique by which he captures his foe (Fig. 27): "When the snake goes into its hole

Figure 26. Detail—"The Unicorn at the Fountain." The Cloisters, Metropolitan Museum of Art.

in the earth, the Hart seeks a spring and takes a deep draft of the spring-water, and fills its mouth, and spits it into the earth hole, and drives the snake out and kills it." (Carlill)

Guillaume le Clerc interpreted the destruction of the snake by the stag as a parallel to Christ overcoming Satan and harrowing Hell.

The *Physiologus* carries this allegory one step further, connecting the hart's destruction of these reptiles with the Crucifixion and baptism. "And, when the Lord suffered the water and blood to stream out of his side, he destroyed the power of the dragon over us through the bath of the second birth and took from us every devilish influence." (Carlill)

This reputation of the stag as a serpent-killer was established by the classical writers, such as Pliny. And because of the reported animosity between the stag and serpents, the stag assumed an important place in Christian symbolism. In the Old Testament, the Forty-Second Psalm reads: "As the hart panteth after the water brooks, so panteth my soul after Thee, O God."

The early Christian allegorists quickly responded to these classical and

Figure 27. "Stag Eating Serpent." Miniature in English bestiary, 12th century. Oxford, Bodleian Library.

Christian sources. In their bestiaries, the stag became symbolic of Christ, the serpent-slayer, and of the soul that longs for the waters of life. A passage from St. Basil's *Exegetic Homilies* provides a good reason for the stag's prominent position in this second tapestry: "Wherever a stag is present, all evil of serpents is banished. The venomous animals do not endure the odor of this animal."

Completing the trio of animals that are antagonistic to the satanic reptiles is the panther. This fine beast is woven next to the genet and under the head of the unicorn.

In all the medieval bestiaries, the panther symbolizes Christ. The attraction of his sweet breath is compared to the multitude who follow Christ: and "the panther's sweet breath is Christ's voice calling out after his resurrection." (McCulloch) Guillaume le Clerc compares the tomb of Christ to the panther's den:

> On the holy cross he fell asleep.
> Then he dwelt until the third day
> In the dear and glorious tomb.
> Then he went straightway
> To harrow hell, and bound the dragon
> Who had held his people in prison.
> And when he was risen from death,
> So strong went forth the sweet odors
> Of his words and of his name
> And so far abroad went the sound of it,
> So far spread out his sweet smell,
> That all the world was the better for it.
> The odor of the resurrection
> Smelled so very sweet
> That all the world was healed.

The *Physiologus* states that the panther "is friend of all animals. . . . Only the dragon when he hears the panther's voice is seized by fear and bolsters itself within subterranean caves where it does not suffer the power of that sweet fragrance" (Fig. 28). Both the snake and the dragon are beasts that are identified with the devil. The dragon's kin in evil is the serpent, who also feared the panther.

> Snakes alone will not stir
> When the panther thus calls out.
> They lie motionless instead in their lairs,
> As if overcome with fears.
> —Elliot

Figure 28. Panther attracting animals with fragrant breath—dragon hiding. Miniature in English bestiary, c. 1170. New York, Pierpont Morgan Library.

The panther completes the benevolent trio of animals that are gathered around the fountain in the second panel of the Unicorn Tapestries.

In the art of the Middle Ages the unicorn was often included in scenes of the Fall. And the weaving of a panther, an icon of resurrection in this particular panel, mirrors the full cycle of Fall and redemption of the Old and the New Testaments. In other words, the entire drama of the Fall and the resurrection is represented in this small segment of the fountain tapestry.

Before we discuss the other animals in this tapestry, a few of the plants woven in the vicinity of the genet, panther, and unicorn need to be interpreted. These are floral icons of Christ and (like the three main animals) are antagonistic to the devil embodied in the image of a serpent. The large sage plant silhouetted so conspicuously against the fountain (next to the scarlet strawberries and wide-eyed rabbit) is woven into this panel because of the important symbolism attached to the plant. Today, we only employ sage as an aromatic seasoning. During the Middle Ages, however, the virtues ascribed to sage were numerous; in fact, it was considered a panacea.

The generic name of sage is derived from the Latin *salvare*, "to save," hence the early Christian iconographers associated the herb with salvation. And the medieval name *Officinalis Christi* makes reference to the many beneficial uses to which sage could be put.

Richard Banckes, writing of sage in his 1525 herbal, states that it is good as an antidote for venom or poison: "Seeth the sage in ale or wine and use to drink it three days, and thou shalt be whole, by the grace of God." In the many books on husbandry, sage was also recommended to be planted in the garden in order to repel poisonous serpents.

The next wildflower is the pimpernel, which—like sage—is antivenomous. A fine specimen of this common wildflower is placed directly under the gaze of the kneeling unicorn. Peter Schoeffer in his popular herbal *Der Gart der Gesundheit,* published in 1485, states that pimpernel "is good for bites of venomous beasts."

An English medieval manuscript relates in verse the following properties of this useful herb:

> The man that beareth it [pimpernel] day or night
> Wicked spirits of him shall have no might;
> It withstands the fiendish power
> And destroyeth venom if it is near.
> —Stephens

In Christian folklore the scarlet pimpernel was said to grow on Calvary. The idea is recorded in the following rhyme—a medieval charm that was recited whilst gathering pimpernel.

> Herbe Pimpernel, I have thee found
> Growing on Christ Jesus' ground
> The same gift the Lord Jesus gave unto thee,
> When he shed His blood upon the tree.
> Arise up, Pimpernel, and go with me,
> And God bless me,
> And all that shall wear thee. Amen.

The herb thus obtained was "good to prevent witchcraft." (Folkard)

The strong connection of the pimpernel with Christ and with the Crucifixion surely necessitates the inclusion of this plant in the second tapestry, as seen at the base of the unicorn's head and also at the base of the fountain. D'Ancona adds that "Because of its salutary properties, the pimpernel symbolized salvation." (1977)

In this particular tapestry are many animals and plants emphasizing the Easter motif. Not least among these is the hawthorn, here woven next to the pheasants' tails. The hawthorn was originally a plant associated with non-Christian rites and practices, but early in the history of the Christian Church it was blessed by theologians, and thereafter symbolized the crown of thorns. With these strong motifs drawn from Christian symbolism, the hawthorn applies in this tapestry to Easter and the Crucifixion.

Sir John Mandeville, a fourteenth-century traveler, wrote: "And ye shall understand, that our Lord Jesus, in that night that he was taken, he was led into a garden; and there he was first examined right sharply; and there the Jews scorned him, and made him a crown of the branches of albespine, that is white thorn, that grew in that same garden, and set it upon his head."

One other small addition to this Easter iconography is the daisy woven under the stomach of the genet. Margaret Freeman points out that in France, the daisy was "the paquerette, flower of Easter, with all of the Easter promise."

As we move away from the immediate fountain area, we will see how clearly all these images connect to one central theme.

The next animal to be considered is the lion, a beast both evil and divine. The benevolent aspect of the lion identifies with Christ, and the malevolent with Satan. Such contrasting symbolism in one icon is very common in the art of the Middle Ages.

This paradoxical beast can be seen in the left-hand margin of the fountain panel, where an open-mouthed lion and his mate are splendidly woven. The bestiaries mentioned the idiosyncratic nature of the lion, and all his contradictions became allegories for Christian iconographers. During the eleventh century, Bishop Theobold wrote in his own bestiary that the lion produces "his offspring without life . . . until the third day of its birth, and then the father of the young thing . . . sends forth a great roar about it, and thus arouses it as if from sleep." Interpreting this phenomenon, the bishop concludes: "since as the lion after the third day rouses its dead cub, so, after the Jews crucified Christ, he himself lay dead in the sepulchre until the third day, and on the third day God the Father aroused him." This resurrection motif connected with the lion cubs appears in nearly all the medieval bestiaries.

Earlier I mentioned that the unicorn was associated with the moon, and the lion with the sun. These are important alliances when we consider the fact that medieval representations of the Crucifixion depict the Cross surmounted with images of the sun and moon. And since this second panel of the Unicorn Tapestries relates—on the Christian mythic level—to the Crucifixion, the appearance of a lion and unicorn makes the intended iconography of the Passion more obvious.

Edward Topsell observes that the lion's head appears like the sun because "the hairs stand out eminent like sunbeams . . . [and] the eyes of a lion are red, fiery and hollow. . . . The pupils or apples of the eye shine exceedingly, insomuch as beholding of them, a man would think that he looked upon fire. . . . Because the lion is also of a hot nature, and seemeth to partake of the substance and quality of the sun, he hath that place in the heavens, the sign Leo, that the sun moves through in July. . . . In his breasts and forepart he is most strong, and in his hinder-part more weak, so the sun, increasing until the noon or fore-part of the year, until the Summer, and afterwards seemeth to languish towards the setting, or later part of the year called winter."

A slight digression from the present discussion, but one that is relevant to this particular tapestry, is another observation made by Topsell when he explains the occurrence of lion heads on fountains and conduits—and no example is better than the one woven into the fountain in this second tapestry. Topsell writes that such lion heads spouting water were customary among Egyptians, "because the Nile overflows the fields of Egypt at that time that the sun passed through the sign Leo."

The lion, as we have seen, was closely identified by all the medieval authors with Christ, and since earliest times had been a symbol of the sun. Because of these associations it would seem that the lion should be placed next to his lunar counterpart; but this is not the case. An explanation for placing the lion far from the fountain is given by one of the Fathers of the Latin Church, St. Ambrose. In his *Hexameron*, written during the fourth century, St. Ambrose mentions that "snake venom kills it [the lion]." (McCulloch) This notion is also repeated by Edward Topsell: "The splendid beauty of a Lion in his long curled mane is quickly abated and allayed when the Serpent doth but lift up his head to his breast; for such is the ordinance of God, that the snake which runneth from a Hart, should without all fear kill a courageous Lion." These accounts helped provide reasons for the depiction of the lion well away from the stream, and the depiction of a stag directly next to the fountain.

The next animal of importance is the wolf, a beast that is placed in this particular tapestry as far away from the lion as possible. Topsell uses the writings of the medieval theologian Albertus Magnus to explain this antagonism between the wolf and the lion. The wolf "has so great a fear of lions . . . that if any part of the lion's grease be cast into a fountain, the wolves never dare to drink thereof, or come near it."

To medieval man, the wolf* was associated with violence, war, winter, and even death itself. And since this animal was a creature of evil, it became a favorite guise of the devil and was a "familiar" of witches. One of the wolf's less attractive traits was its habit of greedily feeding on corpses, even on occasion digging up newly buried bodies. In northern mythology the evil god Loki, the great destructive power of the universe, was pictured in the guise of a wolf. And in the mythology of the Norsemen, there is a monstrous wolf called Fenris, whose ultimate destiny is the destruction of the sun. In the art of the Middle Ages, the representations of Mars as the god of war and violence almost invariably depict him as a fierce man

* For a further detailed discussion of the identity of the wolf, see pages 230–231.

mounted upon a chariot, accompanied by a wolf. The medieval bestiaries also attest to the wolf's unsavory and greedy nature—"The devil bears the similitude of a wolf: he who is always looking over the human race with his evil eye, and darkly prowling round the sheepfolds of the unfaithful so that he may afflict and ruin their souls" (White). More than any other creature depicted in the fountain tapestry, the wolf is identified with evil. Thus this animal represents the negative aspect of the polemical Christian concept of the struggle between good and evil—a battle that is finally resolved by the death and resurrection of Christ during the Easter Passion.

Woven next to the wolf are images of an orange and a marigold— plant icons that symbolize salvation and oppose the wolf as a depiction of evil. Directly under the head of the wolf, the designer has placed the image of a marigold. The Latin name for this flower is *calendula*, derived from *calends*, meaning "the first day of the month." This name is explained in an account given by John Parkinson, the seventeenth-century herbalist: "They flower all the Summer long, and sometimes even in winter, if it be mild, and chiefly at the beginning of those months." (1629) The golden yellow color of the flower and the fact that marigold blossoms open at daybreak and close in the evening helped to identify this plant with the sun. In the mid-sixteenth-century song "A New Ballad of the Marigold," this flower becomes an allegory for the conflict between good and evil, and therefore antagonistic to the evil wolf. The propensity of the marigold's flowers for light was often interpreted as the true Christian's search for Christ.

The other plant positioned next to the wolf is an orange tree—an icon popular with the designer of the Unicorn Tapestries that occurs again as the major tree in the fourth tapestry. Early writers called the orange a "citron," a name shared with limes and lemons. John Gerard, writing about the properties of oranges and lemons, which he collectively calls "citron trees," considered the fruits useful "against deadly poisons," and quotes a poem written by Virgil that attests to the citrus fruit's antitoxic properties.

> If any time stepmothers worse than brute
> Have poisoned pots, and mingle herbs of sute [sweet herbs]
> With hurtful charms: this citron fruit does chase
> Black venom from within each place.

In the wolf, the marigold, and orange, we have a prime example of the careful juxtapositioning of related icons. The orange (because of its solar shape and color) and the marigold are both identified with the sun's radiant light and ability to protect mankind from poison and corruption. This imagery provides a contrast between the benevolent forces of light and the evil forces of darkness, personified by the wolf.

One final mention of this ravenous animal, and perhaps the best with which to conclude this section on the carnivores depicted in this tapestry: there is a passage in Dante's *Divine Comedy* that connects the wolf, the lion, and the leopard. In the various editions of the *Divine Comedy*, translators have rendered Dante's *lonza* as "leopard," "ounce," "pard," "forest beast," and "panther." R. T. Holbrook concludes that "Any accurate determination of the animal meant by Dante seems next to impossible. . . . It is highly improbable that Dante or any ancient or medieval writer had a clear idea as to the various animals now called lynx, panther, and leopard. What Dante beheld was a spotted beast, very swift and light."

After straying from the straight road that led to the mountain of hope, Dante finds himself lost in a terrifying dark wood. Here he encounters three animals, a "panther," a lion, and a she-wolf.

The appearance of these three animals in the second panel of the Unicorn Tapestries is remarkable, for together they present "the three great Dantesque categories of sin." (Holbrook) This is a typically medieval contrast to the three virtuous animals, represented by the unicorn, genet, and stag woven next to the fountain—beasts all identified with the redemption of Christ, which is a central motif of this tapestry. Most scholars of Dante agree that the three animals described in the *Divine Comedy* were included because of a passage in Jeremiah: "Wherefore a lion out of the forest shall slay them, and a wolf of the evening shall spoil them, a leopard shall watch over their cities: every one that goeth out thence shall be torn in pieces: because their transgressions are many, and their backslidings are increased." (Jeremiah 5:6) In the first part of the thirteenth century Hugo a Sancto Caro commented on this passage, and interpreted the animals as symbols of the sins embodied with the three ages of man—lust, pride, and greed—characteristics of youth, middle age, and old age.

Dante obviously meant the lion to signify pride, the wolf to signify greed, and the "panther" to be identified with the lustful sins of youth. "Each of the three beasts represents a demon of sin, and each sin thus embodied in an allegorical beast is more terrible than the preceding sin." (Holbrook)

As I have repeatedly stated, the icons in medieval art often have conflicting meanings and must therefore be interpreted in a pluralistic sense. Thus, the lion and the panther in this particular tapestry are presented at once as benevolent and malevolent creatures. On the other hand, the wolf in most instances represents a vicious creature. The animal depicted in the fountain tapestry is clearly meant to imply the wolf's satanic image—a personification of violence, death, and greed.

This symbolic antagonism between the animals woven into the second panel of the Unicorn Tapestries had a dynamic effect upon the medieval

# The Unicorn Tapestries

I THE START OF THE HUNT

III   THE UNICORN CROSSING THE STREAM

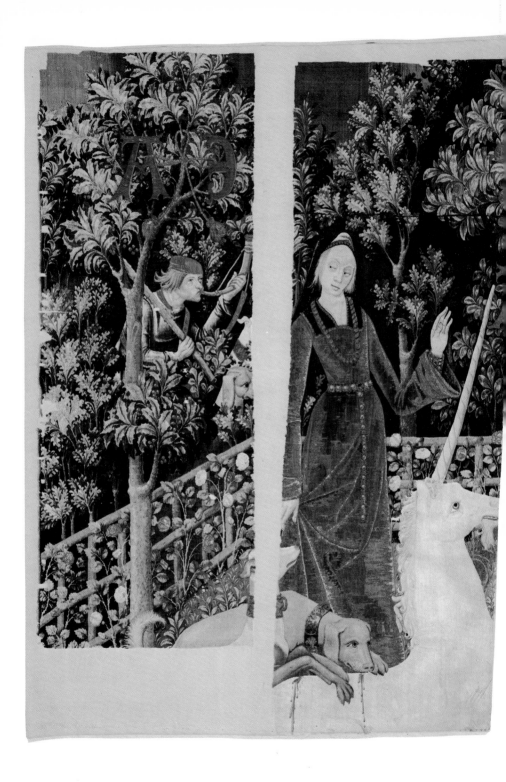

V   THE UNICORN IS TAMED BY THE MAIDEN

VI  THE UNICORN IS KILLED AND BROUGHT TO THE CASTLE

VII  THE UNICORN IN CAPTIVITY

beholder. The interpretation of these images, and the subsequent discovery of the different levels of meaning conveyed by these animals and plants, reveals the vibrancy of the art of the Middle Ages.

As Joseph Campbell states, the medieval scholar and theologian converted "every feature of the locally envisioned order of nature into . . . an icon of . . . Yahweh or of his son Christ." (1969) To these learned men of the Middle Ages, such real or imagined creatures mirrored the nature of God and his antagonist, the devil. This dualistic doctrine was an intrinsic part of medieval theology, which held the fervent belief that the one could not exist without the other.

For example, when the medieval observer viewed "The Unicorn at the Fountain" tapestry, one reality was seen as a reflection of another. The observer would see Christ redeeming mankind as he freed the "Waters of Life" from corruption. This symbolic response was what Ananda Coomaraswamy had in mind when he noted "the representation of a reality on a certain level of reference by a corresponding reality on another." (1977) To the medieval Christian, the unicorn was an icon of Christ; and when other images were annexed to this mythical creature, a more specific and dramatic iconography emerges. The symbolic references abound. For example, to identify the fountain scene with the Crucifixion, the medieval designer placed red roses behind the unicorn, and a pair of goldfinches on the rim of the fountain. According to Christian mystics and theologians, the rose was stained red by the blood of Christ. Albertus Magnus, in his *Opera Omnia*, speaks of "the rose made red by the blood of Christ in his passion." (D'Ancona, 1977)

The two goldfinches on the rim of the fountain in this particular tapestry are iconographically very important. In many ways they are identified with the symbolism of the rose. Goldfinches occur in a number of places in the Unicorn Tapestries. In this second hanging, beside the pair on the rim of the font, another is perched on the medlar next to the fountain. Goldfinches also occur in the third and fourth tapestries. And in the sixth panel of the hunt, two finches are placed in a hawthorn bush directly over the back of the dead unicorn.

The French name for the goldfinch is *chardonneret*, the Scottish "thistlefinch," and the Italian *cardellino*. All these names are of great antiquity— and all connect the bird to the thistle. The names concur with the goldfinch's preference for a meal of thistle, a preference that did not go unnoticed by the early Christian iconographers. According to Christian mythology, when Jesus was carrying the Cross to Calvary, a goldfinch fluttered down to his head and managed to pull out one of the sharpest thorns. The red on the bird's head was believed to be a reminder of the finch's mercy.

Conrad von Megenberg, a medieval canon of the Cathedral of Ratisbon, wrote in his popular encyclopedia *Buch der Natur:* "It is a great wonder that the bird sings so beautifully although it feeds on the sharp spines of the thistle. It is thus a symbol of the good preacher on earth who has to endure greatly, yet even among the thorns of this world joyfully serves God. O, God . . . thou art well acquainted with meals of thorns; yet Thou too hast sung on earth unto the bitter death." (Freeman)

According to Herbert Friedmann in *The Symbolic Goldfinch,* this particular bird represents the soul which is saved with the coming of Christ. The placing of the goldfinch in the hands of the Christ child in religious paintings is no accident, but a deliberate inclusion, a reminder of his ultimate death.

In a less sorrowful vein, the goldfinch was a symbol of fecundity, and hence identified with fertility, the other main motif in this second panel of the Unicorn Tapestries.

Pliny, in his *Natural History,* makes mention of a small bird that is prolific in its egg laying, which he calls the "acanthis." Although the acanthis is not identified for us by Pliny, there is strong evidence that this fecund bird is a goldfinch. During the Middle Ages, Isidore of Seville in his *Etymologiae* referred to the goldfinch as acanthus.

Friedmann, in a very convincing argument, identifies the legendary charadrius with the goldfinch. This mythic bird had the remarkable ability to determine if a sick person was going to live or die. If the illness was not fatal and the patient was to recover, the bird took the disease upon itself, flew toward the sun, and burned away the malady. The bestiaries considered this bird to be symbolic of Christ: "Caladrius [Charadrius] is like Our Saviour. Our Lord is entirely white, having nothing black about him, and he committeth no sin nor was there any deceit in his mouth. Moreover, Our Lord from heaven turns his face from the Jews, because of their disbelief, but turns towards the people of our own sort, bearing our infirmities and taking away our sins. Then he ascends on high, on the wood of the cross, leading captivity captive and giving his gift to men." (White)

In his description of the acanthus (goldfinch), Pliny mentions that the bird produces twelve fledglings. As Friedmann observes: "when we recall that the goldfinch became the substitute for the Charadrius, which in turn was identified by the religious mystics of the Middle Ages with Christ Himself, a parallel between the twelve offspring of the bird and the twelve disciples of Christ becomes possible." (1946)

Following this reasoning, it is not too difficult to conclude that the twelve men grouped around the fountain in the second panel of the Unicorn Tapestries were included by the designer to represent the disciples, and that both the unicorn and the goldfinch are substitutes for Christ.

Another bird, the nightingale, is associated with both spring and serpents. The nightingale has been a long-cherished symbol of spring, and the return of his song is a welcome sound after the long cold winter. The following Provençal prose-poem by Bernard of Ventadour expresses these feelings: "When green herbs and leaves appear, and flowers bud in the green grass, and the nightingale raises her voice, high and clear, and sings her songs, I have great joy in her, and joy in the flowers, joy in myself, and still more in my lady." (Pevsner)

In many instances, the nightingale is described as sitting in its nest with a thorn in its breast. A French poem from the sixteenth century provides the symbolic basis for this image:

> During spring, mild and gracious,
> The nightingale at full voice
> Gives praise to the god among gods
> So much that it makes the woods resound.
> Fear(ing) the snake, it sings loudly
> All night long, and it pulls its breast
> Against some sharp thorn
> Which wakes it up when it falls asleep.
> —Aneau

Thus the nightingale, along with other animals depicted next to the fountain (stag, genet, and weasel), shares antagonistic associations with the serpent.

Before concluding the iconography of this second panel of the Unicorn Tapestries, we must explore a facet of the design that has never been satisfactorily explained. Why is the nobleman in the upper portion of the work pointing toward the holly tree? Some art historians have suggested that this particular gesture is an act of benediction, associated with the unicorn purifying the waters of the fountain. But since the customary Christian gesture requires the use of two fingers, some alternative explanation is needed. And such an explanation may be found in the fact that St. John the Baptist is often depicted using this particular gesture as he points to Christ to indicate him as his successor.

In the fountain tapestry, the pointing noble draws our attention to a large holly tree. This plant, I am certain, is a representation of Christ—who will receive the holly crown. The holly, as mentioned earlier, is associated with the death of Christ. The red berries, the sharp prickles, and the bitter bark all made this evergreen an ideal tree to symbolize the Crucifixion. Considering the Christian icons in this tapestry and the fact that the nobleman is pointing toward the holly, there can be little doubt that much of the iconography corresponds to Christ's martyrdom.

In this remarkable drama, centered upon the unicorn at the fountain, we have iconography that connects both the arrival of spring and the Easter

Passion. The unicorn represents Christ and his Crucifixion, and the action of neutralizing the poisoned waters can be seen as the redemption from sin.

The chronology of March is central to this tapestry, and it is reflected in the trees and animals that are woven into this complex panel. The flora and fauna relate to the vernal equinox and also to the Easter drama of the Christian myth. Indeed, many of the plants and animals relate specifically to the events that surround the Crucifixion. For instance, to reflect the resurrection of Christ, the designer placed the lion in this tapestry—an event paralleled by the genet's restoring her dead cubs with rue, the herb of life. The hawthorn was chosen to represent the crown of thorns. Equally significant icons are seen in the pair of goldfinches—the merciful bird that relieves the suffering of Christ, as well as being identified with the mythic Charadrius, a creature that the bestiaries call "our saviour." And the dozen fledglings connected with the goldfinch are identified with the twelve apostles of Christ, an interesting parallel when we realize that there are twelve hunters standing around the fountain.

The icon of Christ in this tapestry, signified by the unicorn, has the pimpernel under his head—a flower that Christian lore tells us grew on Calvary. In this panel the carnation twice appears in relation to the lion, and is intended to symbolize the nails of the Crucifixion. The fountain itself reflects the idea of the baptism and the cleansing of mankind from sin. In a symbolic sense, two images (one animal and one plant) guard the waters of the fountain during the hours of darkness and daylight. The nightingale keeps watch as he sings his song through the night; and the marigold, a plant held sacred by the Virgin, responds to the new light of day by opening its flowers.

In this tapestry we discover iconography and images that identify with resurrected fertility gods, such as Christ and Narcissus. And we find motifs of mating and fertility that are emphasized by the pairing of animals around the stream and fountain—lion, pheasant, duck, and rabbit. These images forecast the arrival of spring and correspond to the vernal equinox in March. "The Unicorn at the Fountain" is a metaphor for a crucial moment in the cycle of life and nature: barrenness and winter (crucifixion) have begun to lose their grip upon the world, and the earth stirs (redemption) with a new season of growth.

PLATE

# III

# THE UNICORN

# CROSSING

# THE STREAM

On May-day when the lark
began to rise

- - - - - - - -

Within a temple shapen
hawthorn wise.

- - - - - - - -

And forth goeth all the court,
both most and least,
To fetch the flowers fresh,
and branch and bloom,
And namely, hawthorn brought
both page and groom.
—*The Court of Love*
(trans. Walter Skeat, 1897)

I N THIS LIVELY THIRD TAPESTRY, two youths loudly blow their horns
as the actual hunt begins (Plate III). The whole drama depicted in this panel
is a frenzy of activity, as dogs are unleashed and the unicorn emerges from
the stream to be confronted by two huntsmen with threatening spears.

As in the previous panel ("The Unicorn at the Fountain"), the oak is
the predominant tree. And because "The Unicorn Crossing the Stream" is
part of the waxing cycle of the seasons, the oak gains even more prominence
as midsummer approaches. A large oak tree forms the main motif in this
panel, dominating the drama. To the right of this large central tree, another
oak appears in the margin.

Holly is presented in this tapestry twice. The principal weaving of this
tree occurs in the left perimeter (an oak tree of equal stature to this holly
is depicted in the opposite, right perimeter). Another holly tree, though
much smaller, can be seen woven behind the head of the unicorn.

Other trees that are iconographically important in this panel are the
hawthorn and the pomegranate. A neatly depicted tree of hawthorn is

placed so that it silhouettes the body of the unicorn as he makes his way across the stream. And on the near bank of the watercourse, next to the holly, a pomegranate is depicted. Behind this tree, giving the impression that he is oblivious to the fierce ensuing battle with the unicorn, a gentle youth with spear over his shoulder is shown staring into the distance.

The chief drama in this third tapestry centers upon the unicorn fleeing from the hunters. Halfway across the stream, he is confronted by two spears. It is both a perilous and unlikely situation for the unicorn, for according to medieval lore, the unicorn cannot be captured by any conventional means. The designer of the Unicorn Tapestries, aware of this fact and true to legend, includes a virgin in the fragmentary fifth tapestry. In the fable of the unicorn, a young woman pacifies the beast before he is led to his death. Thus in "The Unicorn Crossing the Stream" the huntsmen are not trying to kill the creature, but are attempting to drive him across the stream for a specific reason, a symbolic motive that will be understood when we interpret the icons in this textile.

The second tapestry, "The Unicorn at the Fountain," depicted images that were identified with Easter—chronology that is associated with the vernal equinox of March, the actual blossoming of vegetation, and the return to earth of vegetation gods.

"The Unicorn Crossing the Stream" depicts events, plants, and trees that suggest activities connected with May, a month in which anthropomorphic rites are enacted "to carry out death"—a drama that ritualizes the final defeat of winter and the arrival of summer. Many pre-Christian Europeans believed this to be a very dangerous time for man, animals, and plants. It was a period when the activity of the elements or supernatural agents could upset the delicate balance of nature and so endanger crops, livestock, and even human life.

"The Unicorn at the Fountain" represented the death of Christ during the Easter Passion. "The Unicorn Crossing the Stream" identifies with the events centered upon resurrection. Most fertility gods (Christ included) were ritually killed in early spring, and their imminent resurrection coincided with the time of the greatest fertility of the land. It was an important period in the agricultural calendars of many early cultures, a time when the creative forces of nature needed greatest protection. Rites and sympathetic ceremonies were enacted in order to avert any possible disasters: drought, disease, or blight. The following early Anglo-Saxon charm was used during this period of vulnerability to protect crops from witchcraft:

> Acres a-waxing, upwards a-growing
> Pregnant [with grain] and plenteous in strength;
> Host of [wheat] shafts and of glittering plants!
> Of broad barley the blossoms

And of white wheat ears waxing,
Of the whole earth the harvest!
Let be guarded the grain against all ills
That be sown o'er the land by sorcery men,
Nor let cunning woman [witches] change it nor a crafty
man [male witch]. (Rohde)


The May Day celebrations represented the final defeat of winter, and water—as one of the principal elements of life—played a vital role, being directly linked to the health and benevolence of the community. In order to understand why the unicorn is made to cross the stream in this third tapestry of the series, we must see the unicorn in his full mythological perspective. As well as being an icon for Christ, the unicorn was a creature of magical powers, strength, and fertility; therefore, the entering into the waters of a religious object or icon of the deity in springtime assured health and fertility. As Mircea Eliade points out: "In whatever religious framework it appears, the function of water is shown to be the same; it disintegrates, abolishes forms, 'washes away sins'—at once purifying and giving new life."

This ceremony of the sacred immersion "was generally performed in the cult of the Great Goddess of fertility and agriculture. The goddess's flagging powers were thus strengthened, ensuring a good harvest (immersion as a magic rite was supposed to produce rain) and a rich increase in goods." (Eliade, 1958)

The sacred immersion in Christian mythology is represented in a twelfth-century French sacramentary (Fig. 29). The central drama shows the Baptism of Christ by St. John. The images depicted at the bottom of the painting record another New Testament event, the Marriage Feast at Cana. It was at these nuptial celebrations that Christ transmuted water into wine. Both events in this sacramentary are iconographic references to the union of water and spirit. This amalgam, when it involves a god, provides benevolence for the community.

Fetching summer home was the central theme of the May ceremonies, rituals that on a mythical level paralleled the death of winter. In many of the anthropomorphic mimes of May, the image of death was "drowned," and summer was resurrected from the water. For instance, in the following English May song, the Christianized sun god, St. George, fetches the summer home in a boat.

Awake, S. George, our English knight O!
For Summer is a-come, and Winter is a-go.

--------

Where is S. George: and where is he, O?
He's down in his long-boat upon the salt sea, O.

--------

For to fetch Summer home, the Summer and May, O!
The Summer is a-come, and Winter is a-go.
—*Collectanea, Folklore,* Vol. XVI, 1905

This aquatic mythology is explained by Eliade, who writes that "the symbolism of water implies both death and rebirth. Contact with water always brings a regeneration—on the one hand because dissolution is followed by a new birth, on the other because immersion fertilizes and multiplies the potential of life." (1959)

In a mythological sense, the descent into water (especially when it involved a god or the icon of a god like the unicorn) resulted in benevolence for the entire community. On the mythic level, the immersion or passage through water of the deity, his image, or representative has other important biblical parallels. Joshua, for instance, carrying the most sacred object of the Jews, the Ark of the Covenant, led the Israelites dryshod across the River Jordan. In another Old Testament episode, the prophet Elijah divided the waters of the Jordan with his mantle, and crossed unharmed with his son Elisha. As iconographer Gertrud Schiller notes: "this event is followed by the ascension of Elijah, a prefiguration of the Ascension of Christ. Moses, Joshua and Elijah are types of Christ. They belong to the typology of baptism because all of them—each in a different context—passed unharmed through water, the destructive power of which was tamed so that it became a force for salvation."

The purifying function of water is stressed in the consecration of the baptismal water. Another prototype of baptism in this context is the incident in which the prophet Elisha cured the leprosy of Naaman, the Syrian captain, by instructing him to dip himself seven times in the Jordan. Leprosy represents sin.

In the fourth century, the great preacher of the Eastern Church, John Chrysostom, described baptism as "burying the old man"—and "when we come out of the water, the new man appears at that moment." (Eliade, 1958) It was during the sacred procedure of baptism that the "sinful person is annihilated—as Luther said, the old Adam is drowned—and the baptized person belongs to the new creation grounded in Christ's death and resurrection." (Schiller) Thus the resurrection and purification of the god ensured the necessary fertility for mankind, animals, and vegetation. In other words, this was a mythic drama that explained the appearance of summer. All the iconography of "The Unicorn Crosses the Stream" tapestry is centered upon an important seasonal event of very ancient origin. It was a

Figure 29. Baptism of Christ; Miracle at Cana.   Sacramentary from St. Etienne of Limoges. Paris, Bibliothèque Nationale.

May Day festival of spring that was observed all over Europe—and in some instances is still performed today. The festivities that took place on May Eve and upon May Day signaled the return of summer and the final defeat of winter.

Sir Thomas Malory mentions the month of May in his *Morte d'Arthur*, describing it as a time "when the foliage of herbs and trees is most freshly green, when buds ripen and blossoms appear in their fragrance and loveliness. And the month when lovers, subject to the same force which reawakens the plants, feel their heart open again, recall past trysts and past vows and moments of tenderness, and yearn for a renewal of the magical awareness which is love."

This was the time of orgiastic revels ruled over by an elected May Queen. The ceremonies centered on the Maypoles erected on village greens—venial rites in honor of renewed life and the reappearance of vegetation throughout the land.

In Europe the typical May Day celebrations started the evening before, or, in some instances, early on May morning with the gathering of spring flowers and green branches of hawthorn. The gathering of hawthorn is often illustrated in manuscripts and paintings that depict scenes of seasonal activities from the month of May. And because most medieval devotional books contained a calendar, the illustrations for May provide us with a rich reference of historically revealing images. One particular book from the workshop of Simon Bening (Fig. 30) depicts activities that are central to the May Day celebrations. In the right panel of this illumination, mounted nobles accompanied by their servants, who have gathered hawthorn from the woods, return to the castle to decorate the citadel with the leafy branches. And in the left panel, a boat bedecked with hawthorn conveys a merry group around the castle moat. Within the walls of the citadel the May Day celebrations have already begun, as a group of townsfolk perform a circular dance.

The following passage from Malory's *Morte d'Arthur* provides a word-picture of these joyful activities:

So it befell in the month of May, Queen Guenever called unto her knights of the round table; and she gave them warning that early upon the morrow she would ride on Maying into the woods . . . that ye all be clothed in green . . . and I shall bring with me ten ladies, and every knight shall have a lady behind him. . . . And so upon the morn they took their horses with the queen, and rode on Maying in woods and meadows as it pleased them, in great joy and delights. . . . She had no man of arms with her but the ten noble knights all arrayed in green for Maying. . . . So as the queen had Mayed and all her knights, all were bedashed with herbs, mosses and flowers, in the best manner and freshest.

In northern Europe a queen and sometimes a king, selected from the

Figure 30. Calendar for May, Book of Hours, Bruges. Workshop of Simon Bening, c. 1540. Waddesdon Manor, England, James A. de Rothschild Collection.

community's young people, ruled over the festivities. This merry crowd of revelers, singing the songs of May, proceeded through the village, stopping at each door. In exchange for their songs and antics they expected donations of food and drink. If suitably rewarded by the master or mistress of the household, they would give them the blessings of May. But if spurned or given a meager reward, they would wish ill-luck and a bad harvest upon the ungenerous. These revelers were messengers of the renewal of vegetation, and they assumed the right to punish the niggardly, because avarice (as opposed to generosity) was dangerous to the community's hope for the abundance of nature. At an important time like the coming of summer, "food, the substance of life, must [be ritually] circulated generously within the community in order that the cosmic circuit of life's substance might be kept in motion (trees, flocks, harvests)." The mimers, by announcing the good news of summer, "feel that they are performing a ceremonial action of interest to the whole community, and that such a performance should be rewarded: the group sees spring before anyone else, brings it to the village, shows it to the others and hastens its coming with song, dance and ritual." (Eliade, 1958)

The Maypole, usually decorated the night before, provided the climax of the festivities. "The intention of these customs," says Sir James Frazer (1911), was "to bring home to the village, and to each house, the blessings which the tree spirit has the power to bestow." A puritanical writer, Phillip Stubbes, in his *Anatomie of Abuses,* gives a disapproving account of the May Day celebrations that took place in sixteenth-century England, unintentionally preserving for us a picture of these activities. On May Eve,

all the young men and maids . . . run gadding over night to the woods, groves, hills, and mountains, where they spend all the night in pleasant pastimes; and in the morning they return, bringing with them birch and branches of trees, to deck their assemblies withal. . . . But the chiefest jewel they bring from thence is their May pole, which they bring home with great veneration, as thus. They have twenty or forty yoke of oxen, every ox having a sweet nose-gay of flowers placed on the tip of his horns, and these oxen draw home this May pole (this stinking idol, rather), which is covered all over with flowers and herbs, bound round about with strings, from the top to the bottom, and sometimes painted with variable colors, with two or three hundred men, women and children following it with great devotion. And thus being reared up, with handkerchieves and flags hovering on top, they strew the ground round about, bind green boughs about it, set up summer haules, bowers, and arbors hard by it. And then fall they to dance about it, like as the heathen people did at the dedication of the idols, whereof this is a perfect pattern, or rather the thing itself. I have heard it credibly reported by men of great gravity and reputation, that forty, threescore, or a hundred maids going to the wood over night, there have scarcely the third part of them returned home again undefiled.

In these celebrations the most important tree was the hawthorn, and it was often called May or May tree. The vernacular name was given to hawthorn because May was the month in which this lovely tree was in full flower.

The hawthorn has mixed meanings. On the one hand it was associated with sexuality, particularly female sexuality; on the other, it was considered a tree of ill-fortune and death. The hawthorn's malevolent associations are very ancient, and derive from the tree's connection with the cult of the Greek goddess Maia. This deity, says Robert Graves, "although she is represented in English poetry as 'ever fair and young,' took her name from maia, 'grandmother'; she was a malevolent beldame whose son Hermes conducts the souls to Hell. She was in fact the White Goddess, who under the name Cardea . . . cast spells with the hawthorn. The Greeks propitiated her at marriages—marriage being considered hateful to the Goddess—with five torches of hawthorn-wood and with hawthorn blossom before the unlucky month began." (1966)

The hawthorn's earlier malevolent associations with Maia still survive in England and on the continent. For example, in parts of England, "to sleep in a room, with hawthorn in bloom in it during the month of May is considered by country folk, to be unlucky and sure to be followed by some great misfortune." (Folkard)

Later in history, hawthorn became connected with a much gentler goddess, becoming the symbolic flower of the orgiastic cult of Flora and a plant of the god of love. This association "accounts for the English [and French] medieval habit of going out on May Morning to pluck flowering hawthorn boughs and dance around the maypole." (Graves, 1966)

The antagonistic symbolism connected with the hawthorn evolved as a result of the unification of two differing mythologies. By the Middle Ages, hawthorn was accepted as a symbol for the joyous month of May; nonetheless, some of the earlier sinister associations lingered. In the sixth panel of the Unicorn Tapestries, "The Death of the Unicorn," this macabre aspect of the tree's symbolism will become apparent.

The white and reddish flowers of the hawthorn that deck the countryside during the month of May are indeed a spectacular sight. And equal to the experience of the color of the blossoms is their heady perfume—unless the observer stands too close and is overwhelmed by a fragrance that is unpleasantly strong. For these reasons, and because "for everyone it symbolized the change from spring to summer," Geoffrey Grigson observes that the hawthorn "became above most plants of the far west of Europe a supernatural tree." The May Day activities are a "festival of vegetation and farming, precisely of the bringing in summer. . . . Through the whole month fairies and witches were active, excited no less than humans by the new summer. Milk, butter, and all 'profit,' or farm produce, were liable to be stolen or bewitched. Protection was called for by plants with a powerful 'manna.' . . . In England, and in France, the emphatic plant was the hawthorn, which was among the plants put around the may pole when it was carried in from the woods."

This practice is very ancient, dating back to classical times. The prophylactic properties of hawthorn were recorded by Ovid in the *Fasti*. In a delightful tale, Ovid relates how the nymph Carna [Cardea] was deified and presented with the hawthorn tree:

Near to the Tiber lies an ancient grove of Helernus. . . . There a nymph was born, often wooed in vain by many suitors. . . . If any youth spoke to her words of love, she straightway made him this answer: "In this place there is too much of light, and with the light too much of shame; if thou wilt lead to a more retired cave, I'll follow." While he confidingly went in front, she no sooner reached the bushes than she halted and hid herself, and was nowise to be found. Janus had seen her, and the sight had aroused his passion; to the hard-hearted nymph he used soft words. The nymph as usual bade him seek a more sequestered cave, and she pretended to follow at his heels, but deserted her leader.

Fond fool! Janus sees what goes on behind his back; vain is thine effort; he sees thy hiding place behind him. Vain is thy effort, lo! said I. For he caught thee in his embrace as thou didst lurk beneath a rock, and having worked his will he said: "In return for our dalliance be thine the control of hinges; take that for the price of thy lost maidenhood." So saying, he gave her a thorn— and white it was—wherewith she could repel all doleful harm from the doors.

The practice of placing hawthorn over doorways and other entrances continued through the centuries. The following account records an example in France: "On the calends, or first of May, commonly called May-Day, the juvenile part of both sexes are wont to rise a little after midnight and walk to some neighboring wood, accompanied with music and blowing of horns, where they break down branches from the trees, and adorn themselves with nosegays and crowns of flowers; when this is done they return with their booty homewards, about the rising of the sun, and make their doors and windows to triumph with their flowery spoils." (Thistleton-Dyer, 1875)

Of the many cases of witchcraft that came to the attention of the medieval clergy, adolescent girls seemed more prone to possession by evil spirits than any other group. Because of the high risk of diabolical possession, it was the practice in France during these centuries to place branches of hawthorn outside the windows of young women, particularly during the symbolically critical period of the month of May.

By the Middle Ages the chief association of this tree was with sex and fertility, but, as we have seen, the earlier sinister connections of hawthorn with mortality were not entirely forgotten. And in one sense, this polemical association perfectly suited the morbid medieval mores, in which death and sex were interconnected.

Although hawthorn was a plant considered propitious for engagement and orgiastic revels, in most parts of Europe it was not connected with marriage. The month of June was deemed much more appropriate for marriage vows. In his *Roman Questions*, Plutarch relates that the Romans did not marry in the month of May because it is "in this month that they perform the greatest purification ceremonies." (Graves, 1966)

In the *Fasti*, Ovid mentions an oracle he obtained about the forthcoming marriage of his daughter. The priestess of Jupiter told Ovid to avoid the month of May and wait "until the calm Tiber shall have carried down to the sea on its yellow current the filth from the temple of Vesta." He should hold the marriage in June, "when Vesta's fire shall shine on a clean fire."

By all accounts, May was a month of preparation—a dubious and dangerous time, in which the supernatural agencies antagonistic to man were in full force. This was a period for performing purification rites and a time for enacting sympathetic rituals, the month when the May Queen and Lord "spurred on the creative forces of nature by mating ritually on plowed land." (Eliade, 1958)

It was an enactment that horrified the puritanical and humorless Phillip Stubbes, who describes how "forty, threescore, or a hundred maids [would go] to the forest over night," and after an amorous evening, "scarcely the third of them returned home undefiled." Perhaps it is appropriate that, according to Pliny, the hawthorn was also used as torches "by the shepherds that carried off the Sabine women." (Vol. IV, Book XVI)

The following May carol was sung by the happy revelers as they returned from their nocturnal excursion, symbolically bringing home the summer with them:

> We have been rambling half the night, And almost all
> the day.
> And now, returned—back again, We've
> brought you a branch of May.
>
> --------
>
> O, we were up as soon as day,
> To fetch the summer home-a;
> The summer is a going on,
> And winter is a-gone-a.
> —Furry Day Carol, *Oxford Book of Carols*

And Shakespeare alludes to this custom in *A Midsummer Night's Dream:*

> If thou lovest me, then,
> Steal forth thy father's house tomorrow night;
> And in the wood, a league without the town,
> Where I did meet thee once with Helena,
> To do observance to a morn of May,
> There will I stay for thee.
> —Act I, Scene I

The hawthorn was the main emblem of these lusty times. A French poem dating from the thirteenth century connects the sharp thorns of the hawthorn to the darts of Cupid. In this poem, a wandering scholar calls his lover the "Flower o' the thorn."

> Lovelier than the lily or the rose.
> The Queen of France is not so beautiful.
> And Death is now near neighbor unto me
> Unless she heal the wound she made in me,
> Flower o' the thorn.
> —Waddell

Another interesting French fifteenth-century poem, *L'Amant rendu cordelier,* describes a rather unorthodox monastery where only the martyrs of love were welcomed. Enumerating the orders and obligations, the prior cautions the rejected lover "never to think of bouquets of roses or of violets or pansies strewn on the table, never to sleep under a hawthorn tree." (Freeman) And a medieval poem by Eustache Deschamps, entitled *Lay Amoureux,* explains why the lovelorn were advised never to slumber under the boughs of the hawthorn tree. The poet describes his search through a springtime landscape to discover the flowering hawthorn. When he finds one, he sits under the white blossoms and contemplates the verdant countryside. His tranquility does not last long, however, for soon the poet is amazed to see before him the god of love, riding in a chariot of fire and accompanied by an amorous entourage. Since the lover mentioned in *L'Amant rendu cordelier* was trying to forget his amour, sleeping under a tree that belonged to the god of love would certainly not have helped the youth's distraught condition.

The other amorous plants mentioned in *L'Amant rendu cordelier,* the pansy and the violet, also occur in this third panel of the Unicorn Tapestries. The violet appears a number of times, the most outstanding example being on the riverbank in front of the white duck (Fig. 31). A contemporary of Chaucer's, John Lydgate, was aware of the erotic connections of the violet when he wrote to his lady on St. Valentine's Day, referring to her as "O Violet, O fleur desire," and adding, "since I am for you so amorous, embrace me, lady of the joyous heart." (Skeat, 1897)

The pansy is also woven into this third panel in a number of places, but the most lavish depiction can be seen directly to the right of the hawthorn. The vernacular names of the pansy are similar in all European languages. A few of the common English ones will suffice to reveal why this plant belonged to amorous Venus. They include love-in-idleness, Cupid's delight, and kiss-me.

The pansy was the flower that Oberon describes in *A Midsummer Night's Dream*—the plant that was hit by a "bolt of Cupid" when the arrow missed its target and fell instead

> Upon a little western flower,
> Before milk-white, now purple with love's wound,
> And maidens call it Love-in-idleness.
> Fetch me that flower; the herb I showed thee once:
> The juice of it on sleeping eyelids laid
> Will make a man or woman madly dote
> Upon the next live creature that it sees.
> —Act II, Scene II

Figure 31. Detail—"The Unicorn Crossing the Stream." The Unicorn Tapestries. Franco-Flemish, c. 1500. The Cloisters, Metropolitan Museum of Art.

In the *Booke of Simples,* the sixteenth-century author William Bullein mentions an earlier "monkish written herbal" that gives the name "Trinitaria herba" (herb of the Trinity) for the pansy. Commenting on this medieval herbal, William Bullein objected to the "monkish author" connecting the pansy with the Trinity. "The majesty of God may not with reverence, be compared or lykened, by any allegory, to any base, vayne, venerous flower."

Other images occur in this textile that support the erotic events connected with the merry month of May. Depicted on the near bank of the stream to the left of the central oak tree are a pair of partridges (Fig. 32). These amorous birds were associated by the classical authors with wantonness and sexuality. The Christian iconographers intensified this long-standing erotic symbolism and made the partridge a symbol of lust. The iconography was used by Cranach the Elder in his painting *Recumbent Water Nymph* (Fig. 33). In front of the naked and enticing female, Cranach depicts a pair of frolicking partridges.

According to Pliny, these plump birds were considered so lascivious

Figure 32. Detail—"The Unicorn Crossing the Stream." The Cloisters, Metropolitan Museum of Art.

Figure 33. Cranach the Elder, *Recumbent Water Nymph,* c. 1534. Liverpool, Royal Institution.

that "they become pregnant . . . even with the draft of air from cocks flying over them, and often even merely the sound of a cock crowing, makes them conceive." (Book III, Book X)

The Renaissance iconographer Cesare Ripa depicts lust in his *Iconologia* as an overdeveloped young lady seated on a crocodile, caressing a partridge: "A young damsel with her hair finely curled; in a manner naked; sits on a crocodile, and makes much of a partridge."

Perhaps the partridge is best known for its connection with the Christian carol *The Twelve Days of Christmas.* These cumulative verses describe the gifts given to a maid by her young lover on the twelve days between Christmas Day and Epiphany. The song begins with the first day's gift, the "partridge in a pear tree." In the many versions of the rhyme, the partridge is either on or in a pear tree. As the song progresses through all twelve gifts, the preceding lines are repeated in reverse order after each new stanza. So by the end of the song, the first verse, "partridge in a pear tree" has been sung twelve times. The first gift is thus given special emphasis, as Beryl Rowland points out: "explicators of the carol, while admitting the bad reputation of the partridge, avoided explicitly glossing the partridge in the pear tree. Ornithologically the image is unsound. The partridge does not normally perch. It may rarely do so on a wall but only very exceptionally on a tree. It roosts on the ground and at the bottom of hedgerows." So why "a partridge in a pear tree"? "The image becomes more meaningful when one realizes that the pear tree is a well-known phallic symbol." Rowland concludes that "the lover of the singer is making a gift of himself." (1978)

One final point worth mentioning in connection with the partridges is the tall plant of clary sage depicted to the right of these birds (see Fig. 32). Clary sage was a plant famed in medieval Europe for its curative abilities, and was also used as an aphrodisiac. (Pliny, Vol. VI, Book XXII) The second property would certainly explain why the designer depicted the clary sage next to the partridges, and for that matter why the plant was woven in such a prominent position in this sexually preoccupied panel. Besides the partridge there are other erotic birds woven into this scene of the Unicorn Tapestries. A pair of ducks are depicted swimming in the stream to the right of the central oak tree, and to the left of this central emblem a lone bittern appears.

The duck was given a licentious reputation by medieval authors, thereby proving a good companion for the lascivious partridge. The following medieval poem mentions the duck's amorous behavior:

> Springs about with love again
> With blossoms and with bird's refrain
>
> --------
>
> Wild and wanton drakes abound;
> Their mating calls to lovers sound.
> —Stone, 1964

The medieval scholar and compiler Vincent of Beauvais stated that sometimes in their mating enthusiasm, the drakes killed the females. "The duck usually had a bad reputation," for like all birds that are "said to be over fond of going under water symbolized those who were preoccupied with sex." (Rowland, 1978)

The bittern finalizes this carnal trio of birds. Edward Topsell writes: "The voice of this fowl is most admirable, for . . . he roareth like a Bull, which is usual with him in the Spring when he is stirred with lust for procreation." The solemn and deep-booming voice that is characteristic of the male bittern invested the bird with an uncanny aura. People throughout Europe believed that the sonorous notes of the bittern could be used in both weather and crop prognostication.

The other interesting plants woven into this tapestry include the purple "lady's smocks." These can be seen in front of the partridges (see Fig. 32), one of which is depicted holding down one of the purple stems of this flower. In Europe, the lady's smock appears along the banks of streams in May. Of the countless vernacular names for this plant, those connected with the cuckoo are most numerous. Local English names include cuckoo flower, cuckoo bread, cuckoo's eyes, and water cuckoo. As Gerard notes, "these flowers for the most part [appear] in April and May, when the cuckoo does begin to sing her pleasant note without stammering. They are commonly called in Latin, *Flos Cuculi* . . . and in English Cuckoo flowers." The Flemish name *coeckoecbloem* corresponds to the English term "cuckoo flower." According to Geoffrey Grigson, the early English name, "lady's smock," appears "to have come from the OE lustmoce. The 'smick,' more usual as 'smicket,' of the name 'smick-smock' was another word for smock, and 'smickering,' to 'smicker,' were words of amorous looks and purposes. 'Smock' was used coarsely, especially in the sixteenth and seventeenth centuries, as we use 'skirt,' or 'piece of skirt,' etc. A plant, clearly, which needed Christianizing and handing over to the Virgin."

This transformation was easily achieved insofar as the Virgin's smock was included in the relics found by St. Helena. This fortunate lady (surely the envy of any archeologist!), after an ardent and certainly serendipitous search, claimed to have found the true Cross, the lance, the crown of thorns, and the tomb of Christ in Bethlehem.

However whitewashed the lady's smock had become after the Renaissance, writers like William Shakespeare were aware of the plant's earlier, less delicate associations. In *Love's Labour's Lost*, Shakespeare describes the lady's smock along with the amorous cuckoo:

> When daisies pied, and violets blue,
> And lady-smocks all silver white,
> And cuckoo-buds of yellow hue,
> Do paint the meadows with delight,
> The cuckoo then, on every tree,
> Mocks married men, for thus sings he:
> Cuckoo, Cuckoo, Cuckoo—O word of fear,
> Unpleasing to a married ear.
> —Act V, Scene II

And an early Irish poem associates the cuckoo flower with young girls:

> Tender cress and cuckoo-flower:
> And curley-haired, fair-headed maids,
> Sweet was the sound of their singing.
> —Grigson

This lascivious flower was a perfect companion for the amorous partridge. And as lady's smock was one of the flowers of May, its appearance in this panel of the Unicorn Tapestries is very appropriate. It is my opinion that this flower was woven into the tapestry as an iconographic reference to the cuckoo. James Hardy, author of *The Popular History of the Cuckoo,* writes that "the cuckoo's garland consists of several ingredients. The true cuckoo flower is *Cardamine patensis* [ladies smock]." The botanical reference to the cuckoo supports the strong May motif depicted in this third panel of the Unicorn Tapestries. In all parts of Europe the song of the cuckoo is synonymous with the coming of summer:

> Summer is acoming in
> Loud sings the cuckoo
> Groweth seed and bloweth meadow.
> —Chambers & Sidgwick

The connection of ladies smock with sex, fertility, and the cuckoo provides an ideal icon for this particular tapestry. Another cuckoo flower, the yellow cowslip, can be seen twice in this third tapestry—directly opposite the hawthorn, under the white hound's forepaws; and behind the thighs of the lymerer wearing the red-and-white striped pants. A sixteenth-century English publication, *The Nievve Herball* (a translation of an earlier Flemish text), gives the French names for the cowslip: *Coquu* (cuckoo) and *Brayes de coquu* (cuckoo's hose).

The hawthorn and all the supporting erotic flora that appear in this tapestry are identified with the orgiastic month of May. The other main tree seen here is the pomegranate, depicted next to the spear-carrying youth. This tree, like the hawthorn, is identified seasonally with the May iconography woven into the panel.

According to mythology, during the month of May it was the task of the god Hermes to descend into the underworld and fetch Persephone from that gloomy region. The story is worth describing in brief as the mythology connects Persephone with the pomegranate and suggests an important seasonal myth, the release of the earth from the grip of winter.

After being forcefully abducted by Hades, Persephone was taken to his underworld kingdom. In these gloomy regions she reigned as queen. Her mother Demeter was so distraught at the loss of her daughter that she pleaded with Zeus to release the young goddess from the underworld. Zeus answered the plea, but made it a condition that if Persephone had eaten any of the food of the infernal regions, she would have to remain with Hades. By an unfortunate ruse, Persephone was tricked into eating a pomegranate that had grown in the underworld; by divine decree she therefore had to remain in the realm of the dead.

So enraged was Demeter at the loss of her daughter that as a token of her anger she caused the earth to withhold its fruits and grains. After Demeter had wrought many disasters against mankind, Zeus finally intervened. He declared that Demeter could keep her daughter for six months, while for the rest of the year, because she had eaten the Stygian pomegranate, she would have to remain in hell as the consort of Hades.

In many instances in art and architecture, both from antiquity and the Middle Ages, the pomegranate is symbolic of the beginning of summer—the time when Persephone returns from the underworld to her mother, and Demeter happily covers the earth with green trees and flowers.

Of the many plants depicted in this tapestry, the yellow iris must be mentioned, because when associated with the pomegranate, these flowers present an iconographic reference to Persephone and Demeter. The iris occurs in several of the panels of the Unicorn Tapestries, and on each occasion it is depicted for its rich symbolism. Each time the iris is woven in a different color. Albertus Magnus commented that the flowers may be "white or lemon-colored or sky blue or purple; and because of this variety, they are called iris." (Freeman) As a result of this natural variance in color, the plant was named after Iris, the goddess of the rainbow. This goddess was the messenger of the gods, who traveled between two worlds by means of the bridge created by her rainbow.

It is especially relevant to the mythology of this tapestry that the iris is placed next to the stone bridge. The structure itself is conspicuously woven into the right-hand margin of the panel. A bridge (like its celestial counterpart, the rainbow) connects one world with another; and, as we shall shortly see, both bridge and iris are important images here.

Next to the pomegranate (emblem of Persephone), appears a spear-carrying youth. This figure is walking in the direction of a stone bridge—in the mythological sense, an image of the pathway to another world. Beside the bridge the iris is woven, flower of the goddess who forms the pathway between different realms. And in Greek mythology Demeter, the mother of Persephone, was also known as the "Lady of the Bridge."

Interpreted mythically, then, this bridge would represent the pathway from Hades, the connection between the two worlds in this context; and the youth carrying the spear would identify with Hermes, the escort of Persephone. In a mythological sense, her welcome return to her mother, Demeter, is reflected in the verdant vegetation of summer.

In many parts of Europe, May Eve was the time of a complex ceremonial drama, when death/winter was carried out of the community and the spirit of vegetation escorted back into the village. This was the time when mummers performed anthropomorphic rites, making their plea to the benevolent deities for rain and sun, both essential for the development of food in the field, forest, and stream.

The month of May was a season of charms and talismans, and, as we have noted, protection from malign spirits and other supernatural powers was provided by such trees as the hawthorn. May was also the time of transition from spring to summer. It was a suitable period for auguries, not just from birds like the cuckoo and bittern but from plants as well. And three of the plants depicted in this tapestry—cherry, hazel, and marigold—had rituals ascribed to them that would enable the seeker to foretell if a marriage was imminent, or if the coming season was going to be good for crops.

In this third tapestry the unicorn represents the fertilizing male divinity, and his act of crossing the stream can be seen as a homeopathic rite that ensures rain for the season and a benevolence for the whole ecological realm. The symbol of transition depicted here—the bridge—denotes the change of seasons from spring to summer; or, in respect to the Mother Goddess, it symbolizes the transformation from Virgin to Bride. The summer mythology presented in "The Unicorn Crossing the Stream" comes to a climax in the events iconographically represented in the next panel of the hunt sequence, "The Unicorn Defends Himself." It is highly significant that in the following panels the oak no longer dominates, for the waxing cycle has now come to an end, and a new aspect of the life cycle moves into symbolic focus.

# IV

# THE UNICORN

# DEFENDS

# HIMSELF

I N THE FOURTH PANEL of the Unicorn Tapestries, attention is focused on the unicorn as he violently defends himself against his attackers (Plate IV). At the back a huntsman aims a lethal spear toward the animal, while the unicorn defends himself by kicking with his rear legs and making use of his sharp horn to mortally wound one of the hounds.

An orange tree, with fruit and flowers, provides the central motif in this tapestry; to the left of this tree, an old and a young woodsman are depicted contemplating the scene with great sobriety. Below them a herald is seen blowing a horn, giving the appearance that the sound has scattered all the aquatic birds with the exception of a lone heron, standing next to the peach tree.

"The Unicorn Crossing the Stream" dealt with images that were identified with the month of May—the final defeat of winter and arrival of summer, the time when anthropomorphic rites would protect, stimulate, and encourage the deities of vegetation, and the elemental agencies that governed the rain.

All the iconography connected with the images woven into this next tapestry, "The Unicorn Defends Himself," suggests the midsummer month of June, a time when the marriage of the Oak King with the representation of the earth mother traditionally took place. The central, most significant icons depicted in this panel are trees and flowers that are strongly associated with copulation and the union of the sexes. Yet underlying this theme of propagation is the drama of the death of the Oak King after his midsummer union with the representative of the Mother Goddess. This rite represents the transference of the Oak King's powers of regeneration to a virile successor.

These themes of sexual regeneration and the succession of the earth mother's consorts are the essential ideas of the fourth panel of the Unicorn Tapestries. For instance, there are early seventeenth-century illustrations in a book of alchemy, *Philosophia Reformata,* which reflect similar symbolism that is very ancient. In the engraving (Fig. 34), we see a king and queen preparing to copulate on the newly plowed furrows of a field. A third figure represents a farmer sowing the season's crops. The grain is assured germination and abundance because of the power of the ritual mating of the royal couple. Other prints in this series (Fig. 35) depict the death of the same couple and their resurrection and rebirth as the sun and the moon.

Such sexual rites are common to many primal peoples. As Frazer comments: "To eat and to cause to live, to eat food and to beget children, these were the primary wants of men in the past, and they will be the primary wants of men in the future so long as the world lasts." To these people, "the principle of life and fertility, whether animal or vegetable, was one and individual." Both the primal people of Europe and the population in the Middle Ages believed that "the tie between the animal and the vegetable world was even closer than it really is; hence they often combined the dramatic representation of reviving plants with a real or dramatic union of the sexes for the purpose of furthering at the same time and by the same act the multiplication of fruits, of animals, and of men." (1911)

The other symbolism that is central to "The Unicorn Defends Himself" tapestry identifies the unicorn as an icon of Christ, and reflects actual events in the story of the hunt and capture of this mythical beast. There is a particularly interesting and curious element in the manner in which the unicorn has been portrayed. For instance, the unicorn of the fourth tapestry is depicted without ears. This is no mistake, but a deliberate part of the design, and other icons in "The Unicorn Defends Himself" support the symbol of "silence." As we shall discover, silence is a motif and precursor to the actual betrayal of the unicorn—a drama that is presented in the next panel in the hunt sequence, "The Unicorn is Tamed by the Maiden."

Since the images depicted in "The Unicorn Defends Himself" suggest the midsummer month, a brief summary of the importance of June to medieval people will facilitate our grasp of the events portrayed in this tapestry. Although these seasonal dramas have been dealt with in prior chapters, a brief reminder of the significance of midsummer rituals will help us to follow and interpret the dominant themes of this fourth panel.

Midsummer is the season when the sun reaches its zenith and then starts waning and losing its mythic potency. The primal peoples of Europe thought that the weakening divinity would affect the safety of the world in which they lived. In these cultures, they believed that the course of nature was bound up in the man-god's potency, and to permit the natural

Figure 34. Engraving from *Philosophia Reformata*. Frankfurt, 1622. British Museum.

progression of enfeeblement would result in disaster. In primal societies, the decline of the solar energies was regarded with great anxiety. To rekindle the waning potency of the sun (a man-god), human intervention was necessary.

In his article "The European Sky God," A. B. Cook states that in early Greece the king was held to be a representation of Zeus. The duties that were connected to his high office could only be satisfactorily conducted by a man who was without blemish. Cook illustrates this point by quoting from a speech made by Odysseus: " 'Even as a king without blemish, who ruleth god-fearing over many mighty men, and maintaineth justice, while the black earth beareth wheat and barley, and the trees are laden with fruit, and the flocks bring forth without fail, and the sea yieldeth fish by reason of his good rule, and the folk prosper beneath him.' The king who is without blemish has a flourishing kingdom, the king who is maimed has a kingdom diseased like himself, thus the Spartans were warned by an oracle to be aware of a 'lame reign.' "

If the human incarnation was killed in his prime, his soul could be

Figure 35. Engravings from *Philosophia Reformata*. Frankfurt, 1622. British Museum.

caught and transferred to a virile male, the divine king's successor. This is the reason that in "The Unicorn Defends Himself," the holly tree dominates the floral iconography for the first time—designating the transference taking place from the waxing to the waning cycle. To the left of the central orange tree, there is another holly. This evergreen is one of the largest trees depicted in the panel, and it contrasts sharply with the diminutive oaks. Behind this tall holly an image of an old man is presented. His attention is being directed by his youthful companion toward the fierce battle with the unicorn. The young man points with his left arm; in his right hand he holds a large axe—with which he has just felled a beech tree, an act that has great consequence in this tapestry.

The central emblem in this panel is the orange tree. In the Middle Ages this fruit became strongly associated with the union of the sexes. Although oranges were not known to the ancients and were only established in Europe after the twelfth century, the medieval authors, nevertheless, identified the orange with the mythic apples of the Hesperides. Classical writers such as the Greek author Athenaeus (c. A.D. 208), stated that in honor of the divine wedding of Jupiter and Juno "the Earth brought forth the golden apples of the Hesperides." (D'Ancona, 1977) Literal evidence from the Middle Ages of these associations of the orange with the union of the sexes is presented by the fifteenth-century poet, Hernando del Castillo. This laureate describes love's abode as an island with "a grove of blossoming orange trees." (Freeman) And in a tapestry (Tournai or Brussels?), dating from the end of the fifteenth century, and now on display at the *Musée des Arts Décoratifs* (Paris), Venus is depicted sitting under an orange tree. The orange, like the pomegranate, bears in its fruits many seeds, which is another feature that made medieval authors consider it an emblem of fecundity. The thirteenth-century Italian theologian Armando de Bellovisu, "stated that the orange tree was the most beautiful tree of all . . . because it bears fruit, flowers, and leaves all at the same time. Likewise, the Virgin Mary excelled all women in bearing at the same time the white flower of her virginity and the fruit of her chastity." (D'Ancona, 1977) The religious associations of the orange with the Virgin Mary, Christ's bride, made the blossoms of this tree an ideal emblem in the secular world, as bouquets for the medieval bride.

In this fourth panel of the Unicorn Tapestries a holly is woven at the base of the central orange tree, and to the left of this tree a larger holly is depicted. A newly felled beech is set behind this large holly—apparently the work of the young man with the axe who appears directly behind the stump. Underneath the leafy branches of the toppled beech, the image of an oak is included. The beech tree had a strong association with the oak, for even their religious identities were interchangeable. Like the oak, the beech was "dedicated to Jupiter." During the major religious festivals, the altars of this mighty god were decorated with leaves of beech. Jupiter's holy Alban Mountain contained forests of beech, and nearby in the Alban Hills there existed a sacred grove of these trees. This wood, like the hallowed precinct of Diana at Nemi, was guarded by a king "while he served his term as Diana's husband." (de Vries)

Because of these mythic parallels, the beech was sometimes substituted for the oak. And the close associations between the two trees is revealed by looking into the etymological similarities of their names. The Greek word for oak is *phegos,* phonetically identical with the Latin word for beech, *fagus.* Friedmann points out that to the people of the Middle Ages, "puns and anagrams were looked upon as something not merely accidental but actually suggestive of kindred qualities in the objects represented by the words involved. Behind this tendency was a long and honored tradition." (1946)

Considering the long-standing identification of these two trees, it would not be too far-fetched to conclude that the designer of the Unicorn Tapestries included the felled beech as a substitute for the oak. With these iconographic ideas in mind, we can now make some conclusions about this fourth tapestry. First, the holly placed so conspicuously behind the orange tree is an augury of the midsummer union of the Holly King with the representative of the matriarchal goddess, after the sacrifice of the Oak King. In fact, this tapestry, which depicts the unicorn defending himself, can be seen as representing the unity of the male and female in the bridal month of June. It is the time and the season when the Oak King has reached his prime, and must be sacrificed before his decline. The old man depicted in this panel is an iconographic representation of the enfeebled Oak King, who will be killed and replaced by the "renewed" Holly King, represented by the young man carrying the axe.

Diagonally opposite the two woodsmen and the felled beech is the heron, the ornithological icon of Hermes, the deity who was the messenger of the gods and conductor of the souls of mortals. The heron has other associations derived from its strange way of catching fish. Graves observes that "When they [herons] have speared a quantity of small fish in a river ready to take home to their young, they arrange them on the bank with the tails set together in the form of a wheel." (1966) From earliest times the wheel was identified with the sun, and it played a vital role in midsummer celebrations. Besides being a solar emblem, it also symbolized the turning year. The ancient goddess Fortuna (identified with the Greek Nemesis) held a wheel to indicate that she had control over the annual cycle of time. It was when the goddess's wheel reached half cycle that Hermes would take the soul of the Oak King, and thus the alternative motion from the waxing to the waning cycle would ensue.

In these particular primal cultures, this was the period when the holly was united with the midsummer bride. In a symbolic sense, here in this fourth tapestry the designer realizes this essential union by placing the holly at the base of the orange tree of marriages. And other imagery depicted in the panel reinforces this union. For instance, the unicorn's horn piercing the side of the hound (Fig. 36) presents an interesting drama, if we consider that the horn of this animal has strong phallic connotations. The horn in the wound presents an iconographic image: "as phallus is to vulva. The slit of the vulva appears like the wound made by a spear, and so the spear becomes a phallus." (Thompson) This same phallic imagery applies equally (perhaps even more strongly) to the horn of the unicorn. Furthermore, the blood from the hound's wound is deliberately depicted flowing over the image of a blue violet—a flower that had strong associations with the goddess of love, Aphrodite, and her son Priapus. The latter was a phallic deity of generation and gardens. So closely was Priapus linked to the violet that a Greek name for this flower is *Priapeion*. The erotic associations of the violet are recorded in a number of medieval poems. Sigebert of Gembloux in one of his compositions writes about trying "to make a garland

Figure 36. Detail—"The Unicorn Defends Himself." The Unicorn Tapestries. Franco-Flemish, c. 1500. The Cloisters, Metropolitan Museum of Art.

for the saints." In these verses, the poet lists the flowers that in his opinion should not be allowed, including violets:

> Nor violets wan, to show with pure fire
> The bride for the bride-groom burns.
> —Waddell

The rose also had sexual associations, and in this fourth panel a splendid red rosebush is woven between the unicorn's head and the gored dog. Since classical times roses have been one of the flowers of Venus. The following medieval verse clearly indicates the non-Christian significance of this flower:

> All night by the rose, rose,
> All night by the rose I lay;
> I dared not steal the rose tree,
> But I bore the flower away.
> —Stone, 1964

Several other images woven near the unicorn have strong erotic associations. For instance, to the right of the heron a peach tree is depicted. This is a fruit of Venus and, according to mythologer Ad de Vries, it was much associated with the female principle, specifically the vulva. The German scholar Albertus Magnus wrote that eating peaches "increases intercourse." (Freeman) And the Italian Renaissance scholar Vincenzo Cartari mentions that the peach was sacred to Hymen, the god of marriage, adding that this deity wore a crown of peach flowers on his head.

Diagonally across the stream from the peach tree is the image of cattails or bulrushes. The designer has set this plant just in front of the wounded dog. The phallic morphology of the cattail and the positioning of the "flower heads" in relationship to the hound have the obvious implication of copulation. And beneath this scene is the heron—the bird sacred to Hermes, the phallic deity.

Many other icons associated with the female genitalia are included in this panel. One of the most important is the tall apricot tree, depicted just in front of the cherry in the right margin. The apricot has an ancient symbolic lineage; from Roman times through to the Middle Ages, this fruit has been an icon of the female sex organs. The French satirist François Rabelais, who lived in the first half of the sixteenth century, referred to this association, calling the female organ *"abricot fendu* (slit apricot)." (D'Ancona, 1977)

Another small tree, the medlar, occurs in a number of panels of the Unicorn Tapestries. In this fourth textile, the medlar is depicted just behind the kicking hind legs of the unicorn. Although medlars were popular fruit trees in medieval Europe, the fruit could not be eaten immediately, but had to be left until it was almost rotten. Only then was it palatable. The vernacular medieval names for medlar were quite crude, words that the polite society of later centuries tried to avoid; for instance, the medieval French term was *culs de chien* (dog's arse). Shakespeare, impervious to such niceties, puts a delightful quip into the mouth of Mercutio in *Romeo and Juliet,* preserving for us the lewd associations of the tree:

> Now will he sit under a medlar tree,
> And wish his mistress were that kind of fruit
> As maids call medlars, when they laugh alone.
> O Romeo! that she were, O! that she were
> An open et cetera, thou a poperin pear.
> —Act II, Scene I

(As already mentioned, in the Middle Ages the word "pear" was a euphemism for penis.)

Another important tree in this tapestry is the walnut, which appears to the right of the central orange (Fig. 37). Some of the branches bear nuts.

Figure 37. Detail—"The Unicorn Defends Himself." Left–right: orange, walnut, strawberry tree, and apricot. The Cloisters, Metropolitan Museum of Art.

The walnut has since ancient times been regarded as a tree of ill-omen and as a favorite haunt of witches. But the nuts were considered benevolent: emblems of fertility, and therefore especially propitious to marriages. Said to be of Athenian origin was the custom during wedding ceremonies of throwing nuts at the bride and groom, a practice recorded by Pliny, who wrote that "walnuts have become emblems consecrated to weddings." (Vol. IV, Book XV)

Another botanical emblem that relates to nuptial events is the wall-flower. Two major examples are found in this tapestry. The first can be seen directly in front of the left leg of the huntsman and hind legs of the dog shown on the near bank of the stream. The wallflower appears in other panels of the Unicorn Tapestries, and in all instances, it is represented because it is symbolic of fecundity and procreation. The German *Distilier-buch* (1527), a medieval volume on the art of distillation by Hieronymus Brunschwig, states that the water from the distilled wallflowers, drunk morning, noon, and night for a period of three to four weeks, will "make a woman fruitful."

Another plant, the feverfew, appears only in "The Unicorn Defends Himself" panel, and is depicted between the feet of the huntsman thrusting his spear toward the flanks of the unicorn (Fig. 38). The German herbal *Der Gart* recommends the feverfew for increasing a woman's fertility: "Grind [feverfew] to a powder, and when it is mixed with wine, it will make women fruitful and lighthearted."

One of the most unusual trees woven in the Unicorn Tapestries occurs in this fourth textile (see Fig. 37). This is the strawberry tree, an evergreen native to southern Europe and parts of Ireland. The name is derived from the resemblance of the ripe fruit to strawberries. Francesco Colonna, in the *Dream of Polyphilus,* records an erotic situation involving the strawberry tree. The Venetian edition of this book, published in 1499, provides an illustration for the text (Fig. 39). The narrative describes a sculpture of a sleeping nymph; hovering over this beautiful female image was "a [stone] satyr in prurient lust," depicted bending "an arm of the arbutus tree [straw-berry tree] over the sleeping nymph." (Colonna, English edition, 1592) Because of this association between the strawberry tree and lusty satyrs, there is good reason to assume that to the people of the Middle Ages this tree was an erotic icon.

The French considered that the herbs gathered on the eve of the sum-mer solstice had very strong prophylactic qualities. So widespread was this practice in France that the collecting of these special plants at this time of the year gave rise to a proverb, "To employ all the herbs of St John." (Frazer, 1911) This axiom means that in a difficult situation all resources should be utilized to their utmost.

Figure 38. Detail—"The Unicorn Defends Himself." The Cloisters, Metropolitan Museum of Art.

Figure 39. Francesco Colonna,
"Dream of Poliphilus."
*Hypnerotomachia Poliphilii*
woodcut, Venice, 1499.

One of the principal plants collected by the people during the summer solstice was mugwort, *Artemisia vulgaris*. In this fourth panel of the Unicorn Tapestries, an image of this plant is conspicuously depicted on the near bank of the stream under the woodcock flying in the direction of the heron (Fig. 40). Europeans of the Middle Ages believed that mugwort possessed wondrous virtues if "gathered on the eve or day of St. John . . . hence in France it goes by the name herb of St. John." (Frazer, 1911)

A common practice on Midsummer Eve or Midsummer Day was to wear a crown made from the leaves of mugwort. If purified over the midsummer fire, this chaplet proved a powerful talisman; and the crown, placed in house or barn, would protect the inhabitants of the building from any infernal interventions. The importance of mugwort is stressed in this tapestry by placing it next to another botanical symbol of St. John, the yellow flag iris. This plant became in France the "special herb of St. John's Eve." (Grigson)

One final plant associated with midsummer is the corn marigold, depicted at the bottom left of the panel next to the long-beaked woodcock. The golden yellow flowers of the corn marigold were identified with the disc of the sun, and these flowers were used in the construction of midsummer garlands.

Other iconography besides the midsummer imagery permeates this complex fourth textile—symbols that are identified with the progression of the hunt and that identify the unicorn as an icon of Christ. The most important clue to this symbolism is the unicorn itself. In the fourth panel,

Figure 40. Detail—"The Unicorn Defends Himself." The Cloisters, Metropolitan Museum of Art.

as already mentioned, this animal is depicted without ears (Fig. 41), a curious factor considering that it is the only occasion on which the unicorn appears thus. Bearing in mind all the fine detail in these tapestries, it seems that this omission was not simply an oversight on the part of the weavers. And there is a religious interpretation from the Middle Ages that might help to explain the motif of "silence." Further evidence is found in the mythologies of some of the plants and animals woven into the tapestry. For instance, the heron "symbolizes silence" (de Vries), and according to Ripa's *Iconologia*, the peach was sacred to Harpocrates, the Egyptian god of silence. This symbolism arose because the leaves of the peach look like human tongues.

The following passage, written in the thirteenth century by Guillaume Durand, bishop of Mende, is a strong piece of evidence that provides a further reason for the Unicorn's lack of ears. In his *Rationale Divinorum Officiorum*, the French canonist wrote the following passage on the symbolism of bells, providing an exegesis as to why bells were not rung during the three days before Easter:

on these three days the bells be silent, because the Apostles and preachers, and others who be understood by bells were then silenced. For the sound of bells doth signify the sound of preaching: of which it is said, their sound hath gone out into all lands. . . . After they had sung an hymn they went out with Jesus to the Mount of Olives. To whom when the Lord had said, behold he is at hand that doth betray me, they slumbered for sadness, and ceased from praises. Whence also from Compline, or Vespers, when our Lord was betrayed beginneth the silence of the bells.

We have seen that the unicorn was identified with Christ by the medieval theologians, and that Jesus was called by these churchmen the chief of all preachers. Therefore the absence of ears upon the unicorn is meant to convey the idea that the time for words has ended, and that Christ has accepted his imminent betrayal and subsequent sacrifice.

An incident connected to a New Testament drama reflects these views mentioned by Durand. This particular episode is connected with the arrest of Christ in the Garden of Gethsemane. It was on this occasion that Simon Peter, outraged by the imminent betrayal of Jesus, cut off the ears of the leader of the men who had come to arrest Christ. Because of this New Testament story, figures depicted without ears came to symbolize imminent betrayal.

It seems most likely that the designer of the Unicorn Tapestries was influenced by the writings of Guillaume Durand, or, more specifically, by the particular passage quoted. The *Rationale Divinorum Officiorum* was very well known in the Middle Ages, becoming one of the main sources of Western liturgy. If this was the case, then it would seem probable that the

Figure 41. Detail—"The Unicorn Defends Himself." The Cloisters, Metropolitan Museum of Art.

heron, a long-standing icon of muteness, was placed in this textile to infer silence. For instance, the Norse goddess Frigga wore a crown of heron feathers to indicate that she was privy to all that happened on earth but had to remain silent about it.

We are fortunate that all of the Unicorn Tapestries have survived from the Middle Ages, for the symbolism depicted in the next two panels in the hunt sequence (the unicorn's betrayal and death) explains why silence is so important in this fourth panel. And the absence of ears on the unicorn seems strongly to concur with the interpretation by Durand "that one was at hand who would betray the Lord." It is the use of guile and betrayal, according to medieval myths, that leads to the animal's capture—ploys reflected in the imagery presented in the next two tapestries.

Like the unicorn, the heron has many meanings. Angelo de Gubernatis states that the heron "presents several of the mythical characteristics of the stork." Bartholomaeus Anglicus considered the stork like a heron, "but bigger." (1582) Gubernatis also connects these two birds, and expands their relationship with European folklore.

In these fables the stork, tired of the bachelor's life, seeks the heron to propose marriage, but his proposal is rejected and the stork flies away in great disappointment. As soon as the stork has departed, the heron regrets her rash action. Determined to reverse the situation, she flies to the stork's nest and makes her own proposal. The stork's wounded pride is not mended by the heron's plea, and he rejects her offer. The situation is repeated, with each bird rejecting the other's offer, then countermanding the negative response by a proposal. And though they never marry, the story ends with the heron and the stork continuing to visit each other.

Gubernatis comments that "This fable, although it has a satirical meaning, also implies the intimate mythical relationship between the heron and the stork. The heron and the stork are two birds which equally love the water, and therefore serve to represent the cloudy, rainy, wintry, or gloomy sky . . . the stork personifies the funereal sky, the sky when the celestial hero, the sun, is dead."

The heron is included in this tapestry because it is both an icon of silence and a symbol of the end of the waning cycle—a time that coincides with the approaching death of the solar Oak King and his Greek counterpart, Hercules. The Oak King has reached his prime and is united with the bride of midsummer before his decline. The heron and members of its family are identified with Hermes and Thoth, both messengers of the gods and conductors of the souls of mortals. The great medieval iconographer Rabanus Maurus pointed out that "the heron signifies the souls of the elect which fly above all temporary events to the serenity of heaven, where they behold forever the countenance of god." (Freeman)

The symbolic association of the heron with the dead hero is central to a popular fourteenth-century carol:

> The heron flew east, the heron flew west,
> The heron flew to the fair forest;
> She flew o'er stream and meadows green,
> And a' to see what could be seen:
>
> --------
>
> And in the bower there was a bed,
>
> --------
>
> And in the bed there lay a knight,
> Whose wounds did bleed both day and night . . .
> —Greene

There are some pictorial examples from the Middle Ages that certainly allude to this idea of the Divine King and his immortal counterpart—the spirit of vegetation. These examples provide evidence that this mythology survived in other ways than as simple aspects of folk tradition.

Figure 42. "Summer" manuscript page. *Tacuinum sanitatis*, 1380–1400, Vienna, National Library.

A popular medical manuscript from the Middle Ages, the *Tacuinum sanitatis*, has an interesting illustration representing summer (Fig. 42): a man and a woman hold sickles and are depicted cutting the mature summer wheat. Behind this rustic couple, another figure is included by the artist: a man crowned with stalks of wheat, shown holding bunches of grain in his hands. In his observations on the cutting of wheat and barley, the German scholar W. Mannhardt provides an explanation for this strange image found in the *Tacuinum sanitatis*. "In all these cases the idea is that the spirit of the wheat . . . is driven out of the grain last cut or last thrashed, and lives in the barn during the winter. At sowing-time he goes out again into the fields to resume activity as an animating force among the sprouting corn." (Quoted in Frazer, 1911)

In its original mythic sense, the sickle records the annual death of the old Oak King by his successor. And after the castration, this midsummer emasculation and killing, the Divine King was eucharistically eaten. In this oak cult, the victim became immortal. The successor to the Divine Kingship "inherited the favors of the priestesses of his Goddess mother." The means of death was important, for "reaping meant castration." (Graves, 1966)

The following vivid images taken from a fifteenth-century book on alchemy illustrate the central part of the oak cult—the killing of the enfeebled king by a young and virile successor (Fig. 43). Seated upon a throne, the old god Saturn is depicted holding a sickle, the weapon which he used to castrate and depose his own father, Uranus. Saturn's son Jupiter is presented holding his father's genitals—evidence that he has followed Saturn's example of paternal castration. And Jupiter, wearing vestments made of his sacred oak, holds in his left hand a knife, the implement with which he wounded his father. Completing the mythological coterie, and depicted next to Saturn, is the goddess Ops, a deity who is identified with the Hellenic Rhea, the *Magna Mater,* immortal Mother Goddess and earth mother.

Some of the remaining symbolism depicted in "The Unicorn Defends Himself" adds to the interpretation offered. For instance, the prominent figure depicted blowing the horn in this fourth panel is identified by many art historians as Gabriel. These scholars argue that this is the Angel of Annunciation because the inscription woven on the scabbard of the man's sword reads: "*Ave Regina C[oelorum],*" which translates as "Hail Queen of Heaven." And though the Bible mentions that the actual words spoken by Gabriel at this moment were "*Ave Maria, gratia plena*" (Hail Mary, full of grace), the former invocation, *Ave Regina Coelorum,* "was a popular hymn to the Virgin in the Middle Ages and it could well have been considered an appropriate substitute for 'Ave Maria,' and a more regal salutation." (Freeman)

But this invocation, besides hailing the Virgin, was an address used to honor the pre-Christian goddess of heaven. For example, in Apuleius' *Golden Ass,* the fictitious narrator, Lucius, refers to the Queen of Heaven when bemoaning his transformation into an ass. Lucius prays to the goddess by the sea shore: "Blessed Queen of heaven, whether you are pleased to be known as Ceres, the original harvest mother . . . or whether as celestial Venus . . . who at the time of the first Creation coupled the sexes in mutual love . . . or whether as dread Proserpine . . . whose triple face is potent against the malice of ghosts." (Graves, 1951)

Another prayer to the earth mother, this time from the Christian era of the twelfth century, contains a similar invocation: "Earth, divine goddess, Mother Nature who generatest all things and bringeth forth anew the sun. . . . Guardian of sky and sea . . . Mother of the gods . . . thou art [the] great queen of the gods." (Rohde) Although this is an extreme example in that the prayer is undeniably "pagan," the Virgin Mary, without question, took over the role of the pre-Christian mother goddesses and became ruler of the heavens. The cult of the Virgin not only adopted pre-Christian symbolism but also absorbed some of the liturgical invocations.

Thus "The Unicorn Defends Himself" tapestry can be seen as representing the unity of male and female in the bridal month of June, emble-

Figure 43. Jupiter castrating Saturn. Page from anonymous book on alchemy, 15th century. Rome, Biblioteca Apostolica Vaticana.

matized by the depiction of the holly at the base of the central orange tree, and by the horn of the unicorn piercing the flanks of the dog. Two strong points of action occur in this tapestry: the beech (a pun on oak) has been felled and it is juxtaposed with the two humans representing old age and youth.

The old man depicted here represents the sacrificial victim, the Oak King with his potency waning, who will be replaced by the young man carrying the axe, the Holly King. Diagonally opposite is the heron, a bird that is identified with the wheel of Nemesis—a wheel that reaches half cycle at midsummer, when Hermes (the other god identified with this bird) takes possession of the soul of the Oak King and thus completes the transfer from the waxing to the waning cycle.

PLATE

V

# THE UNICORN
# IS TAMED
# BY THE
# MAIDEN

ALL THAT REMAINS of the fifth panel depicting the dramatic capture of the unicorn are two fragments (Plate V). Fortunately for the purposes
of an accurate interpretation of the imagery, these two portions reveal
important details of the essential elements woven into the complete work.
The unicorn is placed in an enclosed garden, or *hortus conclusus*. In one of
the fragments, the animal is shown staring into what would have been the
face of a maiden in the original hanging. All that remains of this central
female figure is the hand and part of the sleeve of her dress. Both of these
fragments are woven in such a way as to indicate that the lady was depicted
embracing the unicorn in the complete tapestry. So entranced is the unicorn
by this embrace that he is impervious to the wounds inflicted by the hounds
woven next to him in the enclosure.

In the right fragment, a female companion of the central lady has
survived almost intact. The appearance of this maid is not particularly
flattering, as she is depicted with a sly and deceptive expression. It is not
too difficult to conjecture that the lady is presented in this way to indicate
that she is privy to the betrayal of the unicorn. And, as if to announce the
climax of the imminent death of the unicorn, a herald is shown behind a
holly tree, blowing upon his horn.

The fourth tapestry, "The Unicorn Defends Himself," focused upon
imagery connected with midsummer—the June marriage of the Oak King
to the representation of the earth mother, an event that culminates in numerous icons of marriage and copulation which are represented in that
panel, revealing its essential iconographic intent. The other major drama

presented in the fourth panel of the Unicorn Tapestries centers upon the unicorn as a symbol of Christ. And, more specifically, because of the absence of ears on the animal, to the imminent betrayal of Jesus in the Garden of Gethsemane.

This fifth fragmentary tapestry, "The Unicorn Is Tamed by the Maiden," presents the pacification of the fierce and free creature by a virgin, seen under an apple tree. This lady, who once dominated the complete work, is identified with love, death, and rebirth—aspects of both the apple tree and, ultimately, the Triple Goddess. The chronology of this particular tapestry corresponds with the festivals of the mother goddesses Vesta and Diana Nemorensis (Diana of the Grove) held on August 13, a religious celebration adopted by the early Christians to honor the Virgin Mary. The unicorn's submission to the maiden in this walled enclosure corresponds to the Christian myth of Christ's voluntary sacrifice and his acceptance of betrayal.

The enclosure itself is an important feature of this tapestry. From the two fragments, it is possible to conclude that the *hortus conclusus* in the complete work was entirely enclosed. In the middle of this secluded garden, surrounded by a rose-covered fence, the maiden sat—enticement and bait for the unsuspecting unicorn. The enclosure itself is important insofar as it was identified by medieval iconographers as a symbol of Mary's virginity.

An influential and often quoted biblical text identified the Virgin with an enclosed garden. In Solomon's *Song of Songs*, the words "a garden enclosed is my sister, my spouse," appear. In expanding this passage, the twelfth-century poet and theologian Alain de Lille comments: "the Virgin is a garden of delights in which the roses of endurance and the lily of virginity are not lacking. . . . [She] is a garden enclosed because she is a valley of charity that is sealed, into which nothing evil can break . . . since she is surrounded entirely by a guard of angels." (Freeman)

Before undertaking an interpretation of specific images woven into the fifth tapestry of the Unicorn series, it is helpful to explore the medieval description of the capture of the unicorn with which this panel is concerned. In the Provençal version of the *Physiologus,* the anonymous author wrote: "they lead forth a young virgin, pure and chaste, to whom, when the [unicorn] sees her, he approaches, throwing himself upon her. Then the girl offers him her breasts, and the animal begins to suck the breasts of the maiden and to conduct himself familiarly with her. Then the girl, while sitting quietly, reaches forth her hand and grasps the horn on the animal's brow, and at this point the huntsmen come up and take the beast and go away with him to the king." (Poltarnees)

This strange story of the unicorn's capture was probably of Eastern origin, and by the fourteenth century it had become an established allegory of the incarnation of Christ. Albertus Magnus, the great thirteenth-century theologian, wrote that "our glorious Virgin accepted [the unicorn] into her lap when it entered her citadel, that is to say into the womb of her chaste body so that she could nurse it in her bosom and drape it with modest flesh, wherein in accordance with divine decree the unseizeable creature might be captured by its hunters, namely by Jews and Gentiles, and yield voluntarily to death by crucifixion." (Beer)

This rich imagery of the unicorn's capture was not only used by theologians, but also influenced the secular literature of the Middle Ages. Richard de Fournival, in his *Bestiaire d'Amour,* draws the following delightful analogy, comparing himself to the unicorn: "I have been drawn to you by your sweet odor alone, as the unicorn falls asleep under the influence of a maiden's fragrance. . . . [For this] is the woman whom I shall care to possess. . . . But Love . . . has set in my path a maiden in the odor of whose sweetness I have fallen asleep, and I die the death to which I was doomed." (Shepard)

The story of the unicorn's capture is a strange one indeed. And when this tale of the animal's seduction is made into an analogy of the immaculate conception, it seems rather alien to Christian mythology, insofar as it suggests the idea of the Virgin betraying her own son. One of the best ways to understand this perplexing contradiction is to study the actual events that surround the capture of the unicorn.

The drama of a virgin capturing the unicorn is presented in a number of works of art that date from the Middle Ages. In symbolic content, one of the richest sources of this material is a Swiss tapestry altar covering, woven around 1480 (see Fig. 15)—a work already mentioned briefly. This complex panel is concerned with the climax of the hunt of the unicorn, an event envisioned as an allegory of the immaculate conception. The Virgin, accompanied by all her symbols, is the main figure of the enclosed garden— the *hortus conclusus.* The seated Virgin is depicted grasping the horn of the unicorn, while to her right we see Adam with a long spear giving a mortal wound to the helpless animal. Eve is shown underneath the unicorn, catching the blood that gushes from the wound. To clarify the drama, the designer included in his tapestry a number of inscriptions. The scroll under Adam reads: "He is wounded because of our sins." Expanding this redemption motif is the inscription woven near Eve: "And by his blood we are saved." Adam's killing of the unicorn thus parallels the Crucifixion and death of Christ. By his sacrifice, this Christian saviour could then lead Adam and Eve and all other penitent and just souls out of Limbo and into Paradise. According to Albertus Magnus, the unicorn "drove Adam out of the Garden for biting the apple." (Beer) Conversely, as a symbol of Christ, the unicorn leads mankind back into a heavenly Eden—Paradise.

On the outside of the enclosure in this Swiss tapestry, the richly costumed Gabriel, while restraining four hounds, blows his horn and thus announces the mystical impregnation of Mary. Each of the dogs has been identified by the designer: the names of Gabriel's hounds are "Truth," "Justice," "Peace," and "Mercy." These strange companions of the archangel evolved from writings that date from the thirteenth-century mystery plays. In Christian fables, these four virtues are often personified as hounds. They search for the man who is without sin, who will be willing to die in order to save mankind. After an unsuccessful search among mortals, the hound-virtues achieve their goal when Christ offers himself to be sacrificed.

Similar imagery is presented in the fragmentary fifth panel of the Unicorn Tapestries. Both hound and "Gabriel" figures can be seen depicted in the left fragment—images that attest to the voluntary sacrifice that Christ (as the unicorn) will make to redeem mankind.

The fifth panel also contains the image of three trees: oak, apple, and holly. Although we can only conjecture as to the prominence of the oak and the holly in the original tapestry, the argument presented so far would suggest that we are dealing with iconography that relates to the waning cycle of the year. Therefore, the predominant tree in this hanging would have been the holly. In the left panel of this incomplete textile, one of the finest weavings of this tree occurs in the left margin. Furthermore, this particular holly appears inside the *hortus conclusus*, whereas the oak that is visible in this and the other fragment of the tapestry is placed on the outside of the garden.

Like the grail romances of the Middle Ages, the story of the unicorn's capture by a chaste maid has an ancient association, and when we take a close look at pre-Christian fables and images, some semblance of the original drama is revealed. The influential and popular medieval romance of Tristram can help to explain the symbolic drama depicted in the fifth panel of the Unicorn Tapestries, since some carvings and illuminations from the Middle Ages present the romance of Tristram and Iseult as a parallel to the capture and death of the unicorn.

By the twelfth century, Tristram had become fairly well associated with the Arthurian cycle. Joseph Campbell points out that the Tristram cycle of romances was rooted, "like all Arthurian romance, in the most ancient native European mythological tradition—that of the Old Megalithic, Bronze Age goddess of many names, mother of the gods and the immanent power of all nature: the earth, not as dust (Genesis 3:19) but as the source, the living body out of which all things proceed and to which they return at peace." (1969)

Tristram was originally a British sun hero, who passed into the popular medieval romances as a hunter, swordsman, and harper. He is said to have sailed to Ireland to solicit the hand of Iseult for King Mark, the ruler of Cornwall. In this complex mythology, Princess Iseult is a spring fertility deity, the goddess of the dawn, who marries King Mark, the old sun and fading fertility god. After the wedding, King Mark discovers that Iseult is Tristram's beloved, and so the young hero must flee to Brittany, where he marries another lady, "Iseult of the white hands," a lunar and harvest goddess.

This tragic romance provided inspiration for many works of art of the Middle Ages. One of the most popular depicts a meeting between the lovers, with King Mark spying upon them. A French ivory casket dating from the middle of the fourteenth century provides a fine example of this particular episode (see Fig. 10). Significantly, the tryst of Tristram and Iseult is presented on this ivory box alongside a depiction of the killing of a unicorn.

The scene portrayed on the casket shows King Mark spying upon Tristram and Iseult from the vantage of a leafy tree, as the lovers meet beside a pool. A number of art historians have suggested that this romantic scene suggests a contrast between pure love, as exemplified by the unicorn and the maiden, and the adulterous union that is identified with Tristram and Iseult. But on examining a number of similar portraits of the famous lovers, it seems that another meaning was intended. A corbel from Bruges (Fig. 44) dating from the last quarter of the fourteenth century presents the tryst episode in a strange manner; art historian Roger Loomis comments that the corbel presents "King Mark's head surrounded by a sort of Christmas wreath." (1938) There is also a misericord from Chester Cathedral (Fig. 45), in which Tristram and Iseult are carved in such a way that they seem to support the face of the king as he glares from among the oak leaves.

These carvings are but a few of the many surviving examples of art from the Middle Ages that present the tryst between the tragic lovers. In studying these pieces, a number of interesting facts emerge. The wooden misericord, as well as other examples, shows a remarkable resemblance to the "Green Man" architectural carvings found all over Europe (Fig. 46). These sculptures were given this name because they depict a face that is overlaid with foliage. Another interesting feature of these carvings is the predominant use of the oak as the tree from which King Mark spies upon the young lovers, therefore reinforcing the argument that Mark is symbolic of the Oak King.

One further point should be explored before any conclusions can be drawn from the carvings of Tristram and Iseult. This point can be examined by discussing works of art that deal with the death of the unicorn. One beautiful French enamel from the fourteenth century (see Fig. 9) depicts the pacified unicorn kneeling beside the Virgin. While the maid grasps the magical horn in one hand, in the other she holds a round mirror. An oak tree, easily identified by its large green leaves, conceals a hunter who has

Figure 44. "Meeting Between Tristram and Iseult." Stone corbel. Bruges, 1378–87.

Figure 45. "Meeting Between Tristram and Iseult." Misericord, c. 1380, Chester Cathedral.

Figure 46. "Green Man" painted roof boss, Canterbury Cathedral.

just given the coup de grâce to the prostrate unicorn. The use of a mirror plays a conspicuous part in a number of other artworks that present the killing of the unicorn.

The French ivory casket previously mentioned (see Fig. 10) presents, on the right, the death of a pacified unicorn. The animal is depicted sitting in the lap of a maid, while her companion, standing next to an oak tree, kills the unicorn with a long spear. Here the Virgin is shown with one hand on the animal's horn, while the other hand supports a circular mirror above the unicorn's head. The carving on the left side of the casket depicts the secret meeting between Tristram and Iseult, during which the lovers see the face of the spying King Mark reflected in the water of a fountain. Both carvings on this casket share the oak tree, which provides concealment for the old king.

Reflection (mirrored image) is central to the meaning of a set of hangings that is contemporary with the Unicorn Tapestries. In one of the "Lady with the Unicorn" Tapestries—which have been characterized by art historians as dealing with aspects of human perception—the panel devoted to sight shows the unicorn wearing a remarkable expression as he stares entranced at his own reflection (see Fig. 12).

An illumination from a book of hours in which a mirror or reflection plays an important role provides some clues to this magical drama. In the fifteenth-century *Wharncliffe Hours,* there is a page that depicts the drama of St. John and the poisoned cup. Two other events are also represented in this same illumination (Figs. 47 and 48). In the bottom right margin, the artist has included a maiden holding a mirror up to an enraptured unicorn; while in the top right margin of the same page, Samson, like the unicorn, rests in the lap of a beautiful woman. In this illumination, Delilah is shown grasping Samson's locks. The story is a familiar one. Once the hair of this Hebraic Hercules has been shorn, he will lose all ability to defend himself, and, like the pacified unicorn, he can easily be taken by his enemies.

From these examples, it is only a small step to the conjecture that the mirror is in some way connected to the central theme of the capturing of the unicorn. And as we shall shortly see, the mirror—like the reflection of Mark's face in the pool—was included in representations of the Tristram and Iseult tryst for a specific reason.

In his interpretation of the relationship between Tristram and King Mark, Joseph Campbell provides a possible reason as to why the tryst episode of this romance was so important in the secular art of the Middle Ages. Campbell also provides an explanation for the juxtaposition of the tryst with the capture of a unicorn. Tristram was to King Mark "the young year to the old, he was the young god destined to supplant the old in possession of the queen, who in the ritual lore of the old Bronze Age tradition was symbolic of the land, the realm, the universe itself." (1968)

Figure 47. "Unicorn with Maid."
Border miniature in *Wharncliffe
Book of Hours,* by Maître François,
c. 1470. Melbourne, National
Gallery of Victoria.

Figure 48. "Samson with
Delilah." Border miniature in
*Wharncliffe Book of Hours,* by
Maître François, c. 1470.
Melbourne, National Gallery
of Victoria.

Tristram is a solar hero and is therefore also a symbol of the Oak King. In light of this explanation, Mark—the old Oak King—is killed because of his enfeeblement, and he is then replaced by his young successor, Tristram.

To explain the importance in iconographic art of reflections in water and mirrors in general, we need only recall the myth of Narcissus at the fountain. This god of vegetation, enticed by his own reflection in the clear waters, dissolves into oblivion. The fate of the beautiful youth is a mythological explanation for the death that precedes new life. Both the mirror associated with the capture and death of the unicorn and the reflected image of King Mark in a pool of water are explained by Ad de Vries when he comments that the mirror "is the door through which the soul frees itself by passing."

If we accept Campbell's explanation that King Mark is the old god destined to be supplanted by the younger and more vigorous Tristram, and take into consideration that in most works of art King Mark is hidden in an oak tree, we can conclude that in this medieval romance we have the recapitulation of a belief in the Divine King cycle of the Bronze Age.

In the light of these conjectures, we can now explain why the tryst episode between Tristram and Iseult is juxtaposed with the capture and death of the unicorn. If Tristram, Iseult, and Mark are personages identified with the solar oak cycle, then the hunter, virgin, and unicorn logically represent the converse, which is the lunar or holly cycle.

We can never know if the lady in this fragmentary fifth panel of the Unicorn Tapestries was originally woven holding a mirror, but it is a fascinating possibility. What is important is that the unicorn is depicted as being totally enraptured by the central female, and thus pacified, will soon be led off by his captives, like Samson. His death will be violent, as the drama in the next tapestry illustrates. But, like the phoenix, he will be resurrected in all his former glory—in the final panel of the series, this remarkable creature is resurrected and handsomely presented in a wooden enclosure against a *millefleurs* background.

But in order for the unicorn to receive immortality, it is first necessary for him to die. This ritual of immortality through death helps us to get closer to understanding the real identity of the lady who is the central figure of this fragmentary tapestry. And by a stroke of luck, a sufficient part of one of the surviving segments enables the apple tree to be identified as the central plant under which the virgin is depicted in this panel.

Since earliest times the apple tree has been one of the most sacred of trees, the subject of countless myths and legends. For example, the recipient of an apple from a goddess was rendered immortal. But as de Vries points out, "the gift of the apple of immortality automatically includes death." The fruit of this tree provides a passage to immortality, the means by which the possessor can enter paradise, or the Elysian Fields. Such apples were given to heroes by the goddess of the sacred grove of Nemesis, so that they could enter her holy precinct. One of the most popular medieval heroes, King Arthur, when grievously wounded, retired to the magical island of Avalon. This geographical name translates as "Island of the Apples" and had the same meaning as the Elysian Fields. Jessie Weston in *The Quest of the Holy Grail* notes: "in the Isle of Avalon, in a holy house of religion that is placed at the head of the adventurous marshes, there . . . lie King Arthur and Queen Guenevere." (1913)

The apple is connected to other well-known heroes. As Robert Graves points out, the solar hero and divine Oak King Hercules was also called Melon (the Greek word for apple) "because he was given the bough with the golden apples by the Three Daughters of the West"—deities that Graves identifies as the Triple Goddess. (1966) And it was their apple that made Hercules immortal.

The Hebraic equivalent of Hercules is Samson, "a Palestine sun-god who, becoming inappropriately included in the corpus of the Jewish myths, was finally written down as an Israelite hero of the time of Judges. . . . The name 'Samson' means 'Of the Sun' and 'Dan,' his tribe is an appellation of the Assyrian Sun-god." (Graves, 1966)

Earlier, we examined an illuminated page from the *Wharncliffe Hours* and established a connection between the unicorn being pacified by the virgin and Samson being rendered harmless by the wiles of the beautiful Delilah. These two mythic sun heroes, Samson and Hercules, receive their immortality through death, and, like their lunar counterpart the unicorn, they enter the next world by the intervention of a goddess.

We can now begin to perceive the true identity of the lady in the fragmentary fifth panel of the Unicorn Tapestries. The apple tree again provides the answer to this mythic overlay, identifying the lady with the Triple Goddess: love, death, and birth.

We know that the apple was associated with the love goddess, Venus, because she is renowned for having won a contest for her great beauty, receiving from Paris the famous golden apple as her reward. The story of Atalanta and Hippomenes is another myth that connects Venus with the apple. With the help of Venus and three golden apples, Hippomenes tricks Atalanta into marrying him.

One of the most influential pieces of literature that helped expand the Christian symbolism of the apple is found in the Hebrew Canticles. These consist of five books; the first canticle, and the best known since it is part of the King James Bible, is the *Song of Solomon* or *Song of Songs*. The following passage is interpreted by mythologers as a fertility ritual of copulation: "as the apple tree among the trees of the wood, so is my beloved among the sons. I sat down under his shadow with great delight, and his fruit was sweet to my taste." Ad de Vries interprets another passage in this canticle,

"I raised thee up under the apple tree," as an allusion to deflowering the bride.

The apple also has a connection with another, less pleasant goddess. It was because of Eve's enticement to eat this fruit that Adam brought death into the world. The apple has equally malevolent associations in other myths: for instance, the influential pre-Christian apple feast of Halloween was a Celtic festival that honored the dead. In Greek mythology, the fatal apple thrown by Discordia into the assembly of the gods caused the destruction of Troy and the death of many Greek heroes.

From the medieval belief that the apple brought death into the world, theologians wrote that Christ gave mankind immortality by being crucified on the apple tree. The duality of the apple, its life-death aspect, is explained in a passage written by St. Ambrose: "Eve caused us to be condemned by an apple of the tree, Mary wrought our pardon by the gift of the tree; because Christ also hung upon the tree as fruit." (Livius) This symbolism was employed by Berthold Furtmeyer in a missal dated 1481 (Fig. 49). In this sacred book, we see that the Tree of Knowledge is an apple tree. Eve is depicted offering apples to a kneeling group that is presided over by Death. On the left side of the miniature the Virgin is painted as the "new Eve," gathering the sacred host of her crucified son and giving eternal life to the virtuous who kneel beside her.

We can conclude that the apple tree is mythologically identified with love, death, and birth. Therefore, the virgin placed by the designer under the apple tree in this fifth tapestry is the amalgamation of these three moments of human life. In other words, she is the Triple Goddess.

In all the panels of the Unicorn Tapestries examined so far, we have been able to identify each hanging with a specific season. "The Unicorn Is Tamed by the Maiden" is no exception, and the Roman calendar provides a seasonal time frame. This fragmentary fifth panel depicts imagery that associates it with the pre-Christian festival of the Mother Goddess Vesta (or Diana), celebrated on August 13. According to Robert Graves, on this occasion the participants served "Cyder, a roasted kid spitted on hazel twigs and apples hanging in clusters from a bough. Another name of this goddess was Nemesis (from the Greek nemos, 'grove'). . . . In her statues she carries an apple-bough in one hand, and the fifth-century Christian poet Commodianus identifies her with Diana Nemorensis ('of the Grove'). . . . Nemesis carries a wheel in her other hand to show that she is the goddess of the turning year," like her Latin counterpart Fortuna. (1966)

In the Middle Ages, this great festival honoring the Mother Goddess and the deities of the seasons was converted to the Feast of the Assumption of the Blessed Virgin, celebrated two days later, on August 15, because the Virgin, like her divine son Christ, rose to Heaven on the third day.

We now have the possibility of connecting this fragmentary tapestry with the seasonal activities that are associated with August, thus establishing a connection between the apple tree and Nemesis—who is also Diana of the Grove and a goddess of the changing year.

From this vantage point we are in a position to explain the most curious part of the mythology that surrounds the unicorn, its capture by a virgin. The final enslaver and victor over this fierce beast that brave men were unable to capture was the goddess of love. And so it is appropriate that the unicorn falls in love with the maid under an apple tree—the tree of Venus. Under this spell, the unicorn is rendered helpless because of the overpowering amorous instincts aroused in him by the sight of the lovely maiden. And because of this erotic enchantment, the pacified unicorn meets his death. In accordance with events connected with the hunt of the unicorn, this fragmentary fifth tapestry depicts the final episode before the drama of the animal's death, the theme of the next panel, "The Unicorn Is Killed and Brought to the Castle." And in the seasonal context of the waning cycle, the fragmentary fifth panel of the Unicorn Tapestries corresponds to the ritual mating of the Holly King with the representative of the earth mother, the copulation before the winter solstice, when he will be put to death. The rose-covered *hortus conclusus* represents an amorous garden in which the virgin, seated under a tree and surrounded by her principal flower, the rose, is identified with the goddess of love.

This symbolism parallels the description given by Jean de Meun in the final part of *The Romance of the Rose*. In this epic poem, the rose in the center of the walled garden becomes the ultimate quest of the determined lover. After overcoming numerous obstacles and defeating many foes, the lover finally wins the rose; and, as the following lines indicate, the rose is deflowered in more than one sense:

> This much more I'll tell you: at the end,
> When I dislodged the bud, a little seed
> I spilled just in the center, as I spread
> The petals to admire their loveliness,
> Searching the calyx to its inmost depths,
> As it seemed good to me. It there remained
> And scarcely could unmingle from the bud.

In contrast to this obvious secular euphemism for copulation used by Meum, Dante in the *Divine Comedy* spiritualized the same allegory. At the end of his journey, the author finally sees the rose of Paradise. This "radiant white rose" was the flower which Christ with his blood "made his spouse."

It is now possible to grasp the symbolism of the unicorn's capture. The apple represents love, death, and rebirth. Adam and Eve knew death by eating the apple; and as the Bible states, with eating the apple, "Adam knew Eve his wife, and she conceived." (Genesis 4:1)

Figure 49. Berthold Furtmeyer, "The Apple as the Tree of Death and Life."
Miniature from the archbishop of Salzburg's missal, 1481. Munich, Bayerische
Staatsbibliothek.

Figure 50. Apple in cross-section. Illustration by Benjamin Lander in Caroline Creevey, *Flowers of Field, Hill and Swamp*. New York: Harper & Brothers, 1897.

The writers of the Middle Ages believed that it was the apple that brought death into the world, and these same theologians also wrote that Christ gave mankind immortality by being crucified on the apple tree.

The iconographic mystery of the apple can be seen when it is cut in cross-section. The seeds form a five-pointed star, the pentagram (Fig. 50), a symbol that represents immortality, the turning of the wheel from birth to death and back again to birth. So the apple in this connotation becomes the symbol of the goddess of the changing year, Nemesis.

The sacred Holly King, the unicorn—like his mythical human (Oak King) counterparts, Hercules, Samson, and Gawain—meets his fate in the sacred grove of Diana Nemorensis. But each in his own season. The waxing symbols—the various lion/sun associated mortals and deities—are killed at the midsummer solstice, and the waning symbols—those mortals and deities associated with the lunar/unicorn—die at the midwinter solstice.

This fragmentary fifth panel of the Unicorn tapestries corresponds in seasonal context with the month of August, when the Holly King will ritually mate with the chosen representative of the earth mother. After a blissful union, he is led away and is killed as the wheel of Nemorensis reaches full cycle at the midwinter Saturnalia. The *hortus conclusus* depicted in the fifth tapestry is the sacred grove of Diana Nemorensis, and the apple is the fruit of the Triple Goddess. The unicorn is rendered helpless by the power of love, which leads to his capture and violent death. But the tragedy is not final, for ultimately, by entering that dark realm, the unicorn will be reborn into immortality.

PLATE

# VI

# THE UNICORN
# IS KILLED
# AND BROUGHT
# TO THE CASTLE

The holly bears a berry,
As red as any blood;
And Mary bore sweet Jesus Christ
To do poor sinners good.
—Rickert

THE VIOLENCE OF A MEDIEVAL HUNT is captured for us in this sixth panel of the Unicorn Tapestries. Here the pacified unicorn, after being captured by the hunters, is depicted in the final moments of his death agony (Plate VI). In this visual drama, the savage killing of the unicorn is contrasted sharply with the aristocratic assembly outside the walls of an impressive castle. At the head of the noble entourage, waiting to receive the body of the unicorn, are a lavishly dressed lord and lady. These two distinctly different aspects of the hunt are separated by a watercourse, woven into the textile to give the impression of a channel of water running diagonally from the left margin. It passes the hazel tree that conceals a squirrel, and then continues on its way, through the legs of the horse and beyond. This watercourse is particularly important to the symbolism of the panel.

The preceding tapestry, "The Unicorn Is Tamed by the Maiden," depicted a maid under an apple tree, pacifying the unicorn so that he could be easily captured by the hunters. On one, mythic level this lady is identified with the ancient Triple Goddess of love, death, and birth; and on the Christian level, she may be interpreted as the Virgin Mary. The unicorn parallels the betrayal of Christ in the Garden of Gethsemane.

The sixth tapestry, "The Unicorn Is Killed and Brought to the Castle," is the last panel in the actual hunting sequence. The images present a twofold drama: the death of the unicorn; and the presentation of the dead animal to the lord and lady of the citadel. The animals, plants, and figures depicted in this sixth panel are identified with the midwinter solstice, the time when the Holly King meets his death. It is a period when the days begin to lengthen again, and the people rejoice because they believe that this is a celebration of the rebirth of the sun.

When the unicorn finally meets his death, he is juxtaposed with an oak and a holly tree. The latter is depicted directly above the head of the unicorn, while the image of an oak tree silhouettes the two huntsmen delivering the coup de grâce (Fig. 51).

It is remarkable that the only holly depicted in this sixth panel occurs directly behind the mortally wounded unicorn. As I have stressed throughout this book, the holly is associated with the unicorn and the waning cycle of the year; but this evergreen is also the living symbol of the verdant year—the repository of the spirit of vegetation during the months when winter holds sway over the earth and makes the land a frozen wasteland. The English scholar Philippa Tristram points out that "in the natural world green summer' is not erased permanently, and the evergreen holly with its bright berries perpetuates a summer flourish through the dead of winter."

In this sixth panel, we see other oaks woven into the right-hand section of the panel. The largest specimens occur behind the three ladies near the castle. The oak appears again in the citadel precinct, where a large tree is depicted. Behind the castle walls, to the left of the turret and just above the dovecot, there are a number of trees. This wooded arbor looks very much like oak, but is not detailed enough to provide definite identification.

As we have seen from the statements of medieval authors, the death of the unicorn was an allegory of the Crucifixion—the necessary sacrifice of Christ, according to Christian doctrine, that would release the souls of the penitent and the just from Limbo. The New Testament states that after his death and before his ascent into Paradise, Christ descended into the underworld. To the people of the Middle Ages, this underworld was associated with the dark days of December, the landscape of winter, a cold and desolate world.

One fifteenth-century carol expresses this idea of a wintry hell:

> Adam lay bounden,
> Bounden in a bond;
> Four thousand winter . . .
> —Rickert

Another carol from the fifteen century describes the world before the coming of Christ thus:

> It was dark, and it was dim,

> --------

Figure 51. Detail—"The Unicorn Is Killed and Brought to the Castle." The Unicorn Tapestries. Franco-Flemish, c. 1500. The Cloisters, Metropolitan Museum of Art.

Lucifer was all within,

--------

There was weeping, there was woe,
For every man to hell can go
It was little merry so.
      —Rickert

The chorus of this carol repeats in each verse "Till on Christmas Day," referring to the birth of Christ and hence the release of mankind from winter and death.

The winter solstice, the period identified with "The Unicorn Is Killed" tapestry, was an important time to both primal and medieval Europeans. Originally, this had been a time for the worship of Helios—the sun. The allure of such worship was one of the most powerful threats to the Christian Church in its infancy. Comments Marina Warner: "Squarely facing the menace, the Christians of the west fixed Christmas Day on the very feast of *Sol Invictus*, the Unconquered Sun, and invoked Christ by his name as in St. Ambrose's Dawn hymns. . . . Thus the Christian liturgical year commemorates the birth of its god after the winter solstice, on the day when the sun has ended its long hibernation and begun to rise towards the spring; and in the west, celebrates his rebirth from the dead on the day when the sun has finally triumphed over darkness and the days are drawing ahead lasting longer than the nights."

As Philippa Tristram points out, the medieval calendar painters "stress that the death of the year is also the season of Christmas fire and festivity, of Christ's promise through the Incarnation of resurrection, a time at which men anticipate within doors the renewal which Spring will later proclaim without."

The medieval poem *Sir Gawain and the Green Knight* begins and ends in a midwinter landscape, when "fierce winter howls, heavy with snow." (Stone, 1959) Sir Gawain, who is the personification of the vernal forces of nature, has an impact on the imagination that is like "spring's smile summer's glow" (Tristram)

At the beginning of the fourth fit, the poet of *Sir Gawain and the Green Knight* writes: "Now the year neared, the night passed, daylight fought the darkness as the Deity ordained." (Stone, 1959) As Eliade points out, "among Nordic people, Christmas (Yule) was both the feast of the dead and the honoring of fertility and life . . . the time for weddings, and also for attending to the tombs." (1958)

This idea of the exchange of life and death at the winter solstice still survives in our present-day celebration of the New Year. We personify the Old Year as a decrepit elderly man, while the incarnation of the New Year is presented as a newly born child. In the medieval calendar, the Roman god Janus is often seen as the personification of the month of January. For example, in the early fifteenth-century devotional book *Les Belles Heures de Jean Duc de Berry* (Fig. 52), the page devoted to January depicts the god Janus as both youth and old man sitting back to back. The author of *Sir Gawain and the Green Knight* made use of the association of January with this Roman god when he stressed "that the year at midwinter looks, like the double faced Janus, equal to birth and death." (Tristram)

Much of the ribald behavior that we associate with New Year celebrations is a legacy from the Roman Saturnalia. We have a remarkable piece of evidence that attests to the popularity during the Middle Ages of

Figure 52. "Janus as Youth and Age," in *Les Belles Heures de Jean Duc de Berry*. Limbourg brothers, early 15th century. The Cloisters, Metropolitan Museum of Art.

these midwinter revels, which were presided over by a Lord of Misrule. In a letter dated March 21, 1445, sent from the Faculty of Theology in Paris to all the main French ecclesiastical chapters and bishops, we find the following statement: "The preamble sets forth the facts concerning the *festum fatuorum* [Feast of Fools]. It has its clear origin, say the theologians, in the rites of paganism, amongst which this Janus-worship of the Kalends has alone been allowed to survive."

The authors of this medieval document then describe what they considered the atrocious behavior of those clerics who participated in the rites:

Priests and clerks may be seen wearing masks and monstrous visages at the hours of office. They dance in the choir dressed as women . . . or minstrels. They sing wanton songs. They eat black puddings at the horn of the altar while the celebrant is saying mass. They play at dice there. They cense with stinking smoke from the soles of old shoes. They run and leap through the church, without a blush at their own shame. Finally they drive about the town and its theatres in shabby traps and carts; and rouse the laughter of their fellows and the bystanders in infamous performances, with indecent gestures and verses scurrilous and unchaste. (Chambers)

According to Eliade, these festivals in honor of Saturn "symbolize regression to the amorphous condition that preceded the Creation of the World. In the case of a creation on the level of vegetable life, this cosmological-ritual scenario is repeated, for the new crop is equivalent to a new creation." (1959)

This was the time when the representative of the waning year had to be sacrificed, and thus it was the period in which the life of the Holly King would come to an end. The midwinter sacrifice, like that of midsummer, was considered essential to the well-being of all human, animal, and plant life. The blood that came from the sacrificial victim was considered very precious, the essence of the life force. Thus blood was collected during the sacrifice of the Divine Kings and used to anoint both vegetables and animals. This ritual predates and reflects the use of wine in the Christian sacraments, representing the blood of the crucified Christ.

A Middle English poem on the Passion of Christ illustrates this idea of his sacrifice and the preciousness of his blood. In this instance, Christ is likened to a stag slaughtered during the hunt:

> Her Son was drawn
> As deer is torn
> In chase!
>
> --------
>
> Death He bare as Man, for men,
> High upon the Rood,
> All our sins He washed them then
> With His Holy Blood,
> With that flood adown did 'light,
> Brake the gate of Hell forthright.
> —Weston, 1914

One interesting detail in this sixth panel of the Unicorn Tapestries is the careful positioning of the horn sounding the death knell, which is depicted directly in line with the stream of blood issuing from the breast of the unicorn. Upon close examination, some of the blood from the unicorn's wound seems to be captured inside the horn (Fig. 53).

It was the belief of the Christians that the blood of their God would absolve them from original sin and allow departed souls to enter Paradise. This concept is a cornerstone of Christianity and is reflected in many religious works of art dating from the Middle Ages. One of the most famous is the masterpiece by Hubert and Jan van Eyck, *The Ghent Altarpiece* or, as it is also known, *The Mystic Lamb* (Fig. 54). The lamb standing upon the altar in the central panel of this triptych is an icon of Christ. From a wound in the animal's side blood flows into a golden chalice.

Another example of the preciousness of blood in Christian symbolism is found in a Netherlandish sixteenth-century woodcut that depicts Christ in a wine press (Fig. 55). As God tightens the turnscrew, blood flows from Christ's wounds into a wooden tub. Underneath the outlets of the vat, angels gather the blood into a large chalice.

Figure 53. Detail—"The Unicorn Is Killed and Brought to the Castle." The Cloisters, Metropolitan Museum of Art.

Figure 54. Hubert and Jan van Eyck, *The Ghent Altarpiece*, completed 1432. Detail of central panel, *The Adoration of the Lamb*. Ghent, St. Bavo's Church.

Figure 55. *Christ in the Wine Press*. Woodcut. Netherlands(?), 16th century. Washington, D.C., National Gallery of Art.

Similar imagery is also depicted in an earlier work from Bavaria (Fig. 56), but in this painting most of the blood is shown being put into wine casks. The symbolism in the woodcut and in this painting is borrowed from the pre-Christian allegory of Dionysus as the grape turned into wine. In these works Christ appears undisguised, as one of the sacrificed pre-Christian vegetation gods. And around the border of the woodcut, flowers and fruit are depicted—the largesse that a fertility deity would bestow.

Returning to "The Unicorn Is Killed" tapestry, similar imagery can be seen here. The blood of the unicorn is collected in the horn that serves as a chalice. As Jessie Weston points out, the "lance or spear" represents the phallic male, and "the cup, or vase, the female, reproductive energy." Both these objects "are sex symbols of immemorial antiquity."

Weston indicates that in the Grail story, "the lance is borne in procession by a youth, the Grail is carried by a maiden—the sex of the bearer corresponds with the symbol borne." (1920) Furthermore, the lance and

Figure 56. German master, *Christ in the Wine Press*. Central panel, 1500. Munich, Bayerisches Nationalmuseum.

cup are made the central elements of the Grail legend precisely because of their ancient association as sexual symbols.

It is my opinion that, like the goring of the dog in the fourth panel of the Unicorn Tapestries, the carefully chosen drama presented in "The Unicorn Is Killed" is a symbolic representation of copulation—the union of the Holly King with the earth mother before the king's death and later rebirth.

This ritual of the midwinter marriage of the Divine King survives in the ballads, literature, and carols of the Middle Ages. For instance, in the traditional English carol "Tomorrow Shall Be My Dancing Day," Christ speaks in the first person. And in his poetic monologue, the chorus is addressed to Christ's true love:

> Then on the Cross hanged I was,
> Where a spear to my heart did glance;
> There issued forth both water and blood,
> To call my true love to my dance.
> Sing, oh! my love, oh! my love, my love, my love,
> This have I done for my true love.
>
> --------
>
> Then down to hell I took my way
> For my true love's deliverance,
> And rose again on the third day,
> Up to my true love and the dance.
> Sing, oh! my love, oh! my love, my love, my love,
> This have I done for my true love.
> —Rickert

So the iconography of this dramatic sixth panel of the Unicorn Tapestries begins to unfold. Here we have the midwinter death of the Holly King in the symbolic guise of his lunar representation, the unicorn. The death of this god of vegetation will lead to his resurrection into a much more vigorous physique. But his demise must take place before he has passed his prime. The enfeeblement of the unicorn and its subsequent results is mentioned in an influential medieval text, the *Dialogus Creaturarum* (1511): "And when his time was wasted and he himself was made aged, young men despised him."

After his death, the unicorn is carried over the stream to a splendid castle, in front of which appear the lord and lady of the citadel. Because the fabric worn by the noblewoman is the same as the surviving sleeve of the central maid of the fifth panel (the "Virgin Mary" figure), it is highly possible that she is the same lady who appears in front of the castle in "The Unicorn Is Killed" tapestry.

Considering the death theme in this sixth tapestry, and the separation

Figure 57. Detail—"The Unicorn Is Killed and Brought to the Castle." The Cloisters, Metropolitan Museum of Art.

by a body of water of the scene depicting the killing of the unicorn and the scene of the castle, it is possible that the royal figures of the citadel represent the inhabitants of Hades. I also believe that the stream was included by the designer to represent the Styx, the river that surrounds the underworld. If this observation is correct, then the noble couple included here would be identified with Persephone and Hades, the rulers of the nether regions. A survey of the images presented in the panel will support this hypothesis.

In the left-hand margin of the tapestry, there are a number of interesting animal and plant icons. Next to the three dogs is a large hazel tree, in which an alert squirrel conceals itself from the hounds (Fig. 57). To the right of the hazel, a dark blue iris is depicted—one of the largest flowers woven in this tapestry. The iconography of the hazel, iris, and squirrel provides the initial basis for my hypothesis.

Cut branches of hazel have been employed for centuries to make divining rods, used to discover buried treasure and underground water, valuables that are under the auspices of Hades, King of the Underworld.

It was through entangled trees of hazel and hawthorn that Sir Gawain saw the enchanted castle of the Green Knight and his wife, the sorceress Morgan le Fay—a citadel certainly not belonging to this earth. At the base of the hazel, a bramble is entwined. According to European folklore, this bramble was the shrub into which Satan fell when he was cast out of Heaven for his rebellion against God. In writing about this plant, Pliny states that the bramble is one of the "pestilences of the soil itself." (Vol. V, Book XVIII)

Biblical texts are largely responsible for the malevolent associations of brambles. For instance, St. Paul states that the bramble symbolizes evil, the rejected souls that are destined to live in Hell: "That which bearest thorn and briars is rejected, and is nigh unto cursing; whose end is to be burned." (Hebrews 6:8) St. Thomas Aquinas interpreted this passage "as an allusion to the major sins which would lead to damnation." (D'Ancona, 1977) The same message is repeated again in the Book of Isaiah: "For the wickedness burneth as the fire: it shall devour the briars and thorns. . . . Through the wrath of the Lord of hosts is the Land darkened and the people shall be as the fuel of the fire." (Isaiah 9:18–19)

Hidden in the bramble-entwined hazel tree is a squirrel—an animal that in Teutonic mythology was the messenger of the underworld. According to Nordic accounts, the spirits of the underworld congregate around the roots of trees and talk to the squirrel. After receiving these messages, the squirrel climbs the trees and conveys the information to the gods. This connection of the squirrel with the underworld is noted by the art historian Herbert Friedmann: "a squirrel running up and down a vertical tree trunk, as in Cranach's Innsbruck picture of the penitent St. Jerome, may also echo an old Teutonic legend concerning the creature as sowing discord between Heaven and Hell" (1980) (Fig. 58).

In mentioning the squirrel, the French *Ortus Sanitatis* states that if the animal needs to "cross over a body of water in the woods in a tiny boat," it will use its tail by raising it like a sail, so that the wind will blow the squirrel across the water. This amazing feat, ascribed to the animal by medieval encyclopedists, is illustrated in an early thirteenth-century English bestiary. The squirrel is depicted on a nut-laden raft, floating over a tract of water with his tail raised like a sail (Fig. 59). In many European legends the nut is described as a dwelling for the spirits of the dead, and so this medieval belief concerning the nautical ability of the nut-laden squirrel shows a remarkable analogy to Charon, the ferryman in Greek mythology who takes the souls of the dead across the River Styx to Hades.

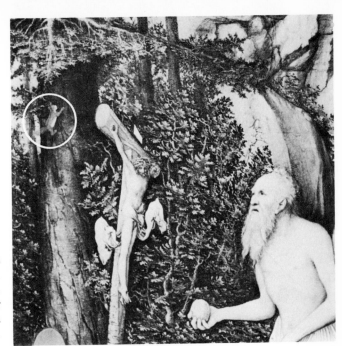

Figure 58. Detail—Lucas Cranach the Elder, *St. Jerome in Penitence*, 1525. Innsbruck, Tiroler Landesmuseum Ferdinandeum.

Figure 59. Illustration in English bestiary, early 13th century. Cambridge, University Library.

The next image to be considered in this section is the dark blue flag iris woven to the right of the hazel, silhouetting the three dogs. As we noted earlier, the iris and the goddess of the rainbow were inextricably united. De Vries points out that this flower was related to the "Triple Goddess in her death aspect." The dark blue flowers were held sacred by Persephone in her aspect as Queen of the Underworld; according to myth, Persephone would make garlands of iris flowers. And on the island of immortality, called Calypso, the iris "was found in the meadows . . . as a death flower."

Like her male counterpart, Hermes, the goddess Iris was not only a messenger of the gods but also a leader of souls from the region of the living to the abode of the dead. In *The Aeneid,* Virgil describes an incident in which Iris acts in this capacity. In one tale, Dido attempts suicide with a knife after her lover Aeneas has departed from Carthage. Because her death was slow and agonizing, Juno took pity on this tragic woman and sent Iris to end the queen's agony:

> Almighty Juno,
> Filled with pity for this long ordeal
> And difficult passage, now sent Iris down
> Out of Olympus to set free
> The wrestling spirit from the body's hold.
>
> - - - - - - - -
>
> At Dido's head she came to rest.
> "This token
> Sacred to Dis I bear away as bidden
> And free you from your body."
> Saying this,
> She cut a lock of hair. Along with it
> Her body's warmth fell into dissolution,
> And out into the winds her life withdrew.
> —Trans. Fitzgerald

This goddess of rainbows "comes and goes without warning, and she cuts the last thread that binds dying souls to their body." (Jobes)

These four images—the hazel, squirrel, bramble, and iris—each of which has unmistakable connections with the underworld, are not the only gloomy icons in this sixth tapestry. The three hounds depicted to the right of the hazel tree are woven in such a way that it is hard not to imagine that they allude to Cerberus, the three-headed dog that guarded the entrance to Hades. Supporting this theory is the positioning of the hounds next to other images that have associations with the infernal region—especially the squirrel as a symbol of Charon. In this panel there is another

Figure 60. Detail—"The Unicorn Is Killed and Brought to the Castle." The Cloisters, Metropolitan Museum of Art.

creature that in legend acts—like the squirrel—as a divine messenger. This is the goldfinch, and two of these birds can be seen upon the branches of the hawthorn tree that is placed directly above the dead unicorn (Fig. 60).

Earlier, I mentioned that the bird called acanthus by the ancients was identified by later medieval authors as the goldfinch. It is this bird, according to Aelian (Book 10:31), that "is sacred to the gods who escort and conduct men on a journey." As Friedmann notes, the goldfinch is closely linked with Christ's Passion on the Cross. The Crucifixion, which in the Christian mythos led to man's resurrection, "is nevertheless, a form of death." (1946)

In one of his notebooks, Leonardo da Vinci states that if the goldfinch sees any of its fledglings imprisoned, it will deliver to them the poisonous juice of the spurge, "preferring to see them dead rather than alive without liberty." From these accounts Friedmann concludes that "the bird was connected with the concept as a death-bringer." (1946)

The hawthorn tree in which the goldfinches are perched is important in this particular tapestry, and in one respect the tree is identified with Cardea in her malevolent aspect. It was under an arbor of hawthorn that this deity wove her hellish enchantments.

We now need to examine the dead unicorn depicted under the hawthorn and the two goldfinches. In this tapestry, the bleeding body of this magnificent creature is being presented by the huntsmen to the lord and lady of the castle. The dead unicorn is depicted with a wreath of oak around his neck as he is carried on the back of a brown palfrey toward the noble couple. This strange garland of oak leaves has never been satisfactorily explained. Some art historians have suggested that the wreath symbolizes endurance, but they have never explained the thorns upon the oak branch. If we compare the wreath with the "Green Man" carvings in Church architecture, some light may be thrown on this perplexing imagery.

A number of studies have been conducted by researchers on the so-called Green Man carvings in medieval churches. As Lady Raglan points out: "If we were about to choose one carving only for the decoration of our church, we should choose the person or the symbol that was in our opinion the focal point of our religious ideals." These faces are most often represented with leaves growing from their mouths and ears.

In the various surveys made, the predominant foliage represented in these carvings is that of the oak (Figs. 61 and 62). C. J. P. Cave points out that "in many instances the oak is depicted significantly, because this was the tree sacred to the Druids and most revered of all trees by the pagan Celts." There is nothing strange about the portrayal of these trees except for the fact that they are placed in a focal position, providing a major icon inside the church.

Rowland Sheridan and Anne Ross suggest that the real explanation is that this "medieval grotesque art stems directly from early pagan beliefs, that the representations are pagan deities dear to the people which the Church was unable to eradicate and therefore allowed to subsist side-by-side with the object of Christian orthodoxy." These two scholars explain that although the carvings vary somewhat in their representation, there is "throughout Europe a remarkable, fundamental consistency which makes it quite clear that whatever their *raison d'être*, their presence in the sacred buildings was not random but deliberate."

Sheridan and Ross believe that the depictions of these remarkable carvings originated in martial practices and in the religion of the Celts. This race, "from whom so many of the later European peoples were descended, were, like the other northern people, head-hunters. But apart from cutting off the heads of their enemies in battle they worshipped the severed head, and believed it to be imbued with every divine power.... Thus, the presence of so many heads in our churches."

Figure 61. Head with wreath of oak leaves. 14th century. Bristol, St. Mary Redcliffe.

Figure 62. Foliate head, roof boss. Hereford Cathedral.

It is therefore highly probable that the oak wreath around the unicorn's neck is derived from this ancient tradition of encircling a deity's head with the leaves of a venerated tree. Even if its original intention had been forgotten by the people of the Middle Ages, the practice was nevertheless perpetuated in their art and in their sacred buildings.

In this sixth panel, the death of the unicorn is an analogy for the Crucifixion. The pre-Christian veneration of the oak and the Christian association of thorns with Christ explain the hybrid garland around the creature's neck. The wreath is both the crown of thorns worn by Christ during the Passion and a symbol of the resurrection of the forces of vegetation—the rebirth of the Oak King during the midwinter solstice.

Let us now consider the other botanical images woven beneath the dead unicorn. Between his head and hooves the yellow cowslip is depicted (Fig. 63). Immediately below the cowslip is the carnation, an iconographic reference to the nails used in the Crucifixion. Completing this trio of botanical images is the red Chinese lantern, a plant that symbolized life in death because the "red bladders" (seed pods) do not fade, but remain bright orange during the winter. The Chinese lantern is placed so conspicuously under the dead unicorn to convey the idea that his death is not final and that he will eventually be resurrected. The cowslip—a plant also called St. Peter's keys because it resembles a bunch of keys—is an iconographic reference to the keys which will open the portals of Heaven. This symbolic association derives from a passage in the Gospel of St. Matthew. Christ presents Peter with the keys of Paradise, saying to his eldest disciple: "And I say also unto thee, That thou art Peter, and upon this rock I will build my Church; and the gates of hell shall not prevail against it." (Matthew 16:18)

Considering that the unicorn is identified with Christ, this New Testament passage is especially relevant, insofar as Jesus descends into the underworld immediately after his death on the Cross, to harrow Hell and release from Limbo all those from the Old Testament who have been given God's grace.

I mentioned earlier that it was probable that the lady presented in this panel is identical to the Virgin in the previous, now fragmentary panel. This maid who captures the unicorn in the fifth tapestry was the Virgin Mary to medieval Christian mystics. And in the art and literature of the Middle Ages, it was not unusual for Mary to be associated with Persephone in her role as Queen of the Underworld.

A fourteenth-century illustration depicts the entrance to Hell as the monster Leviathan's mouth (Fig. 64). Over this nightmarish scene the Virgin is presented along with the Christ child, sitting in glory above Hell's mouth. Commenting on this illustration, Marina Warner points out that the Virgin "becomes queen of hell" because the damned in the realm of Lucifer can

Figure 63. Detail—"The Unicorn Is Killed and Brought to the Castle." The Cloisters, Metropolitan Museum of Art.

Figure 64. The Virgin as Queen of Hell. 14th century. London, The British Library.

only find reprieve through the intercession of Mary.

This association of the Virgin with other realms and deities (beyond her familiar role as Queen of Heaven) is not restricted solely to art. For example, the great French poet François Villon, who died after 1463, addresses the Virgin as "Lady of heaven, regent of the earth, empress of the marshes of hell." (Warner)

A few other plants included in this sixth tapestry are worth mentioning, since they have symbolic associations that connect them either to Hades or to the Christian devil. Under the dress of the lady a large thistle is woven, with only the head of the original flower remaining, the complete plant being obscured by a rather poor nineteenth-century restoration (Fig. 65). The thistle is a symbol of sin and the Fall—indicating the expulsion of Adam and Eve from Eden and the curse put upon the land by God. "Cursed is the ground for thy sake. . . . Thorns also and thistles shalt it bring forth to thee." (Genesis 3:17–18)

Reinterpreting this biblical text, Alcuin stated that "the earth brought forth no thorn or thistles before original sin, but after it the earth produced them." (D'Ancona, 1977)

To the left of this thistle and under the head of the hound, the sinister white campion is depicted (Fig. 65). This is the plant that is woven along with the violet and nettle at the entrance to Hell in the *Last Judgment* tapestry discussed on page 105.

Before summarizing the images represented in "The Unicorn Is Killed" tapestry, one other creature needs mention. Two swans are depicted swimming in the moat of the castle (Fig. 66). According to de Vries, these birds

Figures 65 and 66. Details—"The Unicorn Is Killed and Brought to the Castle." The Cloisters, Metropolitan Museum of Art.

( Swan

are associated with the goddess of death because "at midsummer the swans fly north to unknown breeding grounds." In the mythology of many religions, swans "act as psychopomps, accompanying the souls of the dead (sun heroes) to the Far Northern Other World."

The swan is a sacred bird all over northern Europe and is associated with the Nordic Valkyries, the female war goddesses who collect the souls of brave men who die in battle. Apollo's chariot was drawn by swans as he headed northward to the land of youth. These birds were also thought to embody human souls, and it was considered evil to kill one. The natural coloring of the swan, white with a red neck, is the color of death in many European cultures—hence the familiar notion of the "swan song." A French prose bestiary praises the bird's singing and notes that the "swan that sings so well against its death signifies the soul which has joy in tribulation." (Rowland, 1978)

Aelian, commenting on some observations made by Aristotle, stated that "a flock of swans was once seen in the Libyan Sea and . . . a medley was heard proceeding from them as a choir singing in unison . . . mournful and calculated to move the hearer to pity. And some of the birds . . . when the music was ended were seen to have died."

Considering that nearly all the images presented in this tapestry have some connection to death and the underworld, it would seem highly probable that the castle depicted in this panel is meant to represent Hades, and that the lord and lady are the king and queen of the infernal region.

Behind this noble couple, three ladies are depicted in such a fashion that they present a rather sinister group (Fig. 67). Perhaps they are intended to represent Hecate, the three-headed goddess of witchcraft, who at the dark of the moon became a feared enchantress residing in the underworld. Beneath these three ladies is the image of a young boy who has a sad expression as he embraces a favorite hound and stares into the distance (Fig. 68). Under the child's right leg, the image of a pea plant can be seen. Because it grows in a spiral, this plant (like the bean) became identified with resurrection and rebirth—a token of immortality not unlike the spiral horn of the unicorn.

Perhaps this child, as well as the tall oak behind him and the oak wreath around the neck of the unicorn, are all intended to symbolize the waxing year and its imminent new cycle. In this tapestry, Fortuna's wheel has gone full turn from birth to death and back to birth again. It is the period when the transition takes place between winter and spring. The neck of the unicorn is garlanded with oak as the waxing year's victory wreath—a portent of birth in death. And as a parallel to this concept, under the unicorn's head are various life-in-death flowers.

Swans—the sacred birds of the goddess of death, like the heron in the fourth tapestry—accompany the spirits of the dead to the other world.

Figure 67. Detail—"The
Unicorn Is Killed and
Brought to the Castle."
The Cloisters,
Metropolitan Museum of
Art.

Figure 68. Detail—"The
Unicorn Is Killed and
Brought to the Castle."
The Cloisters,
Metropolitan Museum of
Art.

And the squirrel, as messenger and deathly ferryman, sits in the divining hazel next to the blue iris, an emblem of the goddess of the rainbow in her role as a psychopomp. Considering the coterie of infernal animals and plants in this section, it is hard not to believe that the designer intended the close proximity of the three dog heads as a representation of the three-headed Cerberus.

All the iconography presented in "The Unicorn Is Killed" tapestry concurs with the season of the winter solstice, the end of the agricultural year, and the death of the lunar unicorn. The midwinter solstice was the time of the birth of the Oak King, of his resurrection as the waxing cycle begins and the days start to lengthen after the defeat of winter. The wreath of oak around the dead unicorn's neck would be a victory token, indicating the imminent rebirth of the solar divinities, and the reign of their mortal counterpart, the Oak King. The promise of this fecund season is reflected in the next panel, "The Unicorn in Captivity," which depicts the resurrected unicorn in an enclosure, tethered to an emblem of female fecundity—the pomegranate tree—and placed in a *millefleurs* background of plants that are icons of male virility, botanical elements that ensure successful copulation.

# VII

# THE UNICORN
# IN CAPTIVITY

Most pleasant garden plot, true Paradise of praise . . .
But yet that garden far, exceeding sundry ways
As perfect second works, exceed things wrought before:
All closely walled about, inviolate it stays,
No serpent can get in, nor shall for evermore,
All goodly flowers and fruits, here in perfection grow,
Virtue on stocks of grace, hath them engrafted so.
—Richard Rowlands, *Hortus Conclusus*

T HIS FINAL PANEL of the Unicorn Tapestries presents the resurrected
unicorn in a fenced enclosure, chained with an elaborately decorated collar
to a stylized tree that bears very ripe pomegranates (Plate VII). The captured
unicorn is depicted against a splendid *millefleurs* background. Many of the
plants represented within the *hortus conclusus* are symbolic of fertility, and
are placed in this particular panel to emphasize the sexual prowess of the
unicorn.

The preceding tapestry, "The Unicorn Is Killed and Brought to the
Castle," depicted the violent death of the unicorn. And in that panel there
were images of animals and plants that were identified with Hades and
the winter solstice—the season in which the Holly King meets his death.

The seventh and final tapestry, "The Unicorn in Captivity," depicts
the resurrected unicorn amid botanical images that are icons of copulation
and fertility. Some of these plants, beside being strong aphrodisiacs, were
powerful prophylactics. The "heavenly enclosure" is identified with a fecund paradise, where images of male and female are united. This Eden is
the New Jerusalem, where the evil serpent of Genesis may not enter. To
identify the snake of Eden with this panel, the designer has included in
the *millefleurs* background various plants that possess, among other properties, the ability to repel and destroy serpents.

This seventh panel of the Unicorn Tapestries is not part of the actual
hunt of the unicorn, but rather the apotheosis of the hunt, in which the
resurrected unicorn symbolizes the rebirth of Christian and pre-Christian
vegetation gods. This tapestry is an epigram or coda to the yearly cycle,

mirroring the death and ultimate resurrection of the fecund seasons, and the sexual powers of plants and animals—a reflection of heavenly perfection, where there is perpetual springtime, abundance, and an absence of malign forces.

Before turning to a detailed interpretation of this last tapestry, a common error that concerns the woundlike marks on the unicorn's body must be explained (Fig. 69). Many people think that the red marks on the unicorn are evidence of his violent death, as portrayed in the previous tapestry, "The Unicorn Is Killed." In fact, these crimson stains on the animal's body were included by the designer to indicate that the pomegranates above the chained creature are extremely fertile and ripe; and they are further explained—as indeed are many other images in this tapestry—by passages in the Old Testament canticle, the *Song of Songs*. A careful examination of the weaving reveals that these "stains" are in fact seeds of the pomegranate.

The iconography of this central pomegranate tree is very important, providing the main clue to understanding the symbolism intended by the enclosure in which the unicorn is tethered. The unicorn here is identified with the resurrected Christ, and, in a broader sense, with the reborn, pre-Christian vegetation gods. A number of works of art from the Middle Ages will help to elucidate the iconography in this last tapestry.

For instance, the reason the unicorn is chained to the tree can be explained by examining a fifteenth-century manuscript, *Somme le Roi*. On the page that illustrates the "Paradise of Virtues," Christ is depicted tied to a tree in the middle of a garden (Fig. 70). This central tree is meant to represent the withered Tree of Life that is believed to have dried up after the Fall of man. The tying of Christ to this tree is symbolic of the Crucifixion. The image of Jesus nailed to the Cross identifies with Christ being grafted onto the Tree of Life. When this crucifixion occurs, verdure is restored to the tree again, and mankind, having regained grace by the sacrifice of Christ, can once again enter the heavenly Jerusalem.

Besides being associated with the underworld stories of Persephone and Ceres, the pomegranate tree has strong connections with Hebraic tradition and symbolism.

In the Old Testament, the pomegranate is mentioned as the only tree allowed in the inner sanctum of the temple, the Holy of Holies. One of the reasons for this is that the fruit is never eaten by insects, thus the pomegranate becomes a symbol of incorruptibility. Attesting to the sanctity of this fruit was its use as an embellishment on the robe of the Jewish high priest: "A golden bell and a pomegranate . . . upon the hem of the robe round about." (Exodus 28:34)

In constructing his great temple, Solomon ordered two special pillars to be made, which were to be given a prominent position at the entrance

Figure 69. Detail—"The
Unicorn in Captivity."
The Unicorn Tapestries.
Franco-Flemish, c. 1515.
The Cloisters, Metropolitan
Museum of Art.

Figure 70. The "Paradise
of Virtues," from the
*Somme le Roi*. 15th-century
manuscript. Oxford,
Bodleian Library.

of the temple: "For he cast two pillars of brass. . . . And the chapiters [capitol or head of the column] upon the two pillars had pomegranates also above . . . and the pomegranates were two hundred in rows round upon the other chapter. And he set up the pillars in the porch of the temple: and he set up the right pillar, and called the name thereof Jachin: and set up the left pillar, and called the name Boaz." (1 Kings 7:15–21)

From this description it is obvious that the pomegranate was a very important icon, carved in stone throughout Solomon's temple, and placed on top of the two most important pillars of the temple, Jachin and Boaz.

I. G. Matthews comments: "There are strong reasons to believe that [Jachin and Boaz] were related to the Asherah poles dedicated to Astarte, that stood beside the high places in Canaan. Fertility rites were so prevelant in all the country that, had there been no recognition of them in the temple, many worshipers would have felt the loss as seriously as if all evidence of the cross were removed from Christian churches. . . . Their unquestioned importance is indicated by the fact that on official occasions, such as coronation, and covenant making, the king stood by the pillar."

The importance of the pomegranate is also recorded in the religious images of the Moroccan Jews. This African sect preserved some of the oldest and purest Jewish traditions. For instance, the image of a pomegranate was "placed on the sticks around which the sacred scrolls of the Torah is wound, the sticks being called *Es Chajim*, "the tree of life"; Central European Jews have reduced this pomegranate to the crown formed by its withered calyx." (Graves, 1966)

From these Old Testament texts and symbolic associations with Jewish religion, we can see that the pomegranate was not only thought of as a symbol of fertility, but became identified with the Tree of Life. The abundance of seeds contained in the fruit associated it with the idea of fecundity. Furthermore, in the arid Holy Land this tree produces one of the most succulent fruits—a fact that provides a tangible reason for it to have been singled out for reverence. And the womb shape and numerous seeds contained within the pomegranate have, since antiquity, made this fruit a symbol of female genitalia and fertility in general. In the *Song of Solomon,* the pomegranate is mentioned a number of times because of its importance to the Hebrews as a fecund image. The *Song of Solomon* provides strong motive for depicting the pomegranate tree as the central image in the unicorn's enclosure, and also explains the collar and chain woven around the unicorn's neck.

Fertility is a major theme of this biblical canticle; the whole song makes allusions to a fertile springtime landscape: "For, lo, the winter is past, the rain is over and gone. The flowers appear on the earth; the time of the singing of birds is come, and the voice of the turtle is heard in our land."

The dialogue between Solomon and the Shulamite bride contains many descriptions of fertility. When Solomon praises the woman who is to be his future bride, he compares the various parts of her body with aspects of fertility: "Thy hair is as a flock of goats that appear from Gilead. Thy teeth are as a flock of sheep which go up from the washing, whereof every one beareth twins, and there is not one barren among them. As a piece of pomegranate are thy temples within thy locks."

In one instance this canticle connects the pomegranate tree with the *hortus conclusus:* "A garden enclosed is my sister, my spouse; a spring shut up, a fountain sealed. Thy plants are an orchard of pomegranates, with pleasant fruits."

In another passage, Solomon compares the Shulamite with the palm tree and the pomegranate. "How fair and how pleasant art thou, O love, for delights! This thy stature is like to a palm tree, and thy breasts to clusters of grapes . . . I will go up to the palm tree, I will take hold of the boughs." The bride answers that where "the pomegranates bud forth: there will I give thee my loves . . . I would lead thee, and bring thee into my mother's house . . . I would cause thee to drink of spiced wine of the juice of the pomegranate."

It is my opinion that this particular passage in the *Song of Solomon* provides an explanation for the hybrid tree in the center of the unicorn's enclosure. In this final tapestry we have a tree with palmlike leaves bearing pomegranates "budding forth." The specific reference in the canticle to "the juice of the pomegranate" leaves little doubt as to why the designer depicted the unicorn's body bespattered with pomegranate juice. Furthermore, I think it is highly probable that the designer showed the unicorn chained to the pomegranate-bearing palm tree because of the evocative symbolism presented in the following lines from the *Song of Solomon:* "I have compared thee, O my love, to a company of horses in Pharaoh's chariots. Thy cheeks are comely with rows of jewels, thy neck with chains of gold. We will make thee borders of gold with studs of silver. . . . Thou hast ravished my heart, my sister, my spouse . . . with one of thine eyes, with one chain of thy neck. . . . Thy plants are an orchard of pomegranates, with pleasant fruits." Upon examination, the unicorn is seen to be fastened to the central tree with a chain of gold, and the collar around the animal's neck is indeed studded with silver and jewels.

So, in this last panel we have a powerful male icon (the unicorn), chained to a pomegranate, a tree which in many respects symbolizes the female genitalia. In interpreting and identifying the imagery presented in "The Unicorn in Captivity" with the evocative verses of the *Song of Solomon,* the enclosure becomes the place in which "the pomegranate buds forth" and where a symbolic copulation between male and female images occurs.

In Solomon's words, it is the place of nuptials, in which he will "go up to the palm tree" and "take hold of the boughs."

As I have already mentioned, Solomon and his bride provided the medieval theologians with an allegory for the love of Christ and the Virgin. The mystical language and imagery contained in this Old Testament canticle had a powerful effect on the art of the Middle Ages.

In another French or Flemish tapestry from the sixteenth century, the resurrected Christ is depicted in an enclosure with Mary Magdalen (Fig. 71). Like "The Unicorn in Captivity" tapestry, the central tree in this particular work is a pomegranate. And in both works the tree is depicted with ripe, split fruit. Near the richly robed Christ, in "The Resurrected Christ Appearing to Mary Magdalen" tapestry, numerous fertility symbols—rabbits, violets, daisies, carnations, bluebells—are shown, and at the back of the enclosure is a rose-covered fence.

Another slightly earlier Flemish tapestry from the end of the fifteenth century presents a similar drama (Fig. 72). Christ is seen blessing Mary Magdalen in an enclosed garden. At the edge of the *hortus conclusus* appears a tree that is highly stylized and not unlike the tree in the center of "The Unicorn in Captivity" tapestry.

In a fifteenth-century painting entitled *The Expulsion from Paradise,* by Giovanni di Paolo, an angel forces Adam and Eve from Eden (Fig. 73). Here Adam and Eve are depicted still in the heavenly garden, just about to be expelled. Above them a number of trees appear, recognizable as

Figure 72. "The Resurrected Christ Appearing to Mary Magdalen." Tapestry, Flemish, late 15th century.

Figure 73. Detail— Giovanni di Paola, *Expulsion from Paradise.* Predella painting, Italy, c. 1445. Metropolitan Museum of Art, The Robert Lehman Collection.

Figure 71. (left) "The Resurrected Christ Appearing to Mary Magdalen." Tapestry, Franco-Flemish, 1516–18.

pomegranates by their fruit. Di Paolo has included the familiar icons of fertility, the strawberry and the rabbit, in the Garden of Eden. To indicate the future salvation of mankind, he has also included in this work (behind the angel) a carnation, which is an icon of Christ. And between the angel and Adam a Madonna lily, the flower of the Virgin, is painted.

These various works indicate that the pomegranate is not only associated with fertility, but also identified with Eden and the resurrection of Christ.

Now that we have been able to expand the symbolic implications of the central pomegranate woven into this seventh panel of the Unicorn Tapestries, let us examine the unicorn itself.

This mythical creature has many interpretations and associations. We have already noted that besides being a common lunar symbol, the unicorn stands for chastity, strength, and on many occasions is an emblem of Christ. And because of his great power and phallic horn, he is also an embodiment of fertility and sexual prowess.

The unicorn's erotic motif provides important imagery in a portrait by the sixteenth-century French painter François Clouet. This portrait, of Diane de Poitiers, the powerful mistress of Henry II of France, depicts a beautiful lady in a room filled with images that reflect her sensuous nature (Fig. 74). The great lady is presented naked to the waist; in one hand she holds a carnation, a flower that has amorous associations. Included in this painting are other flowers and fruit that are associated with Venus—rose, cherry, and daisy. And carefully placed on the white tablecloth next to Diane de Poitiers are flowers and fruit that evoke erotic images—pear, apricots, and grapes. At the back of the room the artist incorporates further important symbolism. For instance, a unicorn appears silhouetted against a palm tree on the back of a chair (Fig. 75). Both unicorn and palm tree are associated with fertility and regeneration, and certainly the mythical animal is displayed on the chairback here for its erotic implications.

The next major image depicted in "The Unicorn in Captivity" is the *hortus conclusus*, the enclosure that provides the special precinct confining the resurrected unicorn. In the art of the Middle Ages, these walled gardens were in many instances a reflection of the heavenly Paradise, the New Jerusalem where only the blessed could reside. And to the medieval artist the *hortus conclusus*, with its closed gate, was a symbol of Mary and an icon of her virginity. But these reflections of Eden in works of art were not chaste and sterile. On the contrary, they were intended to convey the image of fertile realms, a land without winter, where flowers and trees and numerous animals lived in eternal fruitfulness.

The symbolic intention of "The Unicorn in Captivity" is reinforced by a marginal illumination from an Italian work, the *Visconti Hours* (Fig. 76).

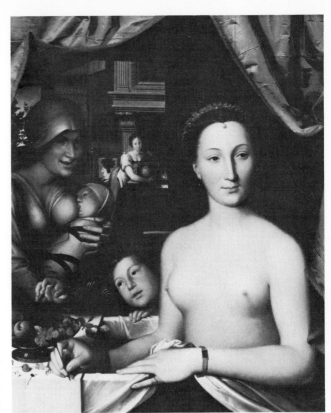

Figure 74. François Clouet,
*Diane de Poitiers*, c. 1571.
Washington, D.C.,
National Gallery of Art.

Figure 75. Detail—Clouet,
*Diane de Poitiers*.
Washington, D.C.,
National Gallery of Art.

Figure 76. Manuscript page from the *Visconti Hours*. Late 14th–early 15th century. Florence, Biblioteca Nazionale.

On the page devoted to Psalm 131, David is depicted kneeling in homage to God. Surrounding this central figure are two vine-covered oaks, each one set in the middle of an enclosure. On the left, a stag is depicted with its head halfway through the wooded fence, and between the two compounds the illuminator has included a hutchful of rabbits. As we shall shortly see, the iconography in this miniature matches the imagery presented in "The Unicorn in Captivity." The particular psalm ("Lord, remember David") refers to David's promise that he will find a "place for the Lord, an habitation for the mighty God of Jacob."

Tertullian, an important theologian of the third century, identified the Tree of Life with the oak. The vine depicted in the Italian miniature was a common symbol of Christ. Thus we have in this illumination an image of Christ "the true vine" growing on the Tree of Life—an allegory of the Crucifixion, which restored to that heavenly tree new foliage that had withered after the Fall. Grace is restored to humankind by this sacrifice, and man can once again enter the heavenly kingdom.

The stag placed in the enclosure provides the key to understanding the relationship between this marginal illustration and the main illumination on this page of the *Visconti Hours.* The psalm contains the promise made by David to transfer the Ark of the Covenant to a permanent site. This he does when he makes Jerusalem the religious capital of all Israel. In discussing the allegory of the stag, the author of the *Physiologus* writes: " 'You are God's temple, and God's spirit dwells in you' [I Corinthians 3:16]. You will never find a dragon in the house where the stag's hair appears or where his bones are burnt. Likewise, if the traces of God and fear of Christ are found in your heart, no impure spirit will enter you." The rabbit hutch depicted between these two enclosures was included by the artist of the *Visconti Hours* as a symbol of fertility.

From the examples cited, it becomes apparent that these enclosures presented in the art of the Middle Ages and Renaissance are meant to imply fertile Edens, realms of abundance—heavenly precincts that are free of any diabolical influence. These were Edens that could not be violated by Satan in any of his disguises.

Now that we have considered the three main images depicted in the seventh panel of the Unicorn Tapestries—the pomegranate, the enclosure, and the unicorn—we can turn to the actual plants woven inside the enclosed garden, as well as those that are prominent in the *millefleurs* background.

One of the most outstanding herbs depicted in this tapestry is the male orchid (*Orchis mascula*), placed so that it silhouettes the unicorn's body (Fig. 69). This orchid has twin roots—and their testicle-like appearance did not go unnoticed by the medieval people of Europe. The sexual association is recorded in the plant's vernacular names; the French *testicule de prêtre,* for instance, translates as "priest's testicle." Even earlier, the Romans called this orchid *satyrion*, for they believed that the plant was the food of satyrs, the drug that "excited them to those excesses which were characteristic of the attendants of Bacchus." (Folkard) The early belief in the prescribed properties of this orchid caused generations of scholars, physicians, and dabblers in the occult to recommend preparations of the orchid as an aphrodisiac.

Pliny notes: "very high on the list of wonders is the plant *orchis*. . . . The root has two tubers like testicles . . . they tell us that sexual desire is aroused if the root is merely held in the hand, a stronger passion, however, if it is taken in a dry wine, that rams also and he-goats are given it in drink when they are too sluggish." (Vol. VII, Book XXVI) And a contemporary of Pliny, Dioscorides, called the orchid *testiculum Satyri* and *Priapiscus*— identifying it with satyrs and with Priapus, the Greek personification of male sexual powers. (Gunther)

In this final panel of the Unicorn Tapestries many herbal aphrodisiacs are woven inside the enclosure, supporting the predominant theme of fecundity. To the right of the orchid there is a cluster of bluebells (Fig. 69). As Geoffrey Grigson points out, the bluebell shares with the male orchid many of the same names and attributes, strongly suggesting that there is a "folk relationship" between these two wild plants. The male orchid and the bluebell are often found growing together. And besides sharing over a dozen vernacular names, both plants flower at the same time—during the weeks from April to June. It seems unlikely that the strong association between the orchid and the bluebell was due to mere error or chance.

When the stem is broken, the bluebell exudes a clear sticky substance that not only provided glue for the early Europeans but gave rise to the identification of the plant with male sexual secretions.

The generic name of the bluebell is *Endymion*, and this name associates it with the lover of the Greek moon goddess, Selene. According to the legend, Selene placed her beloved in a perpetual sleep so that his beauty and strength would not fade. The unicorn was considered by the medieval astrologers to be a lunar creature. Perhaps the designer, aware of this fable, included the bluebell next to the unicorn to make allusions to this erotic legend—an appropriate juxtaposition, considering the nuptial imagery in this panel.

The bluebell was also recommended by Isidore of Seville as a botanical talisman to protect the household. He advised suspending bluebells "above the threshold, and all evil things will flee therefrom." (*Etymologiae*, quoted in Migne)

The other large flower woven into the unicorn's enclosure is the red stock-gillyflower, depicted to the left of the male orchid (see Fig. 69). This plant is in the same family as the wallflower. Because of these close connections, the stock-gillyflower was probably thought to have the same properties as the wallflower—namely, making women fruitful.

Another important herb is woven above the right front knee of the unicorn (Fig. 77). This plant, with its arrow-shaped leaves and a serpentine root, is called bistort. The name comes from the Latin *bis*, meaning "twice," and *torta*, meaning "twisted"—a reference to the shape of the root. Two common vernacular names of this plant, adderwort and snakewort, reflect the morphology of the root system. And because of the root's serpentine form, bistort was considered useful for curing the bites of reptiles.

In the Middle Ages a pudding made from bistort was eaten as a spring rejuvenative. The medieval French herbal *Le Grant Herbier* promises the reader that "an electuary of powdered bistort . . . and of aromatic spices . . . aids conception for it will bring comfort unto the retentive quality of the womb."

Figure 77. Detail—"The Unicorn in Captivity." The Cloisters, Metropolitan Museum of Art.

One of the most interesting plants woven into the unicorn's enclosure is the cuckoopint—an herb that in both appearance and legend is related to the American Jack-in-the-pulpit. This common European flower can be seen framed by the top section of fence immediately to the right of the gate (Fig. 78).

The cuckoopint, or arum, is a strange-looking plant, and because of its peculiar appearance it became shrouded in magic and superstition. The flower consists of a long, club-shaped spadix encased in an outer white sheath called a spathe. The numerous vernacular names connected with this herb give a clue to its symbolism: Adam and Eve, bulls and cows, cuckoo cock, ladies and gentlemen, dog's dibber, kings and queens, lords and ladies, parson's billycock, priest's pintle, bull's pintle, stallions and mares, and wake robin. All these names have equivalents in French, German, and the other European languages. The names suggest couples, both human and non-human, and also, due to the penis-shape of the arum's spadix, other less polite words that associate this plant with the male member. The positioning of the spadix in the spathe of the cuckoopint's flowers was seen by classical and medieval naturalists as a botanical icon for sexual intercourse.

During the first century A.D., Dioscorides wrote in his *De Materia Medica* that cuckoopint drunk in wine "stirs up the vehement desire to conjunction." The aphrodisiac properties of this plant were also noted by John Lyly in his pastoral drama *Loves Metamorphosis* (1601): "They have eaten so much wakė robin [cuckoopint] that they cannot sleep for love."

The medieval herbal *Agnus Castus* calls the arum by the name cokkowyl pyntle. As Geoffrey Grigson points out, though this name initially looks like cuckold's pintle (Old French *coucuol*, Middle English *kokeweld*), there "seems some folk-etymological confusion between cuckoo and cuckold," as well as between the almost identical Latin names for hood and cuckoo, respectively, *cucullus* and *cuculus*. Grigson observes, "here's the penis of the lecherous cuckoo, who cuckolds the birds, and here's the penis inside a hood, or in a cowl—that is to say, the penis of a priest, or monk or friar who goes round cuckolding husbands."

Apart from their amorous associations, many of the plants depicted in the unicorn's enclosure were considered by the classical and medieval authors to be strongly antiviperous. For instance, the arum, if burned, would "keep away serpents, especially asps, or make them so tipsy that they are found in a state of torpor." (Pliny, Vol. VII, Book XXIV) But the predominant connotation of all the flora in this final tapestry is sexuality. The phallic-shaped plant called the *Acorus calamus*, or sweet flag, is depicted behind the unicorn (see Fig. 79). Next to the calamus, a violet is woven—a plant that, like the orchid, is strongly associated with the phallic god Priapus,

Figure 78. Detail—"The Unicorn in Captivity." The Cloisters, Metropolitan Museum of Art.

who presides over the fecundity of gardens and orchards. Often a statue of Priapus was placed in these areas to encourage fertility.

Two carnation plants are also included in the *hortus conclusus*. One is placed by the front hooves of the unicorn, and the other is woven by his tail (Fig. 79). This plant occurs again in a number of places throughout the *millefleurs* background, and is most probably included in this panel because of its association with betrothal. It was fairly common among artists of the Middle Ages and the Renaissance to identify a betrothed couple and their future union by placing in their hands the image of a carnation. A fine example of this custom is presented in an early sixteenth-century Flemish tapestry, "Allegory of Time." The central figure is a richly dressed young man, who is shown offering a bouquet of carnations to a young lady (Fig. 80). In return, the woman is portrayed handing back a single carnation—indicating that she has accepted his amorous advances.

Another icon of fertility that appears in the unicorn's enclosure is the daisy, depicted above the creature's right front hoof. The daisy is the central motif of an anonymous fifteenth-century poet, who describes a castle of love belonging to Queen Venus' lady in *The Court of Love:*

> Within and out it was painted wonderfully
> And many a thousand daisy red as rose
> And white also, this saw I verily,

But what those daisies might signify
Can I not tell, save that the queen's flower,
Alceste it was who kept there her sojourn
Which under Venus lady was queen.
—Skeat, 1897

Occurring within the enclosure and also in great abundance in the *millefleurs* background is a common European flower called periwinkle or, in French, *pervenches*. On the inside of the *hortus conclusus*, periwinkle is woven under the carnation and the unicorn's tail (Fig. 79).

According to Albertus Magnus, this herb was highly venereal. If periwinkle is "beaten unto a powder with worms of the earth wrapped about it . . . love between a man and a woman" will be induced.

A French folksong, "Sur les Marches du Palais," tells of a lover's bed which has periwinkle tied upon the four corners:

On the steps of the palace
is such a beautiful woman

- - - - - - - -

She has so many lovers
that she does not know which one to choose.

- - - - - - - -

The little shoemaker
got the preference.

- - - - - - - -

One day as he was outfitting her with shoes
he made her his demand:
"Beautiful, if you wanted it
we will sleep together.

- - - - - - - -

In a large bed
hung with linen,

- - - - - - - -

And at the four corners of the bed
a bunch of periwinkles

- - - - - - - -

And there we would sleep
to the end of the world."

Figure 79. Detail—"The Unicorn in Captivity." The Cloisters, Metropolitan Museum of Art.

Figure 80. Detail—"Allegory of Time." Tapestry, Flemish(?), 1500–10. The Cleveland Museum of Art.

The Latin name for the periwinkle is *vinca*, which is similar to the verb *vincire* meaning "to tie." Because of this linguistic association, the periwinkle is symbolic of marriage. To the people of the Middle Ages, this was a powerful herb; besides being an aphrodisiac, it was believed that if periwinkle were worn or hung in the house, it would ward off diabolical influences. Another medieval source gives the following description: "[periwinkle] is of good advantage for many purposes, that is to say, against devil sicknesses, or demoniacal possessions and against snakes, and against wild beasts and against poisons." (Cockayne) The periwinkle is also called *violette des sorciers* (sorceror's violet), or *herbe des magiciens* (magician's plant), and was believed to have protective qualities. It was often hung over the lintels of medieval houses to give protection from malevolent forces.

But the periwinkle is here woven into the unicorn's enclosure in its symbolic role as an aphrodisiac—a fit companion for all the other erotic botanical images of the *hortus conclusus*. A large example of a periwinkle to the right of the pomegranate (Fig. 81) conveys its prophylactic properties by its proximity to the floral emblem of evil, the white campion.

Of the many plants that appear outside the unicorn's compound, the

Figure 81. Detail—"The Unicorn in Captivity." The Cloisters, Metropolitan Museum of Art.

most outstanding is the iris, depicted in front of the closed gate (Fig. 82). Both the iris and the locked gate represented images of the Virgin to the Christian iconographers; in combination, they reveal an interesting symbolic meaning. From the evocative verses in the *Song of Solomon*, the gate became an emblem of the virginity of Mary. St. Peter Damian associated the Virgin with the "magnificent door of life through which the hall of heaven is made wide open." He called Mary "the Virgin impregnated by the Word, [who] became the gate of heaven, [and] gave back the Lord to the world and opened heaven for us." (D'Ancona, 1977)

The iris woven in front of the gate of the enclosure carries this symbolism further. The iconography is based upon the fact that the leaves of the iris are shaped like a sword, and the plant's Latin name, *gladiolus,* is the Roman designation for that weapon. In verses praising the Virgin, St. Peter Damian provides an explanation for the depiction of the iris here:

Figure 82. Detail—"The Unicorn in Captivity." The Cloisters, Metropolitan Museum of Art.

"The King of Kings entered her womb . . . hiding there the sword which defeated the enemy." (D'Ancona, 1977) From St. Peter Damian's iconographic interpretations of the gate and the iris, it seems that these two images were placed in front of the unicorn's enclosure to indicate that this particular *hortus conclusus* was a reflection of a heavenly Eden: the precinct that holds the incarnate god. Furthermore, since this seventh panel of the Unicorn Tapestries depicts the resurrected unicorn, the appearance of the iris in front of the enclosure recalls this flower's earlier associations with the pre-Christian goddess Iris, the divinity who leads the dead to the heavenly meadows.

Figure 83. Detail—"The Unicorn in Captivity." The Cloisters, Metropolitan Museum of Art.

A brief survey of the other plants and animals shown outside the *hortus conclusus* will complete this survey of the rich *millefleurs* tapestry. Directly below the gate of the enclosure, appearing almost in the margin, is the blue columbine (Fig. 83), included in this panel for its earlier pre-Christian associations, which identify it with Aphrodite. The columbine's name is derived from the Latin *columba*, or dove, a bird sacred to Aphrodite. Medieval physicians believed that with the aid of this flower they could combat noxious substances. "Against all poisons, take dust of this same wort [and] administer it to drink; it driveth away all poisons." (Cockayne).

Another important botanical image, the dandelion, is shown in the lower right margin of the panel, next to the initials "A.E." The famous sixteenth-century herbalist Mattioli commented that "the juice of this plant [dandelion] is useful for the flow of sperm." (D'Ancona, 1983)

One final plant associated with fertility in the design of this tapestry is the thistle, and a fine specimen is included to the left of the Madonna lily (Fig. 84). In his discussion of thistles, Pliny remarks that, "if we may believe the report, it also affects the womb in such a way that male children are engendered." (Vol. VI, Book XX)

Other plants in the *millefleurs* background of this final panel having important iconography include the Madonna lily. This flower is depicted to the right of the blue iris (Fig. 85). In classical legend, the Madonna lily was associated with immortality. According to Greco-Roman myth, Jupiter prepared a sleeping draft which he gave to his wife Juno, hoping to render the infant Hercules immortal. As soon as she was asleep, Jupiter placed Hercules at Juno's breast. The child imbibed the divine milk of the goddess and became immortal. But a few drops of this precious milk fell to the earth, and where it fell, the lily sprang to life. Thereafter, the lily became

Figure 84. Detail—"The Unicorn in Captivity." The Cloisters, Metropolitan Museum of Art.

Figure 85. Detail—"The Unicorn in Captivity." The Cloisters, Metropolitan Museum of Art.

associated with immortality. And because of its untainted whiteness, it also came to be identified with purity and virginity, becoming the flower of the Virgin Mary, who was in many respects the Christian Juno.

Apart from its aesthetic and religious connotations, the lily was also regarded in the early medieval period as an effective antivenom. In the *Hortulus*, Walahfrid Strabo wrote:

> If a snake, treacherous and wily
> As it is by nature, plants with deadly tongue its parcel
> Of venom in you, sending grim death through the unseen wound
> To the inmost vaults of the heart, then crush lilies with a weighty
> Pestle and drink the juice in wine. Now place the pulp
> On the top of the livid spot where the snake's tongue jabbed,
> Then indeed you will learn for yourself the wonderful power
>     this antidote has.
>     —Trans. Payne

The small creatures woven into the fabric of the *millefleurs* background of this panel are also iconographically significant. A butterfly is depicted upon the carnation that appears to the left of the iris, woven to look as though it has alighted upon one of the flowers (Fig. 86). Since ancient times, the butterfly has been the symbol of the soul. The Greek words for butterfly and soul are the same. In mythology, Eros, the mischievous god of love, had as his companion Psyche, an immortal with butterfly wings; the latter was "the Greek personification of the human soul." (Jobes) In "The Crab and the Butterfly: A Study in Animal Symbolism," the art historian W. Deonna concludes that this winged creature signified "life, human destiny, Renaissance, immortality," and in an analogical sense was identified "with the phallus." The noted mythologer Angelo de Gubernatis also makes this connection, pointing out that in antiquity, Eros—in his aspect as a love god—held the phallic butterfly in his hand. Gubernatis records that "the souls of the departed were represented in the form of butterflies"—a connection that almost certainly arose from the insect's life cycle, in which it turns from caterpillar into chrysalis, then finally emerges as a butterfly, a process that was seen by the classical and medieval writers as an allegory of death and rebirth. Pliny stated that the butterfly was born "from dew at the beginning of spring." (Vol. III, Book XI) It was the observations of writers like Pliny that influenced the literature of the Middle Ages, and helped make this insect an emblem of resurrection.

Similar symbolic connections applied to the dragonfly, and two of these insects are woven into this tapestry. One can be seen on the large iris placed in front of the wooden gate; the other is depicted hovering over the blooms of the Madonna lily (see Fig. 85). Like so many insects that go through a larval stage, the dragonfly represents regeneration, the reborn souls of the dead.

The last small animal that occurs in this panel is a frog. This tiny creature can be observed in front of a white violet that is placed between the Madonna lily and a red carnation bordering the panel's right margin (Fig. 87). The frog was discussed in detail by the classical authors, and their writings influenced the medieval symbolism that surrounded this creature. Pliny suggested that frogs died in the winter and were born again in the spring; he also said that the bones of frogs "worn as an amulet act as an aphrodisiac." (Vol. VIII, Book XXXII)

Aelian makes a similar assertion in his description of the frog: "Men say that there are certain spells to cause love; the frog as a signal for sexual intercourse emits a certain cry to the female, like a lover singing a serenade. . . . When night descends they emerge with complete fearlessness and take their pleasure of one another."

Dioscorides considered frogs to be antiviperous and mentioned that

Figure 86. Detail—"The Unicorn in Captivity." The Cloisters, Metropolitan Museum of Art.

Figure 87. Detail—"The Unicorn in Captivity." The Cloisters, Metropolitan Museum of Art.

they were "an antidote against the poison of all serpents."

And Edward Topsell has much to say about frogs. He writes that "sometimes they enter their holes in autumn before winter, and in springtime come out again. When with their croaking voices the male provoketh the female to carnal copulation." As de Vries notes, frogs were considered an emblem of extreme fecundity because their "embrace takes quite a long time" and "is done openly and promiscuously."

In the sixteenth century, the German scholar Nikolaus Reusner commented: "truly, the frog buried under a (deep) winter returns; thus the dead human being will return to life as another human being." (Friedmann, 1980)

The association of the frog with rebirth was not limited to mortals. Both Christ and Zeus were "born again amid the noise of . . . the croaking of frogs." (Gubernatis) This myth is also noted by Herbert Friedmann: "The reappearance of frogs in the pond in the spring, with their constant noise, made them, like swallows, signs of spring and symbols of resurrection." (1980)

The image of a frog in "The Unicorn in Captivity" tapestry was included as an icon of resurrection—complementing the drama of the central reborn unicorn. And, like the unicorn, "in connection with the 'Resurrection' meaning, the frog became a sexual symbol as well." (Friedmann, 1980)

We have in this final tapestry a wooden enclosure that reflects the Garden of Eden. The unicorn presented in this *hortus conclusus* is identified with Adonis and Christ—reborn gods whose resurrection and transformation bring fertility to the animal and plant kingdoms.

An engraving, dated 1512, illustrates this strong association between sacrifice and fecundity. In this print, the crucified Christ is not presented on the usual wooden cross but nailed to a prolific fruit tree. His suffering produces an abundant crop, which the people, shown beneath Christ, do not hesitate to gather (Fig. 88).

Christianity is by its very nature a religion that centers upon vegetation. The Fall of man and his subsequent return to grace is directly associated with trees. According to myths, the Tree of Knowledge caused the expulsion from Eden, and the wood of the Cross provided the means for man's resurrection. The original Paradise in the Judeo-Christian tradition was a garden. And the New Eden—the heavenly Jerusalem—was to be a place of verdant fields, flowers, and trees.

The many antiviperous botanical elements woven into the unicorn's enclosure identify this *hortus conclusus* as the New Eden—the new Paradise of the blessed, where the serpent, the instrument of the Fall, cannot enter.

The closed wooden gate identifies the enclosure with the holy tabernacle of God, the garden described by Ezekiel in which the "gate shall be

Figure 88. Christ crucified on tree bearing fruit and grapes. Engraving, dated 1512.

shut," an enclosure that "no man shall enter . . . because the Lord, the God of Israel, hath entered in by it, therefore it shall be shut." (Ezekiel 44:2) This was to be an inviolate place, which only a god could enter. "It is for the prince; the prince, he shall sit in it to eat bread before the Lord; he shall enter by the way of the porch of that gate, and shall go out by way of the same." (Ezekiel 44:3)

To provide fruitfulness within this holy precinct, the union of the sexes was essential; but like the subtle language used between Solomon and the Shulamite bride in the *Song of Solomon*, the erotic implications of the tapestry were symbolically disguised as plants and small animals. Nevertheless, it was necessary to produce a sexual cornucopia of imagery, and the designer of "The Unicorn in Captivity" tapestry achieves this result by presenting the unicorn chained to a tree—a pomegranate identified with the biblical Tree of Life, and perhaps more than any other a tree that symbolized the life-giving fertile womb.

According to medieval authors, all the other plants depicted in this seventh panel of the Unicorn Tapestries promote fertility and encourage copulation; and the botanical representations of Priapus and the satyrs are included. The unicorn in this final panel is meant to represent the risen Christ as well as the fertile Adonis, whose copulation with the love goddess, Aphrodite, ensures the abundance of the land and prosperity for the human race.

# CONCLUSION

> I must address myself to the many who still habitually
> mistake pictorial symbols in Renaissance art for
> descriptive naturalism. . . . Renaissance artists . . .
> did not anticipate . . . the retroactive effect that four
> centuries of deepening secularism would have on the
> perception of Renaissance art. They did not foresee that
> the process of demythologizing Christianity would
> succeed in profaning our vision of their sacred art.
>
> —Steinberg

I N ONE SENSE, the Unicorn Tapestries are distinctly medieval, concurring with and capturing the beliefs and religious ideas of the period in which they are woven. But in a broader perspective, the symbolism that imbues these hangings with meaning comes from ideas and mythologies that long predate the era of their creation. The tapestries are the amalgam of pre-Christian, classical Greek and Roman icons, as well as Christian ones.

Art historian Lucy Lippard has used a phrase which is particularly valuable in surveying the visual and plastic arts of the Middle Ages. She calls the impact of the various art idioms upon a succession of cultures an "overlay," by which she suggests that art is not insulated from the continuum of history. One era has a strong conscious or unconscious impact on all successive eras. Thus, the religion, iconography, and symbolism associated with Christianity did not abruptly arise with the founding of the Church. Rather, it has an ancient heritage, one that stretches back into remote antiquity, a continuum from the Asian and Greek interpretations of the world, with many layers of pre-Christian European and North African influence.

The process of acculturation is complex: the early Hellenic mythology was adopted by the Romans, and when Rome was totally Hellenized, it, in turn, Romanized Europe. Clearly, historical periods interact with one another to create a mythology that is suitable to a particular age, but that is inevitably a rich mixture of many far-flung influences.

Twentieth-century scholars such as Sir James Frazer, Jane Harrison, Jessie Weston, Mircea Eliade, and Joseph Campbell realized that Western civilization has gradually concretized its mythology. These visionary historians have been able to turn around and look down the centuries, to rediscover the remarkably wide cultural cosmos of western Europe. It is a heritage that most of us are only now beginning to understand. In 1937, Ezra Pound remarked that "It has taken us two thousand years to get around again to meditating on mythology." (*Guide to Kulture*)

The icon of "the Christ," as we have seen, was derived from various Indo-European religious traditions. Thus our survey of the unicorn (itself an icon of Christ) has reconsidered the source of Christian myth and found it to be a conglomeration of very ancient traditions, which were vividly captured in medieval art such as the Unicorn Tapestries.

These textiles provide a unique iconographic record of the innermost spirit of humankind. At the same time, they present a specific picture of the mythologies and religious ideals of France at the end of the fifteenth century, a time when, as Frederick Artz says, "sorcery, magic, astrology, sun-worship, other-worldly philosophies, and salvation religions were in the air. . . . Everything was moralized and allegorized. . . . No distinction was made between the actual and the fantastic."

The essential sense of animation that brings life to the Unicorn Tapestries is discovered at their iconographic core—in their remarkable kinship with nature. The cycle of the seasons was a vital reflection of human life to the people of the Middle Ages, an intrinsic part of a very ancient agricultural cosmology. The seasonal religions of ancient Europe, in which the oak cult played a major role, was the framework into which Christianity was assimilated and thereby accepted.

The progression of the seasons and the cyclical events of animal and plant life were integral experiences to the people of the Middle Ages. Medieval artists explained such elaborate folk philosophy by depicting the various stages of man as aspects of the "Wheel of Life." For example, an illumination from the fourteenth century depicts, in ten stages, the four ages of humankind (Fig. 89). In the margin, four figures are presented in order, clockwise: youth, prime, middle age, and old age. Starting at infancy and ending in death, the ten illustrations expand this progression of age. Philippa Tristram comments: "When paralleled with the four seasons or the twelve months of the year, the Ages [of Man] can participate harmoniously in the natural cycle, which causes the plants to bud, and the flowers to fruit, and finally to fade."

The Unicorn Tapestries are truly a doorway between our world and the worlds in which our forebears lived. We are hungry for the living, daily reality of the past, because it can tell us something essential about ourselves and our survival. Yet we do not have many sources from which to discover more than inanimate statistics. Clearly, the Unicorn Tapestries bring to life much of the mentality of the era in which they were created. In the truest sense, the Unicorn Tapestries contain the entire cosmology of the age in which they were designed, and summon up vast seas of time that existed long before their creation. It is in this fascinating sense of history—of Europe's most ancient cosmologies—that we have found new meanings in these tapestries, and in ourselves. Implicit to those meanings is the story of Europe itself: of its lost rituals of plants and animals and the fecundity of the earth, and of its fabulous allegory of the divine hunt for regeneration, renewal, and survival.

Figure 89. "The Wheel of Life." A cycle of the four ages in ten stages, c. 1330. London, The British Library.

# DIAGRAMS
# IDENTIFYING
# THE FLORA
# OF THE
# UNICORN TAPESTRIES

**W**HEN IDENTIFYING the medieval depiction of plants, a few facts should be kept in mind. The representations of plants in the art of the Middle Ages and Renaissance are often inaccurate in size, color, and structural detail. Inaccuracies occur in the number of petals shown on flowers, in the positioning of leaves on stems, and in the shape of leaves, as well as less obvious but equally important errors in the veining and scalloping of leaves, the texture of bark, and the shape of fruit.

As Mirella Levi D'Ancona notes: "Some artists combined different plants, using the flowers of one and the leaves of others, giving to the flower the wrong color, or distributing the leaves or branches incorrectly on a stem. Sometimes their knowledge of botany was imperfect and they mistook one plant for another." (1977)

Often when medieval artists wanted to represent a well-known plant of a particular genus, they changed the form of the leaves or the color of flowers; so the modern botanist, with little understanding of medieval art and iconography, misidentifies the species that the medieval artist was portraying. The most common example occurs when botanists identify medieval plant images as rare forms of a common plant, taking too much notice of the artist's embellishments.

One final point concerns the identification of a specific image woven into the second tapestry. In this instance, the weaving is not a plant but an animal, whose identification is much disputed. In discussing "The Unicorn at the Fountain," I identified the snarling creature in the lower right margin as a wolf. In offering this identification, I was differing with an earlier study made by Dr. Richard G. Van Gelder of the Museum of Natural History in New York City. Dr. Van Gelder, who is a zoologist, notes that this animal is "most likely a striped hyena." (Freeman) Two art historians, Herbert Friedmann and Frederick Hartt, draw attention to the confusion in medieval art between the wolf, hyena, and other similar species of canine animals. A painting by Filippino Lippi, *The Exorcism of the Demon in the Temple of Mars*, provides a good example of this confusion in identity between various lupine animals. This particular work, painted by Lippi between 1487 and 1500, was contemporary with the creation of the Unicorn Tapestries. In his painting, Lippi includes a statue of Mars in the temple and places an animal on the stone pedestal of the god. The left hand of Mars can be seen caressing "what is supposedly a wolf, however much it may look like a hyena." (Hartt)

Discussing the wolf in his *Bestiary of St. Jerome*, Friedmann cites another painting, *Meditation on the Passion of Christ*, by Vittore Carpaccio. In this painting there is a depiction of a wolf that, as Friedmann notes, "is zoologically not too accurate; it might be a much enlarged fox(!), but it is more likely that the artist intended it for a wolf, an animal he had never seen, whereas its smaller relative he may have known, and used it as a basis for his rendition."

And the medieval iconographer George Claridge Druce mentions that in carvings of the animal, "the wolf is a difficult creature to identify . . . as it approximates in form the dog, hyena, lynx and other animals." (1919–20)

Considering the sinister associations given to this animal by the medieval compilers—iconography that perfectly suits the intended imagery in the second panel of the Unicorn Tapestries—I think we can conclude that it is most probable the designer of this tapestry intended to depict a wolf, not a hyena.

PLATE I.   *THE START OF THE HUNT*

1. *Prunus avium* (L.) L. Wild Cherry
2. *Fragaria vesca* L. Wild Strawberry
3. *Ulmus procera* Salisb. English Elm
4. *Quercus rober* L. Oak
5. *Tilia x europaea* L. Common Lime
6. *Prunus domestica* L. Wild Plum
7. *Betula pendula* Roth. Birch
8. *Fraxinus excelsior* L. Ash
9. *Narcissus pseudonarcissus* L. Daffodil
10. *Cirsium or Carduus* species. White Thistle
11. *Sagittaria sagittifolia* L. Arrowhead
12. *Mentha arvensis* L. Corn Mint
13. *Dianthus caryophyllus* L. Clove Pink; Carnation
14. *Cheiranthus cheiri* L. Wallflower
15. *Alchemilla vulgaris* L. Lady's Mantle

16. *Briza media* L. ?Quaking Grass
17. *Inula helenium* L. Elecampane
18. *Viola odorata* L. Sweet Violet
19. *Hesperis matronalis* L. Dame's Violet
20. *Silene alba* (Mill.) E. H. L. Krause. White Campion
21. *Trifolium repens* L. White Clover
22. *Centaurea cyanus* L. Cornflower
23. *Rumex acetosa* L. Garden Sorrel
24. *Phoenix dactylifera* L. Date Palm
25. *Chrysanthemum leucanthemum* L. Moon Daisy; Marguerite
26. *Vinca minor* L. Periwinkle
27. *Ruscus aculeatus* L. Butcher's Broom
28. *Bellis perennis* L. English Daisy
29. *Narcissus pseudonarcissus* L. Daffodil (fruit)

PLATE II.   *THE UNICORN AT THE FOUNTAIN*

1. *Fagus sylvatica* L. European Beech
2. *Ulmus procera* Salisb. English Elm
3. *Quercus rober* L. Oak
4. *Ilex aquifolium* L. Holly
5. *Prunus avium* (L.) L. Wild Cherry
6. *Crataegus monogyna* Jacq. Common Hawthorn
7. *Cheiranthus cheiri* L. Wallflower
8. *Mespilus germanica* L. Mẹdlar
9. *Prunus domestica* L. Wild Plum
10. *Rosa centifolia* L. Cabbage Rose
11. *Salvia officinalis* L. Common Sage
12. *Fragaria vesca* L. Wild Strawberry
13. *Ruta graveolens* L. Rue
14. *Dianthus caryophyllus* L. White Carnation

15. *Calendula officinalis* L. Pot Marigold
16. *Anagallis arvensis* L. Pimpernel
17. *Bellis perennis* L. English Daisy
18. *Physalis alkekengi* L. Chinese Lantern; Ground-Cherry
19. *Citrus sinensis* (L.) Osbeck. Orange Tree
20. *Dianthus caryophyllus* L. Clove Pink; Carnation
21. *?*
22. *Viola tricolor* L. Pansy
23. *Silene alba* (Mill.) E. H. L. Krause. White Campion

PLATE III.  *THE UNICORN CROSSING THE STREAM*

1. *Ilex aquifolium* L. Holly
2. *Prunus domestica* L. Wild Plum
3. *Quercus rober* L. Oak
4. *Prunus avium* (L.) L. Wild Cherry
5. *Mespilus germanica* L. Medlar
6. *Adonis vernalis* L. ?Yellow Adonis
7. *Vinca minor* L. Periwinkle
8. *Silene alba* (Mill.) E. H. L. Krause. White Campion
9. *Crataegus monogyna* Jacq. Common Hawthorn
10. *Primula vulgaris* Huds. Common Primrose
11. *Plantago major* L. Common Plantain
12. *Viola tricolor* L. Pansy
13. *Linum usitatissimum* L. ?Common Flax
14. *Iris pseudacorus* L. Yellow Flag
15. *Viola odorata* L. Sweet Violet
16. *Chrysanthemum leucanthemum* L. Moon Daisy; Marguerite
17. *Artemisia vulgaris* L. Mugwort
18. *Cardamine pratensis* L. Lady's Smock; Cuckooflower
19. *Salvia sclarea* L. Clary Sage
20. *Primula veris* L. Cowslip
21. *Corylus avellana* L. European Hazel
22. *Chrysanthemum segatum* L. Corn Marigold
23. *Punica granatum* L. Pomegranate

PLATE IV. *THE UNICORN DEFENDS HIMSELF*

1. *Fagus sylvatica* L. European Beech
2. *Ilex aquifolium* L. Holly
3. *Ulmus procera* Salisb. English Elm
4. *Citrus sinensis* (L.) Osbeck. Orange
   Tree
5. *Mespilus germanica* L. Medlar
6. *Juglans regia* L. Walnut
7. *Arbutus unedo* L. Strawberry Tree
8. *Prunus armeniaca* L. Apricot
9. *Prunus avium* (L.) L. Wild Cherry
10. *Crataegus monogyna* Jacq. Common
    Hawthorn
11. *Quercus rober* L. Oak
12. *Adonis vernalis* L. ?Yellow Adonis

13. *Viola odorata* L. Sweet Violet
14. *Thypha latifolia* L. Cattail; Bulrush
15. *Prunus persica* (L.) Batsch. Peach
16. *Corylus avellana* L. European Hazel
17. *Myosótis scorpioides* L. Forget-me-not
18. ?
19. *Chrysanthemum parthenium* (L.)
    Bernh. Feverfew
20. *Chrysanthemum segatum* L. Corn
    Marigold
21. *Endymion nonscriptus* (L.) Garcke.
    Bluebell
22. *Iris pseudacorus* L. Yellow Flag
23. *Artemisia vulgaris* L. Mugwort

PLATE V.   *THE UNICORN IS TAMED BY THE MAIDEN*

1. *Malus pumila* Mill. Common Apple Tree
2. *Quercus rober* L. Oak
3. *Rosa centifolia* L. Cabbage Rose (red)
4. *Rosa x alba* L. White Rose
5. *Ilex aquifolium* L. Holly
6. *Vinca minor* L. Periwinkle

PLATE VI.   *THE UNICORN IS KILLED AND BROUGHT TO THE CASTLE*

1. *Ilex aquifolium* L. Holly
2. *Quercus rober* L. Oak
3. *Ulmus procera* Salisb. English Elm
4. *Crataegus monogyna* Jacq. Common Hawthorn
5. *Corylus avellana* L. European Hazel
6. *Rubus fruticosus* L. agg. Blackberry
7. *Iris x germanica* L. Common Iris
8. *Physalis alkekengi* L. Chinese Lantern; Ground Cherry
9. *Primula veris* L. Cowslip
10. *Euphrasia officinalis* L. Eyebright
11. ?
12. *Silene alba* (Mill.) E. H. L. Krause. White Campion
13. *Arum maculatum* L. Cuckoopint; Lords and Ladies
14. *Viola tricolor* L. Pansy
15. *Onopordum or Cirsium* species. Thistle
16. *Pisum sativum* L. Common Pea

PLATE VII.  *THE UNICORN IN CAPTIVITY*

1. *Punica granatum* L. Pomegranate
2. ?
3. *Silene alba* (Mill.) E. H. L. Krause. White Campion
4. *Chrysanthemum leucanthemum* L. Moon Daisy; Marguerite
5. *Chrysanthemum segatum* L. Corn Marigold
6. *Matthiola incana* (L.) R. Br. Stock-Gillyflower
7. *Bellis perennis* L. English Daisy
8. *Polygonum bistorta* L. Bistort
9. *Endymion nonscriptus* (L.) Garcke. Bluebell (with fruits)
10. *Cheiranthus cheiri* L. Wallflower
11. *Orchis mascula* (L.) L. Male Orchid; Early Purple Orchid
12. *Endymion nonscriptus* (L.) Garcke. Bluebell
13. *Fragaria vesca* L. Wild Strawberry
14. *Arum maculatum* L. Cuckoopint; Lords and Ladies
15. *Dianthus caryophyllus* L. Clove Pink; Carnation
16. *Vinca minor* L. Periwinkle
17. *Viola odorata* L. Sweet Violet
18. *Acorus calamus* L. Sweet Flag
19. *Primula veris* L. Cowslip
20. *Taraxacum officinale* Wiggers. Common Dandelion
21. *Lilium candidum* L. Madonna Lily
22. *Cirsium or Carduus* species. White Thistle
23. *Calendula officinalis* L. Pot Marigold
24. *Aquilegia vulgaris* L. Columbine
25. *Iris x germanica* L. Common Iris
26. ?Rose or Bramble

# SELECTED BIBLIOGRAPHY

Abraham, Claude K. "Myth and Symbol: The Rabbit in Medieval France." *Studies in Philology*, 60:4 (October 1963).

Adam de Saint Victor. *The Liturgical Poetry of Adam of St. Victor*. Trans. and ed. Digby Wrangham. London: Kegan Paul, Trench & Co., 1881.

Aelian. *On the Characteristics of Animals*. Trans. A. F. Scholfield. 3 vols. Cambridge, Mass.: Harvard University Press, Loeb Classics, 1959.

Albertus Magnus. *The Book of Secrets*. Michael R. Best and Frank H. Brightman, eds. Oxford: Clarendon Press, 1973.

Alexander, J. E., and Carol H. Woodward. "The Flora of the Unicorn Tapestries." *Journal of the New York Botanical Garden* (May 1941).

Allen, Don Cameron. *Mysteriously Meant—The Rediscovery of Pagan Symbolism and Allegorical Interpretation in the Renaissance*. Baltimore: The Johns Hopkins University Press, 1970.

Anderson, Frank J., ed. *The Illustrated Bartsch—German Book Illustration Through 1500*. Vol. 90 (in 2 vols), *Herbals Through 1500*. New York: Abaris Books, 1983–84.

———. *An Illustrated History of the Herbals*. New York: Columbia University Press, 1977.

Anderson, Mary Desiree. *The Mediaeval Carver*. Cambridge: Cambridge University Press, 1935.

Aneau, Barthelemy. *La Déscription philosophale de la nature*. Paris, 1561.

Apuleius. *The Golden Ass*. Trans. Robert Graves. New York: Farrar, Straus & Giroux, 1951.

Aristotle. *Historia Animalium*. Trans. A. L. Peck. Cambridge, Mass.: Harvard University Press, Loeb Classics, 1965.

Armstrong, Edward A. *The Folklore of Birds*. London: Collins, 1958.

Artz, Frederick B. *The Mind of the Middle Ages*. Chicago: University of Chicago Press, 1953.

[St.] Augustine. *The City of God*. Trans. Henry Bettenson. Harmondsworth, Middx.: Penguin Books, 1972.

Banckes, Rycharde. *An Herbal* [Banckes' Herbal, 1525], Facsimile of the 1525 London ed., Stanford V. Larkey and Thomas Pyles, eds. New York: New York Botanical Garden, 1941.

Baring-Gould, Rev. Sabine. *Curious Myths of the Middle Ages* (1866). London: Juniper Books, 1977.

Barnes, Harry. *An Intellectual and Cultural History of the Western World.* Rev. edn, New York: Reynal & Hitchcock, 1941.

Baron, Hans. "Fifteenth-century Civilization and the Renaissance," in G. R. Potter, ed. *The New Cambridge Modern History.* Vol. I, *The Renaissance: 1493–1520.* Cambridge: Cambridge University Press, 1957.

Bartholomaeus Anglicus. *Batman uppon Bartholome, His Booke De Proprietatibus Rerum.* Trans. John of Trevisa. London, 1582. Hildesheim, West Germany: Georg Olms, 1976.

———. *De Proprietatibus Rerum (On the Properties of Things).* (1495). Trans. John Trevisa. 2 vols. Oxford: Clarendon Press, 1975.

St. Basil. *Exegetic Homilies.* Trans. Sister Agnes Clare Way. Washington, D.C.: The Catholic University of America Press, 1963.

Bayley, Harold. *The Lost Language of Symbolism.* 2 vols. New York: Barnes & Noble, 1912.

Beer, Rudiger Robert. *Unicorns—Myth and Reality.* Trans. Charles M. Stern. New York: Mason/Charter, 1977.

Berrall, Julia S. *The Garden—An Illustrated History.* New York: Viking Press, 1966.

"Bestiary" in *An Old English Miscellany.* R. Morris, ed. London: Early English Text Society, 1872.

Branston, Brian. *The Lost Gods of England.* London: Thames & Hudson Ltd., 1957.

Bridge, John S. C. *A History of France.* Vol. II, *Reign of Charles VIII, 1493–1498.* Oxford: Clarendon Press, 1924.

[St.] Bridget of Sweden. *Revelations and Prayers of St. Bridget of Sweden.* Trans. Dom Ernest Graf. New York: Benzinger Brothers, 1928.

Brown, Robert. *The Unicorn: A Mythological Investigation.* London: Longmans, Green and Co., 1881.

Browne, Sir Thomas. *The Works of Sir Thomas Browne.* Ed. Simon Wilkin. London: H. G. Bohn, 1852.

Brunschwig, Jerome (Hieronymus). "The Vertuose boke of Distyllacyon." Trans. L. Andrewe of Brunschwig's *Distilierbuch.* London, 1527.

Bullein, William. "The Booke of Simples," in *In Bulwarke of Defence Against All Sickness.* London: Thomas Marshe, 1579.

Calas, Elena. "Bosch's Garden of Delights: A Theological Rebus." *Art Journal,* XXIX: 2 (Winter 1969–70).

Campbell, Joseph. *The Flight of the Wild Gander.* New York: Viking Press, 1969.

———. *The Hero with a Thousand Faces.* Princeton: Bollingen Foundation, 1949.

———. *The Masks of God: Creative Mythology.* New York: Viking Press, 1968.

———. *The Mythic Image.* Princeton: Princeton University Press, 1974.

———. *The Way of the Animal Powers.* New York: Harper & Row, 1983.

———. "Conversation with Joseph Campbell" by Jamake Highwater. *Quadrant,* Vol. 30, no. 2 (1985).

Carlill, James, trans. *The Physiologus.* In *The Epic of the Beast, Consisting of the English Translations of the History of Reynard the Fox and Physiologus.* London: George Routledge and Sons, 1924?.

Cavallo, Adolph S. *Tapestries of Europe and of Colonial Peru in the Museum of Fine Arts, Boston.* 2 vols. Boston: Museum of Fine Arts, 1967.

Cave, C. J. P. *Roof Bosses in Medieval Churches.* Cambridge: Cambridge University Press, 1948.

Chambers, E. K. *The Mediaeval Stage.* 2 vols. London: Oxford University Press, 1903.

Chambers, E. K., and F. Sidgwick. *Early English Lyrics* (1907). London: Sidgwick & Jackson Ltd., 1966.

Child, Francis James, ed. *The English and Scottish Popular Ballads.* 5 vols. New York: Dover Books, 1965.

Cirlot, J. E. *A Dictionary of Symbols.* Trans. Jack Sage. New York: Philosophical Library, 1962.

Clark, Anne. *Beasts and Bawdy.* London: J. M. Dent & Sons, 1975.

Clark, Sir George. "Introduction," in G. R. Potter, ed. *The New Cambridge Modern History.* Vol. 1, *The Renaissance: 1493–1520.* Cambridge: Cambridge University Press, 1957.

Clark, Sir Kenneth. *Civilization.* New York: Harper & Row, 1970.

Cockayne, Thomas Oswald, ed. *Leechdoms, Wortcunning and Starcraft of Early England.* London: Longman, Roberts, and Green, 1864–66.

Colonna, Francesco. *Hypnerotomachia Poliphili* (*The Dream of Poliphilus*) (Venice, 1499). New York: Garland Publishing, 1976.

————. *Hypnerotomachia: The Strife of Love in a Dream.* Trans. R. Dallington? London, 1592. New York: Garland Publishing, 1976.

*The Complete Grimm's Fairy Tales.* New York: Pantheon Books, 1944.

Conrad von Megenberg, *Buch der Natur.* Franz Pfeiffer, ed., 1861. Hildesheim, West Germany: George Olms, 1962.

Cook, A. B. "The European Sky God." *Folklore,* Vol. XV, 1904.

————. *The Old English Physiologus.* Yale Studies in English, LXIII. New Haven: Yale University Press, 1921.

Coomaraswamy, Ananda K. *Christian and Oriental Philosophy of Art.* New York: Dover Books, 1956.

————. *Literary Symbolism.* In Roger Lipsey (ed.), *Coomaraswamy Selected Papers,* 2 vols. Princeton: Princeton University Press, Bollingen Series, 1977.

Costello, Peter. *The Magic Zoo.* New York: St. Martin's Press, 1979.

Coudert, Allison. *Alchemy: The Philosopher's Stone.* Boulder, Col.: Shambhala Publishing, 1980.

Coulter, Cornelia Catlin. "The Genealogy of the Gods." *Vassar Medieval Studies.* New Haven: Yale University Press, 1923.

Crick-Kuntziger, Martha. "Un chef d'oeuvre inconnu du Maître de la Dame à la Licorne." *Revue Belge d'archéologie et d'histoire de l'art,* Vol. 23 (1954).

Curley, Michael J., trans., *Physiologus.* Austin: University of Texas Press, 1979.

D'Ancona, Mirella Levi. *Botticelli's Primavera.* Florence: Leo S. Olschki, 1983.

————. *The Garden of the Renaissance: Botanical Symbolism in Italian Painting.* Florence: Leo S. Olschki, 1977.

————. *The Iconography of the Immaculate Conception in the Middle Ages and Early Renaissance.* New York: College Art Association of America, 1957.

Dante Alighieri. *The Divine Comedy.* Trans. Laurence Binyon. New York: Viking Press, 1947.

Dawson, Warren R. *A Leechbook, or Collection of Medical Recipes of the Fifteenth Century.* London: Macmillan & Co., 1934.

Deonna, W. "The Crab and the Butterfly: A Study in Animal Symbolism." *Journal of Warburg and Courtauld Institutes,* Vol. 17 (1954).

*Der Gart der Gesundheit.* Mainz: Peter Schoeffer, 1485. (This book is sometimes referred to as the *German Hortus Santitatis.*)

Deschamps, Eustache. *Oeuvres Complètes de Eustache Deschamps.* Le Marquis de Queux de St. Hilaire, ed. Paris: Firmin Didot, 1878–1903.

De Sola Pinto, Vivian, and Allan Edwin Rodway. *The Common Muse.* London: Chatto and Windus, 1957.

*Dialogues of Creatures Moralised.* Kentfield, Calif.: Allen Press, 1967.

*Dialogus Creaturarum.* English translation. Paris, 1511?.

*Dictionary of the Middle Ages.* 12 vols. Joseph R. Strayer, ed. New York: Charles Scribner's Sons, 1982.

Didron, Adolphe Napoléon. *Christian Iconography.* Trans. E. J. Millington. New York: Frederick Ungar, 1965.

Dioscorides. *De Materia Medica.* Trans. John Goodyer (1655). Robert T. Gunther, ed. London: Hafner Publishing Company, 1933.

Doucet, R. "France Under Charles VIII and Louis XII," in G. R. Potter, ed., *The New Cambridge Modern History.* Vol. I, *The Renaissance: 1493–1520.* Cambridge: Cambridge University Press, 1957.

Dronke, Peter. *The Medieval Lyric.* London: Hutchinson and Co., 1968.

Druce, George Claridge. "The Medieval Bestiaries: Their Influence on Ecclesiastical Decorative Art." *Journal of the British Archaeological Association,* 25, n.s. (1919–20):41–82; 26:35–79.

Duncan, Thomas Shearer. "The Weasel in Religion, Myth, and Superstition." *Washington University Studies.* St. Louis: Humanistic Series I:XII (October 1924).

Dunn, Charles W. Introduction to *The Romance of the Rose,* by Guillaume de Lorris and Jean de Meun. Trans. Harry W. Robbins. New York: E. P. Dutton, 1962.

Durand, Guillaume (Gulielmus Durantis). *The Symbolism of Churches and Church Ornament: A Translation of the First Book of the Rationale Divinorum Officiorum.* Trans. T. W. Green. Leeds, 1843. New York: AMS Press, 1973.

Durant, Will. *The Story of Civilization.* Vol. IV, *The Age of Faith.* New York: Simon and Schuster, 1950.

Eisler, Colin. *The Master of the Unicorn: The Life and Work of Jean Duvet.* New York: Abaris Books, 1979.

Eliade, Mircea. *The Forge and the Crucible.* Trans. Stephen Corrin. Chicago: The University of Chicago Press, 1962.

———. *A History of Religious Ideas.* Vol. 2. Trans. Willard R. Trask. Chicago: The University of Chicago Press, 1982.

———. *Images and Symbols.* Trans. Philip Mairet. London: Harvill Press, 1961.

———. *Myth and Reality.* Trans. Willard R. Trask. New York: Harper & Row, 1963.

———. *Patterns in Comparative Religion.* Trans. Rosemary Sheed. New York: Sheed and Ward, 1958.

———. *The Sacred and the Profane.* Trans. Willard R. Trask. New York: Harcourt, Brace, and World, 1959.

Elliot, T. J., trans. *A Medieval Bestiary.* Boston: David R. Godine, 1971.

Ellis Davidson, H. R. *Gods and Myths of Northern Europe.* Harmondsworth, Middx.: Penguin Books, 1964.

Elst, Baron Joseph Julien M. *The Last Flowering of the Middle Ages.* New York: Doubleday, Doran and Co., 1944.

Erlande-Brandenburg, Alain. *The Lady and the Unicorn.* Paris: Editions de la Réunion des Musées Nationaux, 1979.

Evans, Joan. *Life in Medieval France.* London: Oxford University Press, 1925.

Febvre, Lucien. *Life in Renaissance France.* Trans. Marian Rothstein. Cambridge, Mass.: Harvard University Press, 1977.

Ferguson, George. *Signs and Symbols in Christian Art.* New York: Oxford University Press, 1954.

Folkard, Richard. *Plant Lore Legends and Lyrics.* London: Sampson Low, Marston, Searle, & Rivington, 1884.

Franz, Marie-Louise von. *Aurora Consurgens.* New York: Pantheon Books, 1966.

Frazer, Sir James George. *Folk-lore in the Old Testament.* 3 vols. London: Macmillan & Co., 1919.

————. *The Golden Bough.* 12 vols. 3rd edn, London: Macmillan & Co., 1911–15.

Freeman, Margaret B. *The Unicorn Tapestries.* New York: The Metropolitan Museum of Art, 1976.

Friedmann, Herbert. *A Bestiary for Saint Jerome—Animal Symbolism in European Religious Art.* Washington, D.C.: Smithsonian Institution Press, 1980.

————. *The Symbolic Goldfinch.* New York: Pantheon Books, Bollingen Series VII, 1946.

Friend Hilderic, *Flowers and Flower Lore.* London: 1884 (reprinted as *Flower Lore.* Rockport Mass.: Para Research Inc. 1981).

Fulgentius, Fabius Planciades. *Fulgentius the Mythographer.* Trans. Leslie George Whitbread. Columbus: Ohio State University Press, 1971.

Funck-Brentano, F. *The Renaissance.* New York: The Macmillan Company, 1936.

*Funk & Wagnalls Standard Dictionary of Folklore, Mythology, and Legend.* Maria Leach, ed. New York: Funk & Wagnalls, 1972.

Gaskell, G. A. *Dictionary of All Scriptures and Myths.* New York: Julian Press, 1960.

Gerard, John. *The Herball* (1597); 3rd edn, 1633. New York: Dover Books, 1975.

Gobel, Heinrich. *The Tapestries of the Lowlands.* Trans. Robert West. New York: Hacker Art Books, 1974.

Gombrich, E. H. *Symbolic Images—Studies in the Art of the Renaissance.* New York: Phaidon Press, 1972.

Grattan, J. H. G. *Anglo-Saxon Magic and Medicine.* London: Oxford University Press, 1952.

Graves, Robert. *The Greek Myths.* 2 vols. Rev. edn. Harmondsworth, Middx.: Penguin Books, 1960.

————. *The White Goddess.* Em. and enl. edn. New York: Farrar, Straus & Giroux, 1966.

————. Trans. from Apuleius of *The Golden Ass.* New York: Farrar, Straus & Giroux, 1951.

————, and Raphael Patai. *Hebrew Myths: The Book of Genesis.* New York: McGraw-Hill, 1963.

Greene, Richard Leighton, ed. *The Early English Carols.* 2nd edn, revised and enlarged. Oxford: Clarendon Press, 1977.

*The Grete Herball.* London: Peter Treveris, 1526. All entries are from the 1561 edition, retitled *The Greate Herball.*

Grigson, Geoffrey. *The Englishman's Flora.* London: Phoenix House, 1958.

Gubernatis, Angelo de. *Zoological Mythology.* 2 vols. London: Trubner & Co., 1872. Reissued Detroit: Singing Tree Press, 1968.

Guillaume le Clerc. *The Bestiary of Guillaume le Clerc.* (1210–11). Trans. George Claridge Druce. Ashford, Kent: Invicta Press, 1936 (printed for private circulation).

Gundersheimer, Werner L., ed. *French Humanism—1470–1600*. London: Macmillan & Co., 1969.

Hall, James. *Dictionary of Subjects and Symbols in Art*. Rev. edn. New York: Harper & Row, 1979.

Halliwell-Phillipps, James O. *Popular Rhymes and Nursery Tales*. London: John Russell Smith, 1849.

Hardy, James. "Popular History of the Cuckoo." *The Folk-lore Record*, Vol. II (1879).

Harrison, Jane Ellen. *Ancient Art and Ritual*. London: Henry Holt & Co., 1913.

———. *Epilegomena to the Study of Greek Religion* and *Themis: A Study of the Social Origins of Greek Religion*. New Hyde Park, N.Y.: University Books, 1962.

Hartt, Frederick. *History of Italian Renaissance Art*. New York: Harry N. Abrams, 1969.

Hatzfeld, Helmut A. *Literature Through Art*. New York: Oxford University Press, 1952.

Hauser, Arnold. *The Social History of Art*. 2 vols. New York: Alfred A. Knopf, 1951.

Held, Julius S. "Flora, Goddess and Courtesan," in Millard Meiss, ed., *Essays in Honor of Erwin Panofsky*. New York: New York University Press, 1961.

Henderson, George. *Gothic—Style and Civilization*. Harmondsworth, Middx.: Penguin Books, 1967.

Highet, Gilbert. *The Classical Tradition: Greek and Roman Influences on Western Literature*. New York: Oxford University Press, 1949.

Highwater, Jamake. *Dance—Rituals of Experience*. New York: A. & W. Publishers, 1978.

———. *The Primal Mind*. New York: Harper & Row, 1981.

Hirsch, Rudolf. "Printing in France and Humanism," in Werner L. Gundersheimer, ed., *French Humanism—1470–1600*. London: Macmillan & Co., 1969.

Holbrook, Richard Thayer. *Dante and the Animal Kingdom*. New York: Columbia University Press, 1902. New York: AMS Press, 1966.

Holmes, Urban Tigner. *A History of Old French Literature*. New York: F. S. Crofts and Co., 1930.

Holt, Elizabeth Basye, ed. *A Documentary History of Art*. Vol. I, *The Middle Ages and the Renaissance*. 2nd edn. Garden City, N.Y.: Doubleday, 1957–58.

*Hortus Sanitatis*. Mainz: Jacob Meydenbach, 1491.

Huizinga, J. *The Waning of the Middle Ages* (London, 1924). New York: Doubleday, Anchor Books, 1954.

Hulme F. Edward. *The History, Principle and Practice of Symbolism in Christian Art* (1891). Detroit: Gale Research Company, 1969.

Hunter, George Leland. *The Practical Book of Tapestries*. Philadelphia: J. B. Lippincott, 1925.

Husband, Timothy. *The Wildman—Medieval Myth and Symbolism*. New York: The Metropolitan Museum of Art, 1980.

Isidore of Seville. "An Encyclopedist of the Dark Ages." Trans. Ernest Brehaust of passages from the *Etymologiae*. See *Studies in History, Economics and Public Law*, XLVIII: 1. New York: Columbia University, 1912.

Jackson, Kenneth. *A Celtic Miscellany*. Harmondsworth, Middx.: Penguin Books, 1971.

———. *Studies in Early Celtic Nature Poetry*. Cambridge: Cambridge University Press, 1935.

Janson, H. W. *Apes and Ape Lore—In the Middle Ages and Renaissance.* London: Warburg Institute, University of London, 1952.

———. *History of Art.* New York: Harry N. Abrams, 1962.

Jobes, Gertrude. *Dictionary of Mythology, Folklore and Symbols.* 2 vols. New York: Scarecrow Press, 1962.

Joret, Charles. *La rose dans l'antiquité et au moyen age.* Paris: E. Bouillon, 1892.

Jung, C. G. *The Collected Works.* Vol. 12, *Psychology and Alchemy.* Trans. R. F. C. Hall. Princeton: Princeton University Press, 1968.

Keating, L. Clark. *Studies on the Literary Salon in France—1550-1615.* Cambridge, Mass.: Harvard University Press, 1941.

Kelly, Douglas. *Medieval Imagination.* Madison: University of Wisconsin Press, 1978.

Klingender, Francis Donald. *Animals in Art and Thought to the End of the Middle Ages.* Cambridge, Mass.: MIT Press, 1971.

Kuhns, L. Oscar. *The Treatment of Nature in Dante's "Divina Commedia."* New York: Kennikat Press, 1971.

Ladner, B. Gerhart. "Vegetable Symbolism and the Concept of Renaissance," in Millard Meiss, ed., *Essays in Honor of Erwin Panofsky.* London: Phaidon Press, 1961.

Launay, A. J. *Dictionary of Contemporaries.* London: Centaur Press, 1967.

Lawton, H. W. "Vernacular Literature in Western Europe," in G. R. Potter, ed., *The New Cambridge Modern History.* Vol. I, *The Renaissance: 1493-1520.* Cambridge: Cambridge University Press, 1957.

*Le Grant Herbier* (also known as *Arbolayre*). Paris: Jacques Nyverd, after 1520.

Lemprière, John. *A Classical Dictionary* (1788). Originally published as *Bibliotheca Classica.* London: F. A. Wright, 1949.

Levarie, Norma. *The Art and History of Books.* New York: James H. Heineman, 1968.

Lewis, Charles B. *Celtic Myth and Arthurian Romance.* New York: Columbia University Press, 1927.

———. *Classical Mythology and Arthurian Romance: A Study of the Sources of Chrétien de Troyes' "Yvain" and Other Arthurian Romances.* Oxford: Oxford University Press, 1932.

Lippard, Lucy R. *Overlay—Contemporary Art and the Art of Prehistory.* New York: Pantheon Books, 1983.

Livius, Thomas Stivard. *The Blessed Virgin in the Fathers of the First Six Centuries.* London: Burns & Oates, 1893.

Loomis, Roger Sherman. *Studies in Medieval Literature.* New York: Burt Franklin, 1970.

———, and Laura Hibbard Loomis. *Arthurian Legends in Medieval Art.* New York: The Modern Language Association of America, 1938.

———, and Henry W. Wells, trans. and eds., *Representative Medieval and Tudor Plays.* New York: Sheed & Ward, 1942.

Lucretius, *On the Nature of the Universe.* Trans. R. E. Latham. Harmondsworth, Middx.: Penguin Books, 1951.

Mâle, Emile. *The Gothic Image: Religious Art in France of the Thirteenth Century.* Trans. Dora Nussey. New York: Harper & Row, 1958.

Malory, Sir Thomas. *Le Morte d'Arthur.* 2 vols. Janet Cowan, ed. Harmondsworth, Middx.: Penguin Books, 1969.

Malraux, André. *The Voices of Silence.* Trans. Stuart Gilbert. St. Albans, Herts.: Paladin, 1974.

Mandeville, Sir John. *The Travels of Sir John Mandeville.* A. W. Pollard, ed. London: Macmillan & Co., 1900.

Marquand, Eleanor C. "Plant Symbolism in the Unicorn Tapestries." *Parnassus,* X:5 (October 1938).

Martin, Edward James. *A History of the Iconoclastic Controversy.* New York: The Macmillan Company, 1930.

Matarasso, P. M., trans. *The Quest of the Holy Grail.* Harmondsworth, Middx.: Penguin Books, 1969.

Matthews, I. G. *The Religious Pilgrimage of Israel.* New York: Harper & Brothers, 1947.

McCulloch, Florence. *Medieval Latin and French Bestiaries.* Chapel Hill: The University of North Carolina Press, 1960.

McKinney, Howard D., and W. R. Anderson. *Music in History—The Evolution of an Art.* New York: American Book Company, 1940.

Meiss, Millard, ed. *Essays in Honor of Erwin Panofsky.* London: Phaidon Press, 1961.

Mercatante, Anthony S. *Zoo of the Gods—Animals in Myth, Legend and Fable.* New York: Harper & Row, 1974.

Migne, Jacques Paul, ed. *Patrologiae cursus completus . . . Series Prima Latina.* 221 vols. (also known as *Patrologia Latina*). Paris: Sirou-Vrayet, 1841–79.

Miller, Madeleine S., and J. Lane Miller. *Harper's Bible Dictionary.* Rev. edn, New York: Harper & Row, 1973.

Muller, Herbert J. *The Uses of the Past.* Oxford: Oxford University Press, 1952.

Murray, Gilbert. "Daimon and Hero—Excursus on the Ritual Forms Preserved in Greek Tragedy," in Jane Ellen Harrison, *Epilegomena to the Study of Greek Religion* and *Themis: A Study of the Social Origins of Greek Religion.* New Hyde Park, N.Y.: University Books, 1962.

*Natural History.* "Of Birds and a Legend—Truth and Myth Are Woven in Tapestries." (December 1961).

Oakley, Francis. *The Medieval Experience; Foundations of Western Cultural Singularity.* New York: Charles Scribner, 1974.

Odenkirchen, Carl J., trans. *The Play of Adam (Ordo Representacionis Ade).* Brookline, Mass.: Classical Folia Editions, 1976.

*Ortus Sanitatis—translaté de latin en francois.* 2 vols. Paris: Antoine Vérard, c. 1500.

Ovid (Publius Ovidius Naso). *Fasti.* Trans. Sir James Frazer (1929). Cambridge, Mass.: Harvard University Press, Loeb Classical Library, 1976.

———. *Metamorphosis.* Trans. Mary M. Innes. Harmondsworth, Middx.: Penguin Books, 1980.

*The Oxford Book of Ballads.* James Kinsley, ed. London: Oxford University Press, 1969.

*The Oxford Book of Carols.* Pearcy Dearmer, R. Vaughan Williams, and Martin Shaw, eds. London: Oxford University Press, 1964.

Panofsky, Erwin. *Early Netherlandish Painting.* 2 vols. New York: Harper & Row, 1971.

———. *Meaning in the Visual Arts.* New York: Doubleday & Co., 1955.

———. *Renaissance and Renascences.* New York: Harper & Row, 1969.

———. *Studies in Iconography.* New York: Harper & Row, 1962.

Parkinson, John. *Paradisi in Sole: Paradisus Terrestris.* London: Humphrey Lownes and Robert Young, 1629.

———. *Theatrum Botanicum.* London: T. Cotes, 1640.

Patch, Howard Rollin. *The Goddess Fortuna in Medieval Literature.* Cambridge, Mass.: Harvard University Press, 1927.

Pearsall, Derek, and Elizabeth Salter. *Landscapes and Seasons of the Medieval World.* London: Elek Books, 1973.

Peebles, Rose Jeffries. "The Dry Tree: Symbol of Death," in *Vassar Medieval Studies.* New Haven, Conn.: Yale University Press, 1923.

Pevsner, Nikolaus. *The Leaves of Southwell.* London: The King Penguin Books, 1945.

Pliny (Gaius Plinius Secundus). *The Natural History.* 2 vols. Trans. John Bostock and H. T. Riley. London: George Bell & Sons, 1890.

———. *Natural History.* 10 vols. Vols. 1–V and IX, trans. H. Rackham, 1938–52; Vols. VI–VIII, trans. W. H. S. Jones, 1951–63; Vol. X, trans. D. E. Eichholz, 1962. Cambridge, Mass.: Harvard University Press, Loeb Classical Library.

Poltarnees, Welleran. *A Book of Unicorns.* San Diego, Calif.: The Green Tiger Press, 1978.

Power, Eileen. *The Goodman of Paris.* London: George Routledge and Sons, 1928.

Quinn, Esther Casier. *The Quest of Seth for the Oil of Life.* Chicago: University of Chicago Press, 1962.

Rabanus Maurus. *De Universo,* in *Patrologia Latina,* Vol. III. J. P. Migne, ed. New York: AMS Press, 1972.

Raglan, Lady. "The 'Green Man' in Church Architecture." *Folk-lore,* L:1 (1939).

Rahner, Hugo. *Greek Myths and Christian Mystery.* Trans. Brian Battershaw. New York: Burns & Oates, 1963.

*Rationale Divinorum Officiorum.* See Durand.

Read, Sir Herbert. *Art and Society.* New York: Schocken Books, 1966.

———. *Icon and Idea.* New York: Schocken Books, 1965.

*Regimen Sanitatis Salernitanum—The School of Salernum* (originally translated by Sir John Harington, 1607). New York: A. M. Kelly, 1970.

Renaudet, Augustin. "Paris from 1495–1517—Church and University," in Werner L. Gundersheimer, ed., *French Humanism—1470–1600.* London: Macmillan & Co., 1969.

Rickert, Edith. *Ancient English Christmas Carols.* New York: Cooper Square Publishers, 1966.

Ring, Grete. *A Century of French Painting—1400–1500.* New York: Phaidon Press, 1949.

Ripa, Cesare. *Iconology . . . from compositions of C. Ripa, etc.* 2 vols. Trans. George Richardson, London: 1778–79.

Robertson, Durant Waite. "Doctrine of Charity in Medieval Literary Gardens," in his *Essays in Medieval Culture.* Princeton: Princeton University Press, 1980.

Rohde, Eleanor Sinclair. *The Old English Herbals.* London: Longmans, Green and Co., 1922.

*The Romance of the Rose.* Guillaume de Lorris and Jean de Meun. Trans. Harry W. Robbins. New York: E. P. Dutton, 1962.

Rosenberg, Jakob. "On the Meaning of a Bosch Drawing," in Millard Meiss, ed., *Essays in Honor of Erwin Panofsky.* London: Phaidon Press, 1961.

Ross, David J. A. "Allegory and Romance on a Medieval French Marriage Casket." *Journal of the Warburg and Courtauld Institutes,* 11 (1948): 112–42.

Rowland, Beryl. *Animals with Human Faces.* Knoxville: University of Tennessee Press, 1973.

———. *Birds with Human Souls: A Guide to Bird Symbolism.* Knoxville: University of Tennessee Press, 1978.

———. *Blind Beasts: Chaucer's Animal World.* Kent, Ohio: Kent State University Press, 1971.

Russell, Jeffrey Burton. *Witchcraft in the Middle Ages.* Ithaca, N.Y.: Cornell University Press, 1972.

Sanborn, Helen J. *Anne of Brittany.* Boston: Lothrop, Lee & Shepard, 1917.

Schiller, Gertrud. *Iconography of Christian Art.* 2 vols. Trans. Janet Seligman. Greenwich, Conn.: New York Graphic Society, 1971.

Seznec, Jean. *The Survival of the Pagan Gods.* Trans. Barbara Sessions. Princeton: Princeton University Press, Bollingen Series XXXVIII, 1953.

Shapiro, Norman R., trans. *Fables from Old French—Aesop's Beasts and Bumpkins.* Middletown, Conn.: Wesleyan University Press, 1982.

Shepard, Odell. *The Lore of the Unicorn.* Boston: Houghton Mifflin Company, 1930.

Sheridan, Ronald, and Anne Ross. *Gargoyles and Grotesques—Paganism in the Medieval Church.* Boston: New York Graphic Society, 1975.

Shestack, Alan. *Fifteenth Century Engravings of Northern Europe from the National Gallery of Art Washington, D.C.* Washington, D.C.: The National Gallery of Art, 1967–68.

Sichel, Edith. *Women and Men of the French Renaissance* (1901). New York: Kennikat Press, 1970.

Simone, Franco. *The French Renaissance.* Trans. H. Gaston Hall. London: Macmillan & Co., 1969.

Singer, Charles. *From Magic to Science.* New York: Boni and Liveright, 1928.

Skeat, Walter W., ed. *Chaucerian and Other Pieces.* Oxford: Clarendon Press, 1897.

———. ed. *Complete Works of Geoffrey Chaucer.* 6 vols. (1894). Oxford: Clarendon Press, 1900.

Skinner, Charles M. *Myths and Legends of Flowers, Trees, Fruits and Plants in All Ages and in All Climes.* Philadelphia: J. B. Lippincott, 1925.

Smith, Preserved. *A History of Modern Culture.* 2 vols. New York: H. Holt and Co., 1930–34.

Souchal, Genevieve. *Masterpieces of Tapestry—From the Fourteenth to the Sixteenth Century.* Trans. Richard Oxby. New York: The Metropolitan Museum of Art, 1974.

Speirs, John. *Medieval English Poetry: The Non-Chaucerian Tradition.* London: Faber and Faber, 1957.

Steinberg, Leo. *The Sexuality of Christ in Renaissance Art and in Modern Oblivion.* New York: Pantheon, 1983.

Stephens, George. "Extracts in Prose and Verse from an Old English Medical Manuscript." *Archaeology,* Vol. 30 (London, 1844).

Stewart, Stanley. *The Enclosed Garden.* Madison: University of Wisconsin Press, 1966.

"Stockholm Medical MS." *Anglia,* 18 (1896): 325.

Stoddard, Whitney S. *Art and Architecture in Medieval France.* New York: Harper & Row, 1972.

Stone, Brian, trans. *Sir Gawain and the Green Knight.* Harmondsworth, Middx.: Penguin Books, 1959.

———. *Medieval English Verse.* Harmondsworth, Middx.: Penguin Books, 1964.

———. *The Owl and the Nightingale.* Harmondsworth, Middx.: Penguin Books, 1971.

Strabo, Walafrid. *Hortulus.* Trans. Raef Payne. Pittsburgh: Hunt Botanical Library, 1966.

Stubbes, Phillip. *The Anatomie of Abuses.* F. J. Furnivall's reprint. London, 1877–82. (Transliteration, J. W.)

Sumberg, Samuel L. *The Nuremberg Schembart Carnival.* New York: Columbia University Press, 1941.

———. "The Nuremberg Schembart Manuscripts." *Publications of the Modern Language Association,* Vol. 44 (1929).

Swainson, Rev. Charles. *The Folk Lore and Provincial Names of British Birds.* London: Elliot Stock, 1886.

Symonds, J. A. *Renaissance in Italy.* Vol. II, *The Revival of Learning.* London: Smith, Elder & Co., 1877.

Taylor, Henry Osborn. *The Medieval Mind. A History of the Development of Thought and Emotion in the Middle Ages.* 2 vols. 4th ed., Cambridge, Mass.: Harvard University Press, 1951. London: Macmillan, 1911.

Tennant, F. R. *The Sources of the Doctrine of the Fall and Original Sin.* New York: Schocken Books, 1968.

Theobald. *Physiologus—A Metrical Bestiary of Twelve Chapters by Bishop Theobald.* Trans. Alan Wood Rendell. London: John and Edward Bumpus, 1928.

Thiselton-Dyer, Thomas Firminger. *British Popular Customs—Past and Present* (1875). New York: AMS Press, 1970.

———. *English Folk-Lore.* London: Hardwicke and Bogue, 1878.

———. *The Folk-lore of Plants.* New York: D. Appleton & Co., 1889.

Thompson, William Irwin. *The Time Falling Bodies Take to Light.* New York: St. Martin's Press, 1981.

Thorndike, Lynn. *A History of Magic and Experimental Science.* 8 vols. New York: Columbia University Press, 1923.

Tilander, Gunnar, ed. *Livre du roy Modus—Le Livre de chasse du roy Modus.* Paris: E. Nourry, 1931.

Topsell, Edward. *The Fowles of Heaven or History of Birdes.* Manuscript first published, Austin: University of Texas Press, 1972.

———. *The History of Four-footed Beasts and Serpents and Insects.* 3 vols. New York: Da Capo Press, 1967.

Tristram, Philippa. *Figures of Life and Death in Medieval English Literature.* New York: New York University Press, 1976.

Turner, William. *The Names of Herbs* (1548). James Britten, ed. London: N. Trubner and Co., 1881.

———. *New Herball.* 3rd edn, Collen (Cologne): Arnold Birckman, 1568.

Tyler, William R. *Dijon and the Valois Dukes of Burgundy.* Norman: University of Oklahoma Press, 1971.

Virgil. *The Aeneid.* Trans. Robert Fitzgerald. New York: Random House, 1983.

Voragine, Jacobus de. *The Golden Legend.* Trans. Granger Ryan and Helmut Ripperger. 2 vols. New York: Longmans, Green and Co., 1941.

Vries, Ad de. *Dictionary of Symbols and Imagery.* Amsterdam: North-Holland Publishing Co., 1974.

Waddell, Helen. *Medieval Latin Lyrics.* New York: Henry Holt and Co., 1933.

Warner, Marina. *Alone of All Her Sex—The Myth and the Cult of the Virgin Mary.* New York: Alfred A. Knopf, 1976.

Webster, James Carson. *The Labors of the Months in Antique and Medieval Art to the End of the Twelfth Century.* Originally published in *Northwestern University Humanistic Series,* Vol. 4, 1938. New York: AMS Press, 1970.

Weston, Jessie L. *The Chief Middle English Poets.* Boston: Houghton Mifflin, 1914.

———. *From Ritual to Romance.* Cambridge: Cambridge University Press, 1920.

———. *The Legend of Sir Gawain.* London: David Nut, 1897. Reprinted New York: AMS Press, 1972.

———. *The Quest of the Holy Grail.* London: George Bell & Sons, 1913.

White, T. H., trans. *The Bestiary—A Book of Beasts.* New York: G. P. Putnam's Sons, 1954.

Whittlesey, E. S. *Symbols and Legends in Western Art: A Museum Guide.* New York: Charles Scribner's Sons, 1972.

Wijk, H. L. Gerth Van. *A Dictionary of Plant-Names.* 2 vols. Amsterdam: A. Asher and Co., 1971.

Wind, Edgar. *Pagan Mysteries in the Renaissance.* Rev. edn, New York: W. W. Norton, 1968.

Wittkower, R. "The Arts in Western Europe—Italy," in G. R. Potter, ed., *The New Cambridge Modern History.* Vol. I, *The Renaissance: 1493–1520.* Cambridge: Cambridge University Press, 1957.

Wright, Thomas, ed. *Popular Treatises on Science Written During the Middle Ages.* London: R. & J. E. Taylor, 1841.

# Index

# DATE DUE
# REMINDER

DEC 1 9 2010

**Please do not remove
this date due slip.**